ROUTLEDGE LIBR⎰
EDUCATION AN

MW00744901

Volume 9

FOUNDATION SUBJECTS AND RELIGIOUS EDUCATION IN THE PRIMARY SCHOOL

FOUNDATION SUBJECTS AND RELIGIOUS EDUCATION IN THE PRIMARY SCHOOL

Edited by
PETER D. PUMFREY AND
GAJENDRA K. VERMA

Routledge
Taylor & Francis Group

LONDON AND NEW YORK

First published in 1993 by The Falmer Press

This edition first published in 2019
by Routledge
2 Park Square, Milton Park, Abingdon, Oxon OX14 4RN

and by Routledge
52 Vanderbilt Avenue, New York, NY 10017

Routledge is an imprint of the Taylor & Francis Group, an informa business

British Library Cataloguing in Publication Data
A catalogue record for this book is available from the British Library

ISBN: 978-0-367-13819-6 (Set)
ISBN: 978-0-429-05630-7 (Set) (ebk)
ISBN: 978-0-367-17319-7 (Volume 9) (hbk)
ISBN: 978-0-367-17327-2 (Volume 9) (pbk)
ISBN: 978-0-429-05620-8 (Volume 9) (ebk)

Publisher's Note
The publisher has gone to great lengths to ensure the quality of this reprint but points out that some imperfections in the original copies may be apparent.

Disclaimer
The publisher has made every effort to trace copyright holders and would welcome correspondence from those they have been unable to trace.

Cultural Diversity and the Curriculum

The Foundation Subjects and Religious Education in Primary Schools

Edited by

P.D. Pumfrey and G.K. Verma

 The Falmer Press

(A member of the Taylor & Francis Group)
London • Washington, D.C.

UK The Falmer Press, 4 John Street, London WC1N 2ET
USA The Falmer Press, Taylor & Francis Inc., 1900 Frost Road, Suite 101, Bristol, PA 19007

First published 1993

Library of Congress Cataloging-in-Publication data are available on request

A catalogue record for this book is available from the British Library

ISBN 075070 143 9 (cased)
ISBN 075070 144 7 (paper)

Jacket design by Caroline Archer

Typeset in 10/12pt Bembo by
Graphicraft Typesetters Ltd., Hong Kong

Printed in Great Britain by Burgess Science Press, Basingstoke on paper which has a specified pH value on final paper manufacture of not less than 7.5 and is therefore 'acid free'.

Contents

v

Contents

Preface

This series of four books considers contexts, challenges and responses to cultural, ethnic and religious diversity in relation to the school curriculum in this country. The issues identified have a much wider international currency. All nations in which cultural, ethnic and religious diversities exist, will be facing similar tensions within the fabric of their societies and schools.

Any democratic society characterized by cultural pluralism will continually face conflicts involving relationships between cultural, ethnic and religious groups. Minority ethnic groups often suffer unjustly and disproportionately as a consequence of the 'pecking orders' that epitomize social groupings and behaviour. Their concerns, values and aspirations are often neglected. Their potential contributions to society are all too easily ignored or overlooked. Alienations arise and are reinforced.

Whilst the coexistence of social cohesion, cultural diversity and equality of opportunity are not incompatible, such ends are not easily achieved; nor are the individual and collective rights and responsibilities involved in ensuring their coexistence readily acknowledged, established and maintained. Without example, precept and exhortation are soon recognized as but empty words. 'Do as I say, not as I do', sounds a death knell both to social cohesion and equality of opportunity.

Teachers, schools and educational systems can play a key role in establishing an ethos in which the required awarenesses, involvements and reciprocities between individuals and groups can be encouraged and demonstrated, by example, daily. The school curriculum, and the ways in which it is delivered to all pupils, holds major opportunities. Through the curriculum, and the relationships with and between the individuals and groups comprising the community that the school serves, cohesion and coexistence can be fostered. This is not to deny that the task is a challenging one.

Success in such an educational and social endeavour represents a balancing act of the highest order. Any equilibrium achieved is neither stable nor unstable; it is dynamic. There can be no ultimate solution. The nature of society, its priorities and the policies, practices and effects of an educational system are continuously evolving. There is no known pedagogical 'Royal Road' to social harmony. There are a number of educational avenues that represent cul-de-sacs. Beware the individuals or groups claiming absolute certainty concerning either educational policy or practice. No individual, no single group, whether large or small, powerful or otherwise, has a freehold on wisdom. Fortunately, given an acceptance of the importance of the autonomous individual in a democratic society, there are some pointers to promising practices.

Volume 3 consists of thirteen chapters and three appendices. Part 1 comprises three chapters in which societal and curricular implications of cultural diversity in the primary school are considered from complementary viewpoints. Part 2 focuses on Practice in the Content Fields. Chapters on each of the curricular areas of Religious Education and the nine Foundation subjects are presented. Appendices on the Race Relations Act, the Education Reform Act National Curriculum related Publications and revised administrative arrangements governing the funding available through Section 11 of the Local Government Act, are presented.

Volume 3 is complemented by Volume 4 on cross-curricular elements, namely themes skills and dimensions at the primary-school stage. Volumes 1 and 2 parallel the same concerns at the secondary-school stage.

The contributors are all qualified and experienced teachers. Their individual analyses of the challenges of cultural diversity presented by various aspects of the whole curriculum in developing work that capitalizes on cultural diversity, have led to their particular responses. Sometimes the challenges identified are directly addressed. In the majority of cases, the challenges are approached obliquely. Information is provided on resources that may be used in developing a multicultural, equal-opportunity and antiracist curriculum. All contributors involved in this venture are well aware of the considerable curricular flux that exists. The various and rapidly changing Ministers and Secretaries of State for Education have each brought their respective 'visions' to education. Sadly, in their wish to be seen as radical, at times they have mistaken action for progress.

At present, many of the major 'planks' of the curricular 'platform' are established. The cultural, ethnic and religious diversities comprising the population of this country are also in place. The development of a curriculum that is sensitive to the concerns of all groups is essential. It must capitalize on the possibilities inherent in a society that is culturally, ethnically and religiously diverse. Tensions and conflicts between groups cannot be eliminated. The ways in which they are dealt with can be made constructive. If, in education, we move towards this horizon, then the aim of 'Education for All' need not be an impossible dream.

P.D. Pumfrey and G.K. Verma

Acknowledgments

We thank the Office of Population Censuses and Surveys for permission to reproduce the tables and figure in Chapter 3 based on their research.

List of Tables and Figures

Tables

Figures

List of Abbreviations

AIMER	Access to Information on Multicultural Education Resources
AIMS	Art and Design in a Multicultural Society
AMA	Association of Metropolitan Authorities
APU	Assessment of Performance Unit
ARE	Anti-Racist Education
AREAI	Association of Religious Education Advisers and Inspectors
ARTEN	Anti-Racist Teacher Education Network
AT	Attainment Targets
ATEM	Association of Ethnic Minority Teachers
BCPE	British Council for Physical Education
BTEC	Business and Technical Education Council
CARM	Campaign Against Racism in the Media
CATE	Council for the Accreditation of Teacher Education
CDT	Craft, Design and Technology
CPD	Continuing Professional Development
CRE	Commission for Racial Equality
CSE	Certificate of Secondary Education
CTA	Caribbean Teachers Association
DES	Department of Education and Science
DFE	Department for Education
EMAG	Ethnic Minority Advisory Groups
ESRC	Economic and Social Science Research Council
ERA	Education Reform Act 1988
E2L	English as a second language
EFL	English as a foreign language
GEST	Grants for Educational Support and Training
GRIST	Grant Related In-Service Training
HMI	Her Majesty's Inspectorate
HMSO	Her Majesty's Stationery Office
INSET	In-Service Education for Teachers
IT	Information Technology

ITT	Initial Teacher Training
KS	Key Stages (of the National Curriculum)
LARRIE	Local Authorities Race Relations Information Exchange
LEA	Local Education Authority
LMS	Local Management of Schools
LMSS	Local Management of Special Schools
MCE	Multi-Cultural Education
MFLWG	Modern Foreign Languages Working Group
NAME	National Anti-Racist Movement in Education
NAHT	National Association of Head Teachers
NC	National Curriculum
NCC	National Curriculum Council
NCDP	National Curriculum Development Plan
NCMT	National Council for the Mother Tongue
NERIS	National Educational Resources Information Service
NFER	National Foundation for Educational Research
NSC	National Science Curriculum
OFSTED	Office of Standards in Education
PC	Profile Components
PoS	Programme of Study
RE	Religious Education
RI	Religious Instruction
RoA	Records of Achievement
RT	Runnymede Trust
SACRE	Standing Advisory Council on Religious Education
SAIL	Staged Assessments in Literacy
SEAC	School Examinations and Assessment Council
SCAA	School Curriculum and Assessment Authority
SCDC	School Curriculum Development Committee
SoA	Statements of Attainment
SO	Statutory Order
SSD	Social Services Department
TGAT	Task Group on Assessment and Testing
WGARCR	Working Group against Racism in Children's Resources

Part 1

Towards Cultural Pluralism through the Curriculum in Primary Education

Chapter 1

Cultural Diversity and the Curriculum: Context, Challenges and Responses

Peter D. Pumfrey

Context

What type of society do you wish your family, friends and fellow citizens to live in? How can the younger generation be prepared for life in an increasingly multicultural society? What role can education play in such preparation?

In any contemporary society and its educational system, the one constant on which we can depend is change. In the UK, how valid is the assertion that ideological and pedagogical 'Winds of Change' typically blow from West to East? Are not equally strong forces 'blowing' from the opposite (and other) directions? Or are both such assertions no more than direct consequences of the current uncertainties increasingly experienced within all countries and cultures? Are these uncertainties themselves, in part, an almost inevitable consequence of the onward marches of the mass media, of materialism and the mobility of individuals and groups?

The 'Good Life' is increasingly construed in materialist terms by the world's human population. It would be unwise not to acknowledge the tensions between countries, consequent on competition for finite material resources. Within a given country, region, town and locality, individuals, and groups, also compete for limited resources that are seen as desirable and beneficial. These include housing, health care, education and educational and occupational opportunities. This is the case even when there is no cultural diversity in the population under consideration. Ambitious individuals and pressure groups are facts of life, even in ethnically homogeneous societies (if such societies exist). When clearly identifiable subgroups based on, for example, ethnic group, religion, politics, class, sex or age form, either to protect and/or advance their particular interests, a perennial power struggle is exacerbated. The implicit tensions become explicit.

Across the world, large conurbations have been characterized as 'concrete jungles'. Within them, the law of the jungle can be observed in operation.

3

Social Darwinism identifies territorial ambitions, pecking orders and competition for space and resources as processes inherent in the human condition. They are exacerbated as population densities increase. In combination, and over time, it has been argued that these processes result in the survival of the fittest with the weakest going to the wall. Might is right. Or is it?

Fortunately, social animals such as *homo sapiens* also manifest the ability to cooperate, to be concerned with the common good, to subsume short-term material benefits to the individual to those of the group, and to be altruistic. The 'down-sides' of this are the tensions between alienated minorities and a mainstream society that is perceived by minorities as failing to acknowledge and respond to their legitimate aspirations. Current gang warfare in cities is but one manifestation of a long-standing phenomenon. Can the individual and collective intelligence, energies, organization, motivation and alienation clearly manifest in, for example, Manchester's Moss Side and other socio-economically deprived areas, be channelled more constructively? Strategies for constructive change have been developed, are known and have been used successfully (Pumfrey and Verma, 1990).

There are advocates of less concilliatory action. 'All thinking people who have been oppressed are revolutionary. Any time you find somebody today who's afraid of the word "revolution" get them out of your way, they are living in the wrong era, they are behind the times. They haven't awakened yet. This is the era of revolution . . .' This call by the late Malcolm X has been taken up by members of Revolution Youth, an active organization of young black and white individuals who intend to change society. Revolution Youth is associated with *Socialist Challenge*, a weekly paper sponsored by the International Marxist Group (Hercules, Sen and Haddad, 1992).

Other somewhat less extreme and larger organizations involved in addressing the multifaceted concerns of both minority and majority cultural and ethnic groups are listed in Table 1.1.

What positive role can education play in fostering a tolerant and just multicultural society? If education merely mirrors society, the answer is 'Nothing'. Fortunately, there are alternatives. Early interventions can reduce the probability of later alienating social consequences for pupils of all groups. Schools within the educational system can provide the ethos and experiences that encourage tolerance. The value of primary school-linked work with the parents of pre-school children is increasingly recognized. Primary schools matter (Mortimore, *et al.*, 1988; Alexander *et al.*, 1991).

Education is a highly political issue. The content, teaching and assessment of a National Curriculum cannot be politically neutral. In tune with the market economy philosophy of the current British government, those employed in education are seen as providers of services. As the service is funded on the basis of taxation, pupils and their parents are encouraged to consider themselves purchasers having important rights and responsibilities. Increasingly, every educational resource is costed financially. The Local Management of Schools (LMS) and of Special Schools (LMSS) ensures schools' growing

Table 1.1: *Sources of Information and Advice*

Access to Information on Multicultural Education Resources (AIMER),
Faculty of Education and Community Studies,
The University of Reading,
Bulmershe Court,
Earley,
Reading, RG6 1HV.

Commission for Racial Equality,
Elliot House,
10–12 Allington Street,
London, SW1E 5EH.

Commonwealth Institute: Centre for Commonwealth Education and Culture in Britain,
Kensington High Street,
London, W8 6QN.

Institute of Race Relations,
2–6 Leeke Street,
King's Cross Road,
London, WC1X 9HS.

Joint Council for the Welfare of Immigrants,
115 Old Street,
London, EC1V 9JR.

National Association of Racial Equality Councils,
8–16 Coronet Street,
London, N1 6HD.

National Council for Civil Liberties,
21 Tabard Street,
London, SE1 4LA.

National Educational Resources Information Service,
Maryland College,
Leighton Street,
Woburn,
Milton Keynes
MK17 9JD.

The Refugee Council,
Bondway House,
3–9 Bondway,
London, SW8 1SJ.

The Runnymede Trust,
11 Princelet Street,
London, E1 6QH.

Standing Conference on Racial Equality in Europe,
Unit 303,
Brixton Enterprise Centre,
444 Brixton Road,
London, SW1 8EJ.

---

financial independence of LEAs. Increasingly, the governors and headteachers of schools are determining school policies and priorities. With this financial autonomy comes greater financial accountability. Critics argue that there is an escalating danger that we will shortly know the price of everything and the value of nothing. What priority and price will be put on ensuring that a school curriculum adequately addresses multicultural concerns?

One recent development in the USA may well affect the UK in the fulness of time. South Carolina is a State in which the black/white, 'haves' versus 'have nots', divisions in education have been, and still remain, significant. Whilst Governor of South Carolina from 1979–1987, Mr Riley earned a national reputation as a leading education reform governor. He achieved this distinction by constructing a detailed package of sixty-two educational reforms required to address some of the system's manifest weaknesses. Then came the extremely difficult task of obtaining the support of elected representatives. This was, in part, achieved by a concerted political campaign. This campaign ensured that the law-makers became aware of a constituency of concerned voters that they would ignore at their political peril. The proposals required the raising of an extra 240 million US dollars per year (160 millions pounds sterling). This was to be raised by an increase of one cent on the state's sales tax. To British readers, the proposal appears minimalist. Indeed, a much more radical financial policy of adding one penny to the standard rate of income tax in order to fund educational development in the UK was proposed by the Social Democratic Party during the 1992 General Election. As is currently the case in the UK, increasing taxes for public services in the American context is also politically dangerous. Despite this, Riley's proposals to increase taxes were accepted. The Dean of Columbia Teachers' College, Michael Timpane, is reported as saying that Riley's achievement was a pure political *tour de force*. The links between politics and education are important. Mr Riley has been nominated as Education Secretary in President Clinton's Administration.

The strength of an elected democracy rests on an educated citizenry capable of informed reflection about the nature of the society they wish to support. To this end, its teachers must be similarly reflective and they must educate their pupils likewise (see Volume 4, Chapter 15).

Challenges

Does the following quotation ring bells? Is it of relevance to societies and their educational systems across the world? Does it bear on life in general and education in particular in an ethnically, culturally and religiously diverse UK?

> This is our basic conclusion: Our nation is moving towards two societies, one black, one white — separate and unequal . . . This deepening racial division is not inevitable. The movement apart can be

reversed. Choice is still possible. Our principle task is to define that choice and to press for a national resolution.

In May, 1992, one again, the sociological tinder box of Los Angeles exploded literally and metaphorically. The idealistic concept of the USA as a 'melting pot', in which differing groups establish mutually acceptable *modus vivendi*, was once more challenged. The feelings aroused amongst black communities, following the verdict in the first Rodney King trial, can well be understood. The broadcasting of a video recording of King's arrest, during which he was hit fifty-six times in eighty-one seconds by the four police officers involved, led to their being charged and tried. The acquittal of Stacey Koon and his three colleagues employed by the Los Angeles Police Department was the spark that led to race riots in which fifty-eight people were killed and more than a billion dollars of damage to property took place. The reactions were not limited to the USA, but spread to other countries and continents. A re-trial of the accused began in 1993. Was the rioting, looting, arson, mayhem and murder that followed the first trial justified? Was nothing learned from the Watts riots of twenty-seven years before? Apparently not. The quotation with which this section began was taken from the *Report of the USA National Advisory Commission on Civil Disorders*. It was published in 1968!

Can groups with differing cultural histories, religions, belief systems and often conflicting aspirations learn to coexist peacefully within the same country? Is the objective a realistic aspiration? Or is it merely another manifestation of the perennial triumph of hope over experience? The fatalism expressed in Kipling's poem 'The Gods of the Copybook Headings' mocks any endeavour at 'Social Progress'. His ideological descendants survive today. (Readers are asked to accept the anachronistic use of gender by the author. It was of its time).

As it will be in the future, so it was at the birth of Man –
There are only four things certain since Social Progress began: —
That the Dog will return to his Vomit and the Sow returns to her Mire,
And the burnt Fool's bandaged finger goes wobbling back to the fire;
And that after this is accomplished, and the brave new world begins,
When all men are paid for existing and no man must pay for his sins,
As surely as Water will wet us,
As surely as Fire will burn,
The Gods of the Copybook Headings with terror and slaughter return!

Does the re-emergence in many countries, including the UK, of xenophobia, religious extremism, of fascism, of racism in general and anti-semitism in particular, coupled with the tragic examples of interethnic power struggles in the former Yugoslavia and many other countries, confirm this view? (Breslau *et al.*, 1992). Are there no alternatives to such a pessimistic analysis of human behaviour? If not, does despair, and all the miseries that flows from it, become self-fulfilling prophecies?

Acknowledging the existence of such powerful challenges to social cohesion is an essential, but not sufficient, condition to addressing them. A contrasting viewpoint, succinctly expressed by Woolf, summarizes the optimist's position concerning progress to social cohesion in the face of the problems listed above. It challenges the despairing views of Kipling and his ideological heirs. Woolf's assertion has much to commend it on the basis of both individual and collective experiences in groups ranging in size from that of a dyad to a country. 'It is more contemptible to be intimidated by distrust of human nature than to be duped by believing in it'. Values are vital! Such an assumption leaves open the possibility of progress towards greater social cohesion, whilst not denying the manifest difficulties involved in approaching and maintaining such a state. Any equilibrium between the competing aspirations of individuals and groups within a society is always dynamic, always changing.

In any pluralist society there will inevitably be many deeply held moral, religious and political disagreements. Within an elected democracy, the convention that divergent opinions should be respected, is a central tenet. Changes can be achieved by the ballot box, if not by consensus, and without violence or bloodshed. In reality, there are certain viewpoints that are not accorded this protection. Censorship does exist. 'It should not be allowed' is a rallying cry that can be extremely potent in determining what is accepted as 'Politically Correct' at any point in time in any society. Within this complex and confusing social matrix, the education of future generations of citizens is acknowledged as an important seedbed. In it, the potential of tolerance between groups of all descriptions must be nurtured. That is why the content and delivery of a multiculturally sensitive curriculum is essential.

In most elected democracies, teachers and schools are charged with enabling students to become members of one nation within which the strengths of cultural, ethnic, religious and ideological diversity can be utilized to the benefit of all groups. Viewed from a reconstructionist philosophy of education, schools have a key role to play. Education may not be as rapid in its effects as a revolution, but it represents one avenue whereby the difficult mutual learnings, on which social cohesion and equity depend, can be constructively approached in a society. Allegiances need not alienate. Siren cries for ideological conformity, irrespective of the charisma of the caller, must be treated with great caution.

There are crucial lessons for individuals and institutions to be learned from the latest manifestations of minority ethnic, religious and cultural group alienation by all members of any given society. No country, no ethnic, religious or social group, can afford to adopt a 'holier than thou' attitude. In the UK, the riots in Manchester, London, Bristol, Liverpool and Leeds during the 1980s and the ethnic, religious and social tensions that exist in the 1990s, show the fragilities inherent in our own social cohesion. They underline the importance of multicultural education if the concept of 'One Nation' is to be approached. In this endeavour, the nature of the school curriculum and its delivery are of the essence.

Approximately 2,620,000 people from minority ethnic groups live in Britain. They comprise 4.8 per cent of the population. Of these, approximately 1,200,000 are Muslims, 500,000 Sikhs, 300,000 Hindus and 300,000 Jews. Over 50 per cent live in the South East. The remainder tend to be located mainly in the North West and the Midlands. 75 per cent of the members of minority ethnic groups live in metropolitan areas whilst only 33 per cent of Whites do so. In Britain today, excluding English, there are thirteen living languages that are spoken by a minimum of 100,000 persons. These languages are Arabic, Bengali, Chinese, Greek, Gujarati, Hindi, Italian, Polish, Spanish, Turkish, Urdu and Welsh (Commission for Racial Equality, 1992). Further demographic details are given in Chapter 3.

Responses

> I believe deeply that all men and women should be able to go as far as talent, ambition and effort can take them. There should be no barriers of background, no barriers of religion, no barriers of race. I want . . . a society that encourages each and every one to fulfil his or her potential to the utmost . . . let me say here and now that I regard any barrier built on race to be pernicious. (Prime Minister John Major, September, 1991)

The evidence of institutional racism in relation to the law, housing and education is, sadly, substantial (CRE, 1991). According to the results of a survey reported by the CRE, when asked 'Is Britain Racist?', 67 per cent of Whites, 79 per cent of Blacks and 56 per cent of Asians answered 'Yes'. In 1988, 4,383 racial attacks were reported to the police in England and Wales. By 1990 the figure had risen to 6,459. On average, a racial attack takes place every thirty minutes with individuals from ethnic-minority groups being sixty times more likely than white people to be the victims. Asian women and children are the most likely to suffer, although members of many other groups are attacked because of their race, colour, ethnic origin, nationality and/or religion (CRE, 1992). The murders of 13-year-old Ahmed Ullah by Darren Coulbourn at Burnage High School, Manchester, on 17 September 1986, of Rolan Adams in 1991 by a gang of white youths on his way home, and the alleged murder of Arif Roberts at Gladesmore school in Tottenham by a 16-year-old Vietnamese youth represent tragedies of intolerance. In July 1992, Rohit Duggal, an Asian boy, was stabbed to death in Well Hall Road. Stephen Lawrence, a black sixth form student was mortally stabbed in Well Hall Road, Eltham, south-east London by a gang of white youths in April, 1993. In May, they were charged with the crime.

Such antipathies typically have their genesis in much earlier stages of pupils' lives. A study into the use of racist name-calling involved discussions with 160 pupils aged 9, 10 and 11 years attending three mainly white primary schools in which overt racism was not readily apparent. According to the research workers, name-calling was perceived as offensive and damaging by the non-white recipients. The researchers considered it likely that racism in mainly white primary schools is probably more prevalent and more complex than many teachers, parents and governors would like to admit. On the constructive side, the authors describe strategies enabling children to understand and address such issues (Troyna and Hatcher, 1991).

Elsewhere, it is reported that, in reply to the question 'Do schools treat ethnic minorities worse? (than white pupils), 13 per cent of Whites, 38 per cent of Blacks and 15 per cent of Asians answered 'Yes'. The importance of role models with whom pupils can identify is subverted when teachers from minority ethnic groups are under-represented within the educational system. A study of some 20,000 teachers employed within the state educational systems of eight cities revealed that only one in fifty was drawn from ethnic minorities and, of these 400, 80 per cent were at the lowest levels of the salary scales (CRE, 1992). Britain has a long history of deeply hostile attitudes towards foreigners (Holmes, 1991). In this, Britain is not unique. Despite this xenophobia, the country is one to which citizens of many other countries wish to come for a multitude of reasons. Possibly in recognition of continuing antipathies, coupled with a governmental intent to minimize these, we also currently have important legislation protecting minorities. It is probably superior to parallel legislation in the vast majority of countries (CRE, 1992).

To individuals in other countries, what is currently taking place in the schools of England and Wales can be looked upon as an important case study of a country and an educational system attempting to develop a multicultural education based on an entitlement curriculum (DES, 1989; 1991; DFE, 1992; NCC, 1990). To teachers in England and Wales, the creation and implementation of such a National Curriculum has led to the identification of challenges at many levels. The contributions to this series specify some of the many constructive responses that are being developed.

Education for All was the title of the report of the Committee of Inquiry into the Education of Pupils from Minority Ethnic Groups chaired by the late Lord Swann (Committee of Inquiry, 1985). Achieving this objective represents an educational horizon towards which we can move, but which can never be finally reached. Life is not that simple. Despite this, in principle, the aspiration has much to commend it. As with most such objectives, agreement in principle is (relatively) easy. The 'devil' is in the details of translating a policy into practice. A common technical terminology has been developed in relation to the National Curriculum (see Chapter 3). This is an important first step towards the delivery of that multiculturally informed and sensitive National Curriculum to all pupils.

Those involved within the educational system, whether as professionals, parents, pupils or politicians, whether as developers, deliverers or consumers of the National Curriculum, bear heavy and complementary responsibilities. Ensuring that the direction of curriculum reform, development and delivery keeps an acceptable balance between the interests and concerns of majority and minority groups is easily espoused, but less readily attained. One constructive response is to gather together teachers who are concerned with such matters and ask them to consider the educational issues raised in delivering a National Curriculum in their respective fields of expertise.

This is the third in a series of four books that adopts this strategy. Volumes 1 and 2 concern secondary schools. Parallel volumes 3 and 4 concern primary schools.

Volumes 1 and 3 address the implications of the National Curriculum foundation subjects and religious education in relation to cultural diversity at the secondary and primary school levels, respectively. Volumes 2 and 4 consider the implications of cross-curricular elements in relation to cultural diversity at the secondary and primary school levels.

The series has two major purposes. The first is to describe and discuss cultural diversity and the curriculum from various contextual and curricular perspectives. The second is to consider how the legitimate educational concerns of minority ethnic groups, and those of larger groups, can be constructively addressed within the framework of the National Curriculum and those equally important aspects of the curriculum subsumed under the broader headings of the 'Basic' and 'Whole' curriculum respectively. To this end, specialists in the key components of the curriculum have considered some of the challenges and describe promising practices in a number of specific subjects and cross-curricular fields.

In education, theory and practice are equally important to the teacher. Being an effective teacher, but not being able to reflect upon and communicate the reasons for such success, is professionally insufficient. The bases of effectiveness must be made explicit in order that expertise can be developed and disseminated. The nature, causes and effects of particular patterns of behaviour are of crucial importance in education. The central objectives of any profession considering any phenomenon are sixfold:

- conceptualizing its nature;
- describing aetiologies;
- operationalizing symptoms;
- making prognoses;
- devising effective interventions; and
- evaluating responses to various interventions.

In all of the above, the *assumptions* made concerning the nature of individuals, groups and society determine, in part, what is looked at by the observer and how what is seen is interpreted. Extreme hereditarians and extreme environmentalists are likely to interpret the same data somewhat differently.

Religious and scientific beliefs can come into conflict on issues such as creation and evolution (Desmond and Moore, 1991). Assumptions are themselves typically underpinned by value systems of which the holder may, or may not, be aware.

Should the contributors to an edited book in a series such as this be required to write from either a common ideological position concerning the nature of society or a common theoretical position concerning how change is best achieved? It would certainly be one means of ensuring coherence, but this apparent gain could easily be offset in the present state of knowledge. 'Political Correctness' is an ever present danger in the social sciences.

J.D. Saxe wrote a poem entitled 'The Blind Men and the Elephant'. It began with the following lines.

> There were six men of Hindustan
> To learning much inclined,
> Who went to see an elephant
> Though each of them was blind . . .

Their comments, consequent on their respective encounters with different parts of an elephant's anatomy, demonstrated six conflicting interpretations concerning the nature of the phenomenon under scrutiny.

Disputes between individuals trained in the many differing disciplines interested in theoretical and applied aspects of education are well known. To conceptualize and describe 'Contexts', identify 'Challenges' and advocate 'Responses' in relation to cultural diversity and the National Curriculum, are important objectives. Each discipline and profession has something to contribute towards these ends, as has each subject specialist in relation to the National (and whole) Curriculum. In the quest to do this in a field as complex and controversial as that covered in this series, it is almost inevitable that individual contributors will hold differing theoretical positions. In this respect, no one has a freehold on 'truth'. The same applies to the variety of policies and practices that are advocated.

Consideration of hypotheses and their antitheses, of their related policies and practices in the dialectic, can be a constructive activity. Presenting and evaluating theories and evidence matters. The absolute certainty of the fundamentalist, whether secular or otherwise, is typically less than helpful in any search for the disinterested resolution of conflicting views. Consensus about cultural diversity is analogous to the pursuit of a chimera (Lynch, Modgil and Modgil, 1992).

When social scientists consider a phenomenon, they all too frequently and easily suffer from a conceptual 'tunnel vision' imposed by whichever disciplines and sets of beliefs have influenced their modes of thinking. Recognizing this is mutually beneficial to improved communication. By reading the four books in this series, colleagues will be able to make judgments concerning whether the contributors' present insights and/or illusions.

The analyses, evidence, suggestions and reflections of highly experienced educators on key curricular aspects of cultural diversity and the effective delivery of the National Curriculum, cannot lightly be dismissed. The contributors provide many practical suggestions for improving education in a multicultural society and for improving delivery of the National Curriculum to all pupils. As such, the varied contributions merit the attention of all citizens in our multiethnic community. Fortunately, for pupils, parents, professionals, schools and communities within our country, the messages contained in the series *are* increasingly being received, considered, modified to fit specific circumstances, and implemented. The last line of Saxe's poem puts the central point concerning both theory and practice that we ignore at our peril. 'Though *each* was *partly* in the right, they *all* were in the wrong.'

Each contributor in each of the four volumes comments under three headings on that aspect of the curriculum in which the contributor has specialist experience and expertise, in relation to cultural diversity. The headings used by all contributors are identified as Context, Challenges and Responses. The views expressed, the analyses of Contexts, the identification of Challenges and the suggestions for Responses represent the considered opinions of the individual contributors.

Volumes 3 and 4 in the series address the primary stage of education. Figure 1.1 shows the NC foundation subjects being taught in the primary school during 1992–3.

These nine subjects comprise up to 540 Statements of Attainments. Does such a curriculum sacrifice depth in order to achieve breadth and balance? In primary schools, the pressures generated by the National Curriculum are leading to a rethinking of the teacher preparation and pedagogy required to deliver such a curriculum. The subject knowledge of primary-school teachers is increasingly being seen as a central issue. The Chief Primary HMI and Deputy-Director of Inspections at the new Office for Standards in Education (OFSTED), Mr J. Rose, is reported as believing that primary teachers should spend more time as specialists in an effort to raise standards. Mounting evidence from inspections was cited as showing that more coherent planning with specialist teaching would benefit pupils. 'It is not the children who have the difficulty in keeping up. We could chance our arm in Primary schools with better divisions of labour' (Nash and Hofkins, 1993). As this increasing specialization takes place, it is vital that subject specialists consider seriously and systematically the implications for the teaching and learning of their subject in a multicultural society.

The thirteen chapters, by sixteen contributors, that comprise this book are divided into two major parts. Part 1 consists of three chapters each addressing ideas central to the theme of the series. In Part 2, consideration is given to the implications of cultural diversity in teaching the nine foundation subjects (and RE). (Although it is an integral part of the National Curriculum, RE is not included in Figure 1.1 as it is not one of the foundation subjects). Additionally, there are three important appendices.

Figure 1.1: *National Curriculum Subjects Being Taught (1992–93)*

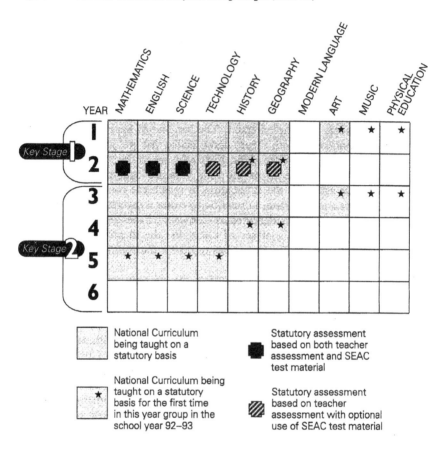

Source: adapted from *Schools Update*, Autumn, 1992

Appendix 1 concerns the implications of race-relations legislation. It has been written by a member of the Commission for Racial Equality (CRE). Appendix 2 lists pertinent curricular publications by the National Curriculum Council (NCC), the Department of Education and Science (DES) and the Department for Education (DFE), the School Examinations and Assessment Council (SEAC) and Her Majesty's Inspectorate (HMI). Appendix 3 includes information on the recently revised Section 11 Funding.

Much remains undecided concerning the structure, content, pedagogy and assessment of many components of the primary-school curriculum. Despite these considerations, and virtually irrespective of the decisions reached concerning them, the multicultural nature of the population and of schools will develop. Demographic data presented in Volume 1, Chapter 3, in Chapter

2 of Volume 2 and in Chapter 3 of this volume, confirm this point and provide indications of the demographic changes that are likely to take place in the future. These demographic changes, and their educational implications, must be considered if the educational system is to respond adequately and fairly.

The editors and contributors have deliberately ventured into this controversial field whilst the 'rules of the curricular game' in state primary schools are still being negotiated in relation to certain aspects of the curriculum. We do so because of the importance with which we view the increasing ethnic, cultural and religious diversity of the school population and of the country. Janus-faced, that diversity represents both problems and opportunities for all parties involved. To deny either would be a disservice to the pupils and the communities that the educational system exists to serve. It would also limit the chances that an education meeting the requirements of the Education Reform Act 1988 would ever be provided.

Our contributors are drawn from various cultural, ethnic and professional backgrounds. Consequently, their respective philosophical and theoretical stances vary. To have sought only individuals operating from a single agreed ideological, philosophical, or theoretical position concerning the nature and curricular implications of cultural diversity, would have implied that the editors considered such a position existed and was the most tenable. Irrespective of the authors' respective ideological, philosophical and theoretical positions, all are clearly concerned with ensuring that the whole curriculum is effectively delivered in our multicultural society. The claim that good practice can help to drive out poor theory, has something to commend it. Belief in the importance of both theoretical analyses of, and the curricular implications and practices deriving from, cultural diversity, unites our contributors.

Let us end this chapter by recalling the concerns with which this chapter began.

- What type of society do you wish your family, friends and fellow citizens to live in?
- How can the younger generation be prepared for life in an increasingly multicultural society?
- What role can education play in such preparation?

References

ALEXANDER, R., ROSE, J. and WOODHEAD, C. (1991) *Curriculum Organization and Classroom Practice in Primary Schools,* London, HMSO.

BRESLAU, K., SULLIVAN, S., NOGORSKI, A. and VIVARELLI, N. (1992) 'Europe's New Right', *Newsweek*, CXIX, 17, pp. 6–11.

COMMISSION FOR RACIAL EQUALITY (1991) *Second Review of the Race Relations Act 1976: A Consultative Paper,* London, CRE.

P.D. Pumfrey

COMMISSION FOR RACIAL EQUALITY (1992) *Race through the 90s*, London, CRE.

COMMITTEE OF INQUIRY INTO THE EDUCATION OF PUPILS FROM MINORITY ETHNIC GROUPS (1985) *Education for All*, Cmnd., 9453, London, HMSO.

DEPARTMENT FOR EDUCATION (1992) *Your Child and the National Curriculum: A parents guide to what is taught in schools*, London, DFE.

DEPARTMENT FOR EDUCATION, NATIONAL CURRICULUM COUNCIL AND SCHOOLS EXAMINATIONS AND ASSESSMENT COUNCIL (1992) 'National Curriculum Subjects being taught 92–93', *Schools Update*, Autumn 1992.

DEPARTMENT OF EDUCATION AND SCIENCE (1989) *National Curriculum: From Policy to Practice*, London, DES and WO.

DEPARTMENT OF EDUCATION AND SCIENCE (1991) *The Parent's Charter: You and Your Child's Education*, London, HMSO.

DESMOND, A. and MOORE, J. (1991) *Darwin*, London, Michael Joseph.

HERCULES, K., SEN, A. and HADDAD, W. (1992) *From Rebellion to Revolution: a strategy for black liberation*, London, Socialist Challenge.

HOLMES, C. (1991) *A Tolerant Country? Immigrants, Refugees and Minorities in Britain*, London, Faber.

LYNCH, J., MODGIL, C. and MODGIL, S. (1992) *Cultural Diversity and the Schools, Vol. 1 Education for Cultural Diversity: Convergence and Divergence*, London, The Falmer Press.

MORTIMORE, P., SAMMONS, P., STOLL, L., LEWIS, D. and ECOB, R. (1988) *School Matters — The Junior Years*, Exeter, Open Books.

NASH, I. and HOFKINS, D. (1993) 'Chief HMI urges greater specialization'. *Times Educational Supplement*, 3933, 8 January, p. 7.

NATIONAL ADVISORY COMMISSION ON CIVIL DISORDERS (1968) *Report of the National Advisory Commission on Civil Disorders*, New York, Bantam Books.

NATIONAL CURRICULUM COUNCIL (1990) *The Whole Curriculum, Curriculum Guidance No. 3*, York, NCC.

NATIONAL CURRICULUM COUNCIL (1990) *The National Curriculum: A guide for parents of primary children*, York, NCC. (translated into Bengali, Chinese, Greek, Gujerati, Hindi, Punjabi, Turkish and Urdu).

PUMFREY, P.D. and VERMA, G.K. (1990) *Race Relations and Urban Education: Contexts and Promising Practices*, Basingstoke, The Falmer Press.

TROYNA, B. and HATCHER, R. (1991) *Racism in Children's Lives*, London, Routledge/National Children's Bureau.

16

Chapter 2

Cultural Diversity in Primary Schools: Its Nature, Extent and Curricular Implications

Gajendra K. Verma

Context

The role of formal education in the increasingly technological complexity and interdependence of modern societies is undoubtedly an important one. Access to education, once the privilege of a small section of the population, is now a basic 'right' for all in many countries. In most developed societies children are required to undergo a stipulated minimum period of compulsory schooling. As societies are becoming more complex, greater reliance is being placed on formal educational structures, going beyond those of compulsory schooling into those of further/higher education.

Educationalists might find it easier to develop the curriculum and achieve explicit educational objectives, equality of opportunity and access to the curriculum if children came from similar socio-economic, cultural, religious and linguistic backgrounds. In a multicultural, multiethnic society the population is composed of a number of distinguishable, albeit overlapping, groups and this inevitably affects the process of education. The educational system thus faces the challenge of a complex reality because of the diversity of the school population. The need for an appropriate 'raft' of responses to achieve the objectives of the ERA (DES, 1988) is a daunting task.

Few would disagree that education is an important vehicle to bring about behavioural and attitudinal changes. Education itself, without the structuring of inputs, is unlikely to have a lasting influence on values.

Over the last three decades or so there has been an increasing awareness of the unequal treatment in the UK of ethnic minorities. There is sufficient evidence to suggest that ethnic minorities have suffered from all sorts of disadvantages in terms of education, careers advancement, welfare, employment and other fields. There are many reasons for their disadvantaged position in society (Pumfrey and Verma, 1990).

Hyman and Wright (1979) in a review of data from thirty-eight national surveys in America, showed that exposure to education had an enduring effect on the values of Whites in matters such as support for civil liberties and equality of opportunity for minorities. Indeed, it would be surprising if education could not have such lasting effects on the values of both its recipients and providers.

Ethnic-minority disquiet about relatively low achievement of their children in the British state educational system is long established: the Rampton report (DES, 1981), the Swann report (DES, 1985) and several government and EEC reports attempted to explain factors contributing to underachievement of ethnic-minority pupils. These include:

- stereotyped attitudes of teachers;
- low expectation among teachers;
- the lack of relevance of the curriculum to ethnic minorities;
- a Eurocentric/Anglocentric curriculum;
- biased assessment and testing procedures;
- poor communication between school and parents;
- racism in the educational system; and
- racial prejudice and discrimination in society at large.

The educational responses since the 1960s to the presence of ethnic minorities in British schools can be seen as movements through three overlapping philosophies based, in turn, upon concepts of assimilation, integration and pluralism. In this process, many strategies and models have been adopted to deal with the disadvantaged position of many ethnic-minority pupils. 'Assimilation' refers to educational strategies designed to make all groups of people adopt the culture of the mainstream. The outcome of such a strategy might be like America, where many minorities have been fully assimilated into the essentially white, middle-class lifestyles that exist today. In such a model there is apparent conflict between cultural values. With the majority group dominating: 'When in Rome, do as the Romans do'. Integration refers to the policy of coordinating the goals of each cultural group, but allowing each group to maintain its culture. It would seem that integration is preferred by some groups in every society. For example, Canada has an integration policy which seems to have the support of many cultural groups. Pluralism regards each ethnic group as having the right to develop and maintain its distinctive cultural and traditional characteristics within a national identity framework.

The development of pluralistic education carries a number of difficulties including the actual identification of ethnic and cultural groups in society, and assessing in a democratic and open manner what the values and aspirations of those group members are (Smolicz, 1980; Lynch, Modgil and Modgil, 1992).

Perhaps the most popular approaches used to provide equality of opportunity are multicultural and antiracist education. These have featured increasingly widely in research reports and in the media, and thence into everyday language of those interested in the educational process. Yet the nature and process of these complementary approaches have rarely been fully explained to, and discussed by, a majority of practitioners.

Multicultural and antiracist ideas in education have undoubtedly made most people aware of many of the issues facing children and adolescents from minority groups. It is also true to say that such ideas do not seem to have met the challenges that face society in the dramatic changes in today's world. However, they have at least helped us to come to terms with the existence and experience of discrimination on the grounds of race or ethnicity and helped us to challenge some of the basic premises in the educational process antithetical to equality of opportunity. Despite this, multicultural and antiracist models of education have failed to change the ideological perceptions of society as a whole. The Swann report (DES, 1985) rightly comments that

> The fundamental change that is necessary is the recognition that the problem facing the education system is not how to educate children of ethnic minorities, but how to educate *all* children — Britain is a multiracial and multicultural society and all pupils must be enabled to understand what this means. (DES, 1985, p. 363)

In recent years, there have been a number of studies published — both large and small-scale — on ethnic-minority educational performance which have produced a variety of results. Encouragingly, some have suggested that the performance of certain subgroups of British Asian youngsters have begun to match that of their white peers (e.g. Chughti, 1993). However, we ought to remain cautious about such findings since the criteria used in assessing performance are subject to wide variations. The vast majority of research findings indicate that ethnic-minority pupils in the UK are underachieving (see Vol. 2, Ch. 12).

In some respects, there has been improvement in recent years with regard to ethnic record keeping at school, LEA and DFE levels, and in other avenues of educational and public life. The inclusion of a question on ethnic origins in the 1991 Census makes the point. The rationale for ethnic monitoring as a tool is that it is a means towards the end of ensuring equal opportunities. It is hoped that ethnic record keeping is the starting point for working towards social justice and for complying with anti-discrimination legislation. In time, this should contribute towards a better understanding of the plural reality of education in Britain.

Analyses of ethnic diversity and the demands for a pluralist approach to education take us into the broader framework of mainstream services catering for *all* children. A framework of appreciation of diversity, with recognition of the potential for enhancement of opportunities for all, is essential to the development of pluralist approaches and methods. The creation of such a framework is the implicit aim of many equal-opportunities policies and practices. As we all know however, reality falls far short of theory. Unfair discrimination and racism remain potent everyday realities to members of many minority ethnic, religious and cultural groups.

A common ambiguity inherent in the concept of cultural pluralism is the confusion and interchangeable use of the concepts of 'race', 'ethnicity' and 'culture'. Consequently, in any discussion concerning education in a culturally pluralist society this is exemplified by the frequent use of interchangeable terms such as 'multicultural', 'multiethnic', 'multiracial' and so on, indicating degrees of cultural differentiation. In such usage an ethnic group is usually defined on the basis of cultural criteria. Unlike the term 'race', which has its foundations in physical distinctiveness, the term 'ethnic group' is associated with social structures and shared values, implying the existence of an 'ethnic identity'.

It would seem more appropriate to describe contemporary Britain as a society of ethnic communities, each with its distinct culture or ways of thought and life. They are not just cultural groups but ethnic communities. Thus, the various Asian and Caribbean communities are ethnic in nature, that is, physically distinguishable, bonded by social ties arising out of shared customs, language and practice of intermarriage, and having their distinct history, collective memories, geographical origins, views of life and modes of social organization.

One of the theoretical aspects which has given rise to confused thinking in the area of multicultural education is the notion of defining culture primarily in terms of ethnicity. Such a perspective assumes that there are single Chinese, Indian, West Indian, Pakistani or English cultures. Such an oversimplified and stereotyped definition does not allow for two important factors. First, a 'culture' is not a static entity. It is dynamic and changes over time in interaction with political, economic, ecological and social factors. Second, a 'culture' is not objective; any attempt to describe it must allow for the way in which it is perceived by different individuals living in that particular culture. Personal experience may well dictate a different attitude to, or perception of, some specific aspect of a shared culture. Collectively, these differences may well be of considerable importance to individuals or subgroups within those having what seems superficially to be a 'shared' culture.

Challenges

How did the Education Reform Act (DES, 1988) respond to the ethnic diversity of late-twentieth century Britain? The opening section of the Act states that the curriculum of a school meets the requirements of the Act if 'it is a balanced and broadly based curriculum which:

    (a) promotes the spiritual, moral, cultural, mental and physical development of pupils at the school and of society;
        and

(b) prepares such pupils for the opportunities, responsibilities and ex-periences of adult life.'

The 1988 Act was followed by the DES Circular 5/89, dated 22 February 1989 pointing out that this Act 'emphasises the need for breadth and balance in what pupils study' and that 'cultural development and the development of society should be promoted'. The Circular further added that: 'it is intended that the curriculum should reflect the culturally diverse society to which pupils belong and of which they will become adult members.'

A document by the DES titled 'DES Guidance for Schools: From Policy to Practice, 1990' was produced to guide headteachers and governors to im-plement the new legal requirements. This document made it clear that 'More will . . . be needed to secure the kind of curriculum required by Section 1 of the ERA. The whole curriculum for all pupils will certainly need to include . . . coverage across the curriculum of gender and multicultural issues.'

Another DES Circular 16/89, dated 25 July 1989, was issued concerned with the collection of ethnically-based data. It stated that the purpose of col-lecting such data is 'to help secure equality of opportunity for ethnic minority pupils'. The Circular emphasized the importance of learner-centred approaches to curriculum planning.

In 1990 the National Curriculum Council (NCC, 1990) produced a docu-ment entitled 'Guidance Document on the Whole Curriculum'. This docu-ment also emphasized, like the DES document, 'a commitment to providing equal opportunities for all pupils, and a recognition that preparation for life in a multicultural society is relevant to all pupils, should permeate every aspect of the curriculum.'

In February 1991 the National Curriculum Council (NCC, 1991) pub-lished an article in *Schools Update*, its regular newsletter, entitled 'A Pluralist Society in the Classroom and Beyond'. In this article the NCC stated that the National Curriculum 'contributes to multicultural education by broadening the horizons of all pupils so that they can understand and contribute to a pluralist society'. The NCC has issued other circulars and newsletters since 1990 dealing with other issues such as equal opportunity, equal access, bilin-gualism, cultural pluralism etc. (See Appendix 2).

It is clear from the above that the introduction of a centralized common National Curriculum was intended to provide guidance as to the nature of a curriculum which all pupils are entitled to receive. It can be assumed therefore that, if certain pupils are unable to receive this curriculum for one reason or another, they could be said to be treated unequally.

An in-depth analysis of the curriculum suggests that minority cultures *have* been neglected in the development of core and foundation subjects, and therefore, ethnic-minority pupils *are* at a disadvantage. The fundamental question as to what curricular knowledge is essential to provide equal chances of success for minority pupils is still open to debate. Many children and young people are presented with an Anglocentric curriculum which is not only alien and exclusive, but one which obliterates the reality of their ethnic identity and experience. The identity of such groups is usually referred to as their culture and may be defined as a pool of values, attitudes, beliefs and behaviours to which its members largely subscribe. They are transmitted by the group, primarily but not exclusively by their parents, to children maturing within it and form the major influence on the development of their individual identities. The extent to which particular individuals see themselves as members of that cultural or 'ethnic' group and the extent to which they are accepted as members of that group is determined by the relative importance of the cultural identity to the individuals in respect of their own identity formation.

Britain, particularly in certain urban areas, is demographically multicultural, with a variety of ethnic-minority groups practising cultural values, beliefs, attitudes and behaviours which differ from those of the largely Christian white British majority. This situation raises important questions over the identity formation of children and young adults who are in regular contact with more than one cultural group. The introduction of the National Curriculum was an excellent opportunity to recognize differences in terms of ethnicity and culture in our society. This could have made a positive contribution to the development of pluralist goals. We have instead a curriculum which might have been thought to eliminate cultural differences — not by denying the values, beliefs and customs of other cultures but by assuming that they do not even exist!

A glance through the explicit goals of the National Curriculum suggests that it seeks

- to improve the quality of the education received by *all* children and young people in the maintained sector;
- to achieve a greater balance in the scope of the education received than was available before; and
- to achieve a high degree of uniformity in the education as received in different areas of the country.

Few would disagree that such goals would have a high level of acceptance amongst people since these would seem to be common sense goals, and to be fair.

The controversy has developed with regard to the detailed statements on content, purpose within the individual subject areas and on methods of assessment in behavioural terms. At the heart of the assessment process are nationally prescribed tests to be taken by all pupils. Despite legitimate concerns about aspects of their work, English primary schools remain the envy of much of the world, and had certainly developed new approaches to teaching, generally recognized as highly effective. In the National Curriculum there is an obvious attempt to force subject-based teaching back into the upper primary school. People have to wait and see as the impact of the National Curriculum comes to play an ever-increasing part in education, and what is still largely a blueprint becomes a reality. It is a tragedy that the research required to explicate processes and evaluate outcomes in relation to equal opportunities is woefully neglected by the government.

Responses

The implementation of the 1988 Education Reform Act — a catalyst for major change in education policy and practice — has inevitably brought concerns and challenges in the realization of pluralist goals, particularly in terms of addressing pupils' cultural, religious and linguistic diversity. It is rather early to determine the impact of national and local educational change on equality in education for pluralism. Some believe that the introduction of the National Curriculum will give our system a much needed metaphorical shot in the arm; that no reform can guarantee quality unless the educational system undergoes a revolution of expectations (Figueroa, 1991).

Whilst the ERA has instituted central direction over the National Curriculum content and the assessment process, management and finances have been devolved to schools with an increased parental choice. This policy has obviously generated new controversies and issues.

It is clear that the objectives, content and assessment procedures in the National Curriculum of primary education are not only monocultural and narrow, but largely assimilationist in their orientation. Analysis of various reports and comments show that very little, if any, account has been taken of cultural, linguistic and religious diversity represented by minority groups in our society. The National Curriculum has largely ignored the contributions by non-western countries to English, mathematics, science, technology, history, music, art and physical education.

It is not possible within the scope of this chapter to discuss all the issues relating to the content and assessment of the National Curriculum in primary education. Nonetheless, a few key issues taken from individual subjects will be mentioned here. They illustrate the argument about the curriculum's overall character and offer a foretaste of the range of issues raised by individual 'subject' authors in this volume.

Religious education is always a controversial issue within the educational system in a plural society. In the National Curriculum all state schools are required to make Christianity the basis of religious education and give children a 'broadly Christian' act of daily worship. Given the religious diversity of many of the urban schools, it is unfortunate that the Act has set schools and certain religious communities on a collision course. Many headteachers and teachers in primary schools are uncertain how to deal with the issue of religious education, particularly where the school population is composed of children from differing religious backgrounds.

The wide spectrum of religious beliefs in Britain today is an example of the diversity of a multicultural society. The multifaith approach would seem to be the only teaching strategy that accords with the basic principles of cultural pluralism and the philosophy of 'Education for All'. A primary aim in a school's religious-education curriculum should be to create an ethos where children develop respect for others' beliefs. Religious experience is often a central element in 'ethnic identity' which is essential to cultural maintenance (see Chapter 4 in this volume). The question has been raised by many ethnic communities as to whether the religious traditions of all children are treated with equal respect!

Few would deny the significance of language in ordering one's social and cultural experiences. Yet, analysis of the English National Curriculum shows that little has changed, despite efforts by many teachers and schools to provide equality of opportunity in the presence of linguistic and cultural diversity (see Chapter 5 in this volume). It is well-known that English texts in schools are dominated by white English writers. Many of their writings have often perpetuated negative cultural stereotypes of Africans, Asians, Chinese, Japanese and many others.

The terms of reference to the working group of the National Curriculum in English did not specify cultural diversity but asked them to consider the multicultural nature of British society. The working group was also asked to present the English subject proposals into workable PoS and SoAs for schools.

In spite of receiving minimal guidance from the National Curriculum Council, many teachers, particularly in multiethnic schools, have been trying to adopt methods and materials to meet the linguistic and cultural needs of their school (see Chapter 5 in this volume). However, there are primary schools where linguistic diversity is still minimally encouraged and thereby children's home cultures are either marginalized or ignored. Many educationists believe that without coherent and systematic school policies relating to linguistic diversity in the English curriculum, the efforts of individual teachers, however committed, are likely to be ineffective (see Chapter 5 for a detailed discussion as to how challenges posed by the English National Curriculum can begin to be met by teachers and schools). The indications are that the 1993 revision of the English curriculum is likely to make a difficult situation worse insofar as the acceptance of cultural diversity is concerned.

There is a naive assumption by many people that mathematics is a culturally free subject. Chapter 6 in this volume discusses many of the examples of biases in the development of the mathematics National Curriculum. It also shows how teaching of mathematics can be done within a multicultural context. Such an approach of teaching will develop positive images of students from all cultures and provide real contexts for pupils in achievement.

The science National Curriculum has adopted a more positive approach to cultural diversity. Although the science curriculum for primary education makes reference to cultural and linguistic backgrounds of children, there is confusion and misunderstanding amongst the teaching profession (see Chapter

7). Furthermore, as some commentators point out, the shortage of primary-school science teachers coupled with a requirement that cultural-diversity aspect of the subject be addressed in the curriculum, the task is indeed challenging for the school and teachers.

Technology, like any other subjects, offers the potential for a multicultural and antiracist approach within the framework set out in the National Curriculum for primary schools. It is interesting to note that 'The 1990 Order for Technology in the National Curriculum contains, within the Statements of Attainment, many references to consideration of the multicultural dimension' (see Chapter 8 for a more detailed discussion). However, much depends on the exploitation of the aims of the syllabus (PoS). Success in attaining the goals of pluralism also depends on the resources, experience of the individual schools and teachers, and on the professional and material support offered. That would enable school staff to translate the NC contents into practice, adopting a pluralist approach, that facilitates achieving the objectives of the whole curriculum.

It should be mentioned at the outset that the history curriculum was designed by a group of people who had never taught in primary schools, and it was they who largely determined the content of the history syllabus. Analysis of the history syllabus shows that it does not foster cultural diversity. Although the history working group accepted in principle the multicultural nature of British society, they argued the case for including a substantial element of British history within primary education. The fundamental issue within the curriculum is that of Anglocentrism, which concentrates heavily on proclaiming the glory of Britain, and the way it affects the delivery of a balanced curriculum (see Chapter 9). It is widely accepted that the history syllabus adopts an assimilationist perspective.

Many geography teachers in primary schools have expressed their concern that the content of the National Curriculum makes it difficult for them to relate their classwork to fast changing events, nationally and globally. The curriculum heavily concentrates on Britain and largely ignores the rest of the world. Pupils at Key Stages 1 and 2 are required to study their own locality. A problem arises with all white schools where children will have no opportunity to study the culturally diverse nature of British society. Furthermore, analysis of the geography content indicates that teachers are expected to teach pupils about a world which is largely white, middle-class British (see Chapter 10). Concern has also been expressed that requirements to teach the names of specific places in the geography syllabus could reinforce stereotypes and negative images of the developing world.

An examination of the music National Curriculum for primary schools shows that there is a lack of understanding as to what music education is about. Music is a very personal experience and understandably the argument as to the 'legitimacy' of what constitutes 'music' is largely unresolved in the National Curriculum. The music of other cultures is unfamiliar to most British teachers. There is also a shortage of useful material for the teaching of world music in primary schools. All too often the esoteric values of what is 'culture' overlook the important dimension of personal experience (see Chapter 11 for further discussion).

One of the underlying assumptions of the National Curriculum is that it is a curriculum for *all*. Yet, it is obvious that the multicultural dimension was an afterthought in the design of National Curriculum art. Art is also an area of subjective experience. Aesthetics tend to be largely culture-specific. Commentators have expressed the concern that statements about cultural diversity reflect a superficial token coverage of the subject. The final report of the art working group sets out what is common in cases of good practice. There is no mention of multicultural art, but there is emphasis on the development of primary-school children's confidence and skill and the valuing of the individual's responses (for a more detailed discussion, see Chapter 12).

The recommendations of the physical education working party included little reference to cultural diversity. On the face of it the physical education curriculum seems to have the potential to cater for cultural diversity. A closer examination of the relevant documents and reports suggests that physical education like other foundation subjects is largely monocultural, narrow and nationalistic (see Chapter 13). However, this does not mean that the committed teacher is not able to adopt non-racist teaching strategies whilst teaching PE at Key Stages 1 and 2.

In the context of the pluralist nature of British society, key national-policy statements can be highlighted to support cultural diversity. For example, one of the aims of the ERA for a curriculum which 'promotes the . . . cultural development of pupils at school and of society' should be more strongly emphasized by the NCC. It should also be highlighted that British culture may be enriched by utilizing the viewpoints of the many minority cultures that exist in society today, rather than trying to force pupils to adopt a monocultural, parochial viewpoint which may in the long run reduce creativity and the chances of effective adjustment in a fast changing world.

Another aspect of the teaching process is the 'hidden curriculum'. The formal changes are likely to come from the prescribed curriculum process which may teach knowledge, facts and competencies, but the hidden curriculum has a complementary and powerful part to play in bringing about the changes in values and attitudes to complete the process of personal adaptation. For example, it may be damaging to the self-esteem of ethnic minorities if school expectations are insensitive to, and dismissive of, cultural and religious backgrounds with respect to school uniform, girls' dress for physical education and meals. Pastoral arrangements must not force pupils and parents into a position of conflict between the requirements of the home and those of the school.

Educational change rarely takes place in a tidy or uniform fashion. When issues of culture and schooling are involved, it would be naive to think that it could. Such issues have generated debate and discussion about the nature of our society and its future social cohesion, and they will continue to do so. There is, however, a sense that a climate of acceptance of Britain as plural society is slowly emerging. It may be argued that this is due, in part, to the persistence of minority groups who are determined to make educational institutions and structures more responsive to their needs. There is evidence, too, to suggest that minority groups are developing political skills to effect changes they seek.

Acknowledging the ethnic, religious and cultural diversity of the population of the UK is a *contextual* imperative for all citizens. Awareness of the *challenges* this presents in the delivery of the whole curriculum to all pupils is another. In all aspects of the curriculum, teachers are beginning to develop constructive *responses* based on the principle of equality of opportunity. We have far to go; but the 'long march' has begun.

References

CHUGHTI, I. (1993) 'Dialect interference and the reading attainments of Asian bilingual children in England', unpublished Ph.D thesis, University of Manchester School of Education.

DEPARTMENT OF EDUCATION AND SCIENCE (1981) *West Indian Children in Our Schools: Report of the Committee of Inquiry into the Education of Children from Ethnic Minority Groups* (The Rampton Report) Cmnd., 8273, London, HMSO.

DEPARTMENT OF EDUCATION AND SCIENCE (1985) *Education for All: Report of the Committee of Inquiry into the Education of Children from Ethnic Minority Groups* (The Swann Report) Cmnd., 9453, London, HMSO.

DEPARTMENT OF EDUCATION AND SCIENCE (1988) *The Education Reform Act 1988*, London, HMSO.

DEPARTMENT OF EDUCATION AND SCIENCE (1990) *Guidance for Schools: From Policy to Practice*, London, HMSO.

FIGUEROA, P. (1991) *Education and the Social Construction of 'Race'*, London, Routledge.

HYMAN, H. and WRIGHT, C. (1979) *Education's Lasting Influence on Values*, Chicago, University of Chicago Press.

LYNCH, J., MODGIL, C. and MODGIL, S. (Eds) (1992) *Cultural Diversity and the Schools. Vol. I. Education for Cultural Diversity: Convergence and Divergence*, London, The Falmer Press.

NATIONAL CURRICULUM COUNCIL (1990) *Introducing the National Curriculum*, York, NCC.

PUMFREY, P.D. and VERMA, G.K. (1990) *Race Relations and Urban Education: Promising Practices*, London, The Falmer Press.

SMOLICZ, J. (1980) *Culture and Education in a Plural Society*, Adelaide, Curriculum Development Centre.

Chapter 3

The Whole, Basic and National Curriculum in Primary Schools: Context, Challenges and Responses

Peter D. Pumfrey

Context

Headlines, such as 'Secretary of State for Education slates teachers', are resented by members of the profession when the basis of the criticism is suspect. Fewer proverbs are metaphorically more suspect that 'Sticks and stones may break my bones, but words can never hurt me'. 'The word is mightier than the sword' is its counterpart. We are all vulnerable.

Irrespective of the curriculum, name-calling in schools (and in society generally) is common. It has acceptable and unacceptable faces. In schools within a multicultural society, racist name-calling as a form of verbal harassment is one of its unacceptable forms. Unfortunately, it is frequent in secondary schools (Cohn, 1988; Kelly, 1990) and also in primary schools (Troyna and Hatcher, 1991) (see Chapter 1).

As teachers in primary schools looking at the youngsters in one's class, we are looking at the nation's future. It is salutory to bear in mind that the following individual is but one product of our educational and social systems. 'You were driven by an evil, senseless, barbaric and gloating hatred of Pakistanis.' Thus spoke Mr Justice Moreland when sentencing 25-year-old Wayne Lambert to two life sentences at Manchester Crown Court in January 1993. Lambert had pleaded guilty to the murder of Mohammed Dada, a 60-year-old Withington shopkeeper, and Mohammed Ansari, a 47-year-old taxi driver and father of six. Both victims died from head injuries caused by blows from a metal tube. Also in the dock were three others: a 22-year-old woman and two youths aged 17 and 18 years respectively. It is reported that, after his arrest, Lambert said 'I hate Pakis. I'll only be 43 when I get out and I'll kill another one.'

The potent reality of xenophobia is highlighted by such extreme cases. Fortunately, they are rare. Sadly, there is evidence that the harassment of members of minority ethnic groups is severe and extensive (Commission for

Racial Equality, 1992). The individual racism manifest in Lambert's acts and the less visible but pervasive institutional racism that permeates society has to be acknowledged, if it is to be addressed (Evans, 1992).

As an agent of society, the educational system has an important role to play in helping to produce citizens who can live relatively harmoniously in a multicultural society. Each individual, family, community and society shares this responsibility. It is one cost of the valued rights of citizenship in a democratic society. Whilst the formal educational system is but one means of socialization, the values it transmits contribute significantly to the cohesion of society.

The Education Reform Act 1988 represents radical political pressure for change. The whole endeavour is an act of political faith in the efficacy of market mechanisms in improving systems and making them responsive to the wishes of the 'consumer'. Its purpose is to change the state system of education because of its perceived inadequacies. For many years, the management and financing of education will be in a state of flux. In this period of continuing change, it is imperative that those involved in education have a sense of direction concerning where education in this multicultural society can lead us. It is possible that the content and delivery of a curriculum can increase understanding between ethnic, religious and cultural groups. It can also achieve the opposite, despite the best intentions.

Objectives of the Whole Curriculum

Under the provisions of Section 1 of the ERA 1988, all maintained schools are required to provide

a balanced and broadly based curriculum which —
(a) promotes the spiritual, moral, cultural, mental and physical development of pupils at the school and of society: and
(b) prepares such pupils for the opportunities, responsibilities and experiences of adult life.

The inclusion of the word 'cultural' in the above list of five key facets of development merits comment. It denotes an explicit political acknowledgment of the importance of cultural diversity in our society, and of the complex interactions between all five aims in the context of education.

Let us turn from Parliament to the primary school. Listen to Sybil Marshall, teacher, teacher-trainer and the author of *Experiment in Education* and *Adventure in Creative Education*, two extremely influential books on primary education. The words come from her preface to a book based on the experiences of a white teacher working with pupils from minority ethnic groups.

The advent of a significant number of coloured immigrants, and their accumulation in large cities . . . has presented a new situation to which we have previously not been accustomed. As the numbers grew, we were aware of questions that needed answering, of differences and difficulties; these were human questions about day to day existence, and the difficulties of adjusting to each other's cultures, when people of different races, colours and beliefs had to live in close proximity. Then politics — on both sides — stepped in, and common-sense departed. 'Questions' have become 'problems', to which solutions are 'demanded'; arguments have turned into 'causes' and 'difficulties' spell 'trouble'. 'Differences' changed to division, and controversy such as 'freedom' and 'equality' have become dangerous in the mind and dynamite on the tongue, for they generate an impassioned oratory, virulent journalism, banner-waving 'demos' and private violence in the back streets. (Scott, 1971)

In the UK in the 1990s, there is little doubt that we are now a multicultural society. In any society, fear and mistrust between groups whether ethnic, cultural, religious or social, breeds further antipathies. During a recession, when unemployment is high, xenophobia rapidly raises its head.

There are potential dangers in the identification of individuals by ethnic group. When the issue was discussed prior to the 1991 census, the reasons adduced for collecting such data included the following points:

- To facilitate policy planning and resource allocation by local government, particularly in the areas of education, housing, environmental health, personal social services and employment.
- To ensure that the particular needs of minority ethnic groups are met and the effectiveness of programmes monitored.
- To ensure that programmes could be targeted appropriately.
- To provide a data base for local authorities to use in local surveys.
- To assist in the allocation of finance to local authorities under the 1966 Local Government Act in general and Section 11 in particular (see Appendix 3).
- To help in allocating finance to local authorities under the Urban Programme.
- To assist in determining investment in housing.
- To help in implementing race-relations and equal-opportunity legislation.
- To develop a demographic database for use in combatting racism.

A widespread ignorance exists concerning the sizes of minority ethnic groups in relation to each other and to the majority. Teachers in training and qualified teachers in the UK have been shown to lack correct information (Cohen, 1989; Pumfrey and Verma, 1990). Would you be able to list, by size, the rank order of the minority ethnic groups resident in this country? Do *you* have an appreciation of the relative sizes of these groups?

Challenging misinformation with facts is a sound strategy. An apprecia- tion of the estimated sizes of various ethnic groups in the population is one starting point. A knowledge of demography is essential. There exists wide- spread ignorance of such basic information. Its interpretation requires con- siderable care.

The Office of Population Censuses and Surveys regularly collects demo- graphic data including that on the sizes and distributions of ethnic groups (Haskey, 1990; 1991). Table 3.1 estimates changes in the sizes of various ethnic-minority groups over the period 1981–8. The annual average increase in the ethnic-minority population was estimated at 'just over 80 thousand per year'. (ibid., p. 35). 51 per cent of the total ethnic-minority population was of Indian, Pakistani or Bangladeshi ethnic origins. Those of West Indian ori- gins comprised about 20 per cent and approximately one in nine was of mixed ethnic origins. The numbers and proportions of each group change over time.

In view of the history of this island, the apparent assumption that the ethnic white majority is *not* of mixed ethnic origins, is intriguing and chal- lenging! For example, individuals remain proud of their origins as English, Scottish, Welsh, Irish, or any combination of these and myriad other nation- alities. Can the UK become an ethnic, religious and cultural 'melting pot' in which the stages of immigrant and minority ethnic-group assimilation, inte- gration and multiculturalism can coexist?

The distribution of ethnic groups by age bands is presented in Table 3.2. The implications for educational provision and for future demographic changes are considerable. There are significant variations between the ethnic groups in the proportions of children who are under school age, of school age and also of those over the age of 60 years.

A minimum of 90 per cent of ethnic-minority children under the age of 5 years have been born in the UK. There are marked variations in these proportions between ethnic groups. Ethnic-minority populations with the oldest age profiles have, unsurprisingly, been resident in the UK for longer than those groups with the younger age profiles. Irrespective of minority ethnic group, the younger the individual, the greater the probability that he/ she was born in the UK. For many reasons, the proportions of ethnic-minority groups born in the UK and elsewhere, vary considerably. The effects of policies in Uganda in 1972 and of an exodus of Asians from Kenya during the 1960s and 1970s contribute towards the 18 per cent of Indians who were born in East Africa. The impending return of Hong Kong to China is already having an effect on migration to other countries, including the UK.

Minority ethnic groups often form communities in particular locations. These groups cohere and grow as new members arrive and as children are born. The density of distribution of minority ethnic groups by county across this country is consequently uneven. The reasons for this are important. A demographic overview is shown in Figure 3.1. The so-called 'White Highlands'

Table 3.1: Population by Ethnic Group, 1981–88, Great Britain

Ethnic group	Percentage 1981	Estimated population (thousands) 1981	1986	1987	1988	1986–88 (average)	Sample numbers 1986–88 (average)	Percentages* 1986–88 (average)	Percentages*	Change in population 1981–1986/88 Thousands	%
West Indian†	25	528	526	489	468	495	1,340	19	0.9	– 33	– 6
African	4	80	98	116	122	112	298	4	0.2	+ 32	+ 39
Indian	35	727	784	761	814	787	2,138	31	1.4	+ 59	+ 8
Pakistani	14	284	413	392	479	428	1,169	17	0.8	+144	+ 51
Bangladeshi	2	52	117	116	91	108	289	4	0.2	+ 56	+109
Chinese	4	92	113	126	136	125	343	5	0.2	+ 33	+ 36
Arab	3	53	73	79	66	73	188	3	0.1	+ 20	+ 38
Mixed	10	217	269	263	328	287	801	11	0.5	+ 70	+ 32
Other	3	60	164	141	184	163	429	6	0.3	+103	+173
All ethnic minority groups	100	2,092	2,559	2,484	2,687	2,577	6,994	100	4.7	+485	+ 23
White	—	51,000	51,204	51,573	51,632	51,470	144,745	—	94.4	+470	+ 1
Not stated	—	608	607	467	343	472	1,540	—	0.9	–136	– 22
All ethnic groups	—	53,700	54,370	54,524	54,662	54,519	153,279	—	100.0	+819	+ 2

* Derived from grossed-up estimates (column 6)
† Includes Guyanese
Note: averages have been calculated using unrounded figures
Sources: 1981, 1986, 1987, and 1988 Labour Force Surveys quoted in Haskey, 1990.

Table 3.2: Population by Age and Ethnic Group, 1986–88, Great Britain

percentages

Ethnic group	Age-group											All ages		Males per 100 females
	Under 1	1–4	5–9	10–14	15–19	20–24	25–34	35–44	45–59	60 and over	Pensionable age*	%	Thousands	
West Indian†	2	8	7	7	10	14	16	9	20	7	5	100	495	94
African	(2)	8	8	8	8	13	20	17	12	3	(2)	100	112	120
Indian	2	9	10	8	9	10	20	14	14	5	4	100	787	100
Pakistani	2	13	15	11	10	9	16	10	11	2	2	100	428	107
Bangladeshi	3	17	14	13	9	7	15	8	13	2	(1)	100	108	124
Chinese	(1)	7	10	10	8	9	23	18	9	5	4	100	125	101
Arab	(2)	8	7	(4)	5	12	28	17	11	6	(4)	100	73	163
Mixed	5	18	17	12	13	10	11	7	6	3	3	100	287	93
Other	2	9	9	7	7	10	20	18	11	6	5	100	163	100
All ethnic minority groups	2	10	11	9	10	10	18	12	13	5	4	100	2,577	102
White	1	5	6	6	7	8	14	14	17	21	19	100	51,470	95
Not stated	3	7	8	9	9	9	14	12	13	18	16	100	472	95
All ethnic groups	1	5	6	6	8	8	14	14	16	20	18	100	54,519	95

* 65 and over for men. 60 and over for women
† Includes Guyanese
Note: Figures in brackets are based on a sample of fewer than 30
Sources: 1986, 1987, and 1988 Labour Force Surveys quoted in Haskey, 1990

Figure 3.1: Ethnic-Minority Population as a Percentage of the Total Population, by County, 1986–1988

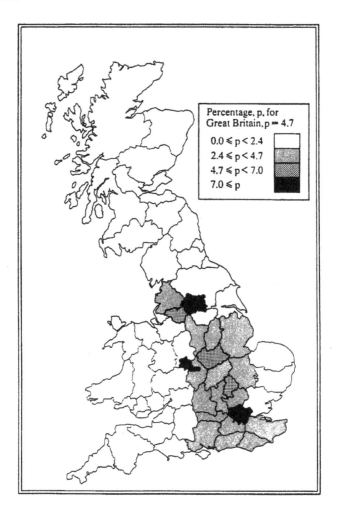

Source: Haskey, 1991
Notes: Percentage is estimated — Region instead of County for Scotland

can be broadly identified. This does not mean that education for cultural diversity is the concern of *only* a part of Great Britain.

A more detailed analysis of the information presented in Figure 3.1 is given in Table 3.3. Estimates of minority ethnic populations in various regions of Great Britain are presented. There are great variations from area to area. Within the London boroughs, Brent has the highest concentration

Table 3.3: *Estimated Ethnic Minority Populations in the Control Areas* of great Britain, 1986–1988 (standard regions, metropolitan counties, regional remainders, and countries)*

thousands

Control areas* (SRs/MCs/RRs/countries)	Ethnic group										All ethnic minority groups	White	All ethnic groups‡
	West Indian†	African	Indian	Pakistani	Bangladeshi	Chinese	Arab	Mixed	Other			
North	1.8	0.6	5.1	14.2	6.5	4.2	1.6	6.0	1.6	42	2,982	3,042
Tyne and Wear MC	0.5	0.3	2.5	5.7	5.6	2.3	1.2	2.2	0.5	21	1,094	1,124
Remainder of North	1.3	0.3	2.6	8.5	1.0	1.9	0.4	3.8	1.2	21	1,887	1,918
Yorkshire and Humberside	24.1	3.7	44.2	86.9	5.7	7.8	5.5	19.9	6.9	205	4,610	4,847
South Yorkshire MC	6.1	0.4	2.5	6.9	0.5	2.8	1.9	4.8	2.3	28	1,247	1,286
West Yorkshire MC	17.5	2.0	38.0	79.7	5.2	2.1	3.4	10.6	3.9	162	1,856	2,031
Remainder of Yorkshire and Humberside	0.5	1.3	3.7	0.2	0.0	2.9	0.1	4.6	0.7	14	1,508	1,530
East Midlands	16.4	1.4	88.0	15.3	3.5	7.0	2.0	17.2	5.9	157	3,708	3,899
East Anglia	3.4	1.0	6.3	10.8	0.3	4.6	0.1	9.3	5.2	41	1,925	1,982
South East	322.8	86.8	418.0	119.5	66.0	71.1	39.8	152.6	118.4	1,395	15,438	16,997
Greater London	288.2	77.4	333.3	72.0	51.2	50.8	31.4	103.5	91.8	1,100	5,462	6,640
Inner London LBs	187.9	57.8	67.6	27.2	42.5	25.1	19.6	55.1	47.6	530	1,876	2,434
Outer London LBs	100.3	19.6	265.7	44.7	8.7	25.7	11.8	48.4	44.2	569	3,586	4,205
Remainder of South East	34.6	9.4	84.7	47.5	14.8	20.4	8.3	49.1	26.6	295	9,976	10,358

Table 3.3: (Cont.)

thousands

Control areas* (SRs/MCs/RRs/countries)	Ethnic group										White	All ethnic groups‡
	West Indian†	African	Indian	Pakistani	Bangladeshi	Chinese	Arab	Mixed	Other	All ethnic minority groups	White	All ethnic groups‡
South West	13.5	2.2	10.9	1.0	1.4	6.4	2.9	12.5	3.4	54	4,406	4,494
West Midlands	83.8	3.1	147.6	82.6	17.8	4.1	4.1	26.0	8.1	377	4,729	5,140
West Midlands MC	77.1	3.1	130.4	70.4	17.0	1.5	3.7	17.5	5.0	326	2,256	2,600
Remainder of West Midlands	6.7	0.0	17.2	12.2	0.8	2.6	0.4	8.4	3.1	51	2,473	2,539
North West	24.6	9.7	56.5	75.4	4.9	12.4	7.2	27.7	10.1	228	5,989	6,289
Greater Manchester MC	20.0	2.3	36.0	46.8	3.5	5.2	3.3	13.2	3.5	134	2,397	2,560
Merseyside MC	0.4	5.4	2.8	0.5	0.8	4.0	2.7	8.4	3.0	28	1,395	1,435
Remainder of North West	4.2	2.0	17.7	28.1	0.5	3.2	1.2	6.1	3.6	67	2,197	2,294
England	490.5	108.4	776.6	405.6	106.0	117.5	63.2	271.1	159.6	2,499	43,788	46,690
Wales	3.1	1.3	5.1	5.4	1.2	3.4	5.0	9.6	1.0	35	2,739	2,804
Scotland	0.9	2.3	4.8	17.0	0.9	4.1	4.6	6.1	2.4	43	4,943	5,025
Central Clydeside Conurbation	0.1	0.0	2.4	15.5	0.6	2.4	2.5	1.3	0.1	25	1,609	1,635
Remainder of Scotland	0.8	2.3	2.4	1.5	0.4	1.7	2.1	4.8	2.2	18	3,334	3,390
Great Britain	494.6	112.0	786.5	428.0	108.1	125.0	72.7	286.8	163.0	2,577	51,470	54,519

Components may not add to totals. because of rounding
* See text for definition of control areas — for completeness, other areas have also been included above.
† Includes Guyanese.
‡ Includes not stated ethnic group.
Source: 1986, 1987 and 1988 Labour Force Surveys, quoted in Haskey, 1991

Table 3.4: *Ethnic-Group Size Provisional Estimates for England and Wales Based on the 1991 Census*

(thousands)	N.	%
White	46,940	94.1
Black Caribbean	496	1.0
Black African	209	0.4
Black Other	175	0.4
Indian	828	1.7
Pakistani	455	0.9
Bangladeshi	161	0.3
Chinese	143	0.3
Other groups		
(a) Asian	189	0.4
(b) others	280	0.6

estimated at 27 per cent. Gateshead, in Tyne and Wear metropolitan county has the lowest concentration of minority ethnic groups at 1 per cent. The information contained in Tables 1–3 and Figure 3.1 represent estimates based on Labour Force surveys. In time, the 1991 Census results will provide updates on the figures.

Thanks to the cooperation and permission of the Office of Population Censuses and Surveys (OPCS), it is possible to present some preliminary information obtained from the 1991 census concerning the ethnic composition of the population of England and Wales. The categories used to group individuals by ethnicity were agreed between representatives of interested parties prior to the census. These categories are somewhat different from those used in the preceding tables and from the overview presented in Chapter 1. Table 3.4 summarizes the overall position in England and Wales. Provisional estimates exist for each of the OPCS fifty-five geographical areas in England and Wales. The Centre for Research in Ethnic Relations has recently published a paper on the settlement patterns of ethnic minorities in Great-Britain based on the 1991 Census data (Owen, 1992).

The above patterns will continue to change in predictable ways. Accepting and maintaining ethnic identities, beliefs and values in a culturally diverse democratic society requires tolerance and understanding by all parties. All too readily we claim highly valued rights as members of a democratic society; all too easily we forget our reciprocal and inevitable responsibilities on which such hard won rights depend. Further analyses based on the 1991 census will be presented in Volume 4.

The Legal Context

In the United Kingdom, we have some of the most forward looking race-relations legislation in Europe. It aims to prohibit both individual and institutional manifestations and operations of racism. Teachers and schools must consider the ethical and legal contexts of race relations if they are to understand how the National Curriculum can incorporate cultural diversity. Fortunately, readily available discussions of these issues are available (Kloss, 1990; Lee, 1990; Commission for Racial Equality, 1992).

Challenges

Whether in Britain or the Balkans, in all countries, national identity is likely to remain a potent concept. The 'whole' of that identity is much more than the sum of its ethnic, religious or culturally distinctive 'parts'. In the UK, the dynamic equilibrium between the values, beliefs and behaviours of a wide range of interest groups are dealt with through democratic processes. The later are far from perfect, but they appear to have considerable advantages to all concerned over currently available alternatives based on bullets, bombs and totalitarianism.

'Coming events cast their shadows before', says an ancient proverb. As they always have been, the 'seeds' of the nation, society and cultures that will develop here in the UK, are already sown and sprouting. Will the social fruits of present and future harvests be bitter or sweet? What social legacies are we leaving to our children and their children's children: communality; cooperation; coexistence; competition, conflict or confusion? In their turn, what 'seeds' will our children inherit, propagate and reap?

Can the rank weeds of institutional and individual racism be acknowledged, identified, rooted out and replaced with tolerance in primary schools and in society? Can amity arise from the ashes of acrimony and animosity between ethnic, religious and cultural groups within the UK? Do such assertions smack of 'Political Correctness'? The cynics respond: 'And pigs can fly'. Can the many examples of cooperation and tolerance between ethnic, religious and cultural groups offset the negative aspects of diversity of values, interests and power in its various forms? On reflection, probably only partially; but moving in that direction holds more hope for the future than doing otherwise. Primary schools, with their generally excellent home–school liaison, are in a powerful position to further this end.

Tensions between Ethnic Groups in the UK

In the UK conscious and unconscious prejudices and suspicions exist mutually between ethnic groups, whether large or small. Politicians are well aware of the possibility of racist reactions from the white British public if policies are perceived as unduly favouring ethnic minorities. Suspicions that many ethnic minorities are not a part of the British national identity are fostered by some right-wing politicians and writers. For example, Norman Tebbitt's question concerning which cricket team one supports during a Test Match is one suspect example. It is suspect because the concepts of national identity and ethnic distinctiveness are not necessarily mutually exclusive.

The widely reported comments made in 1992 by Kalim Siddiqui, leader of the self-styled Muslim parliament, when interviewed by Ludovic Kennedy on Radio 4's programme 'Beyond belief', aroused considerable critical reaction from both Muslim and non-Muslim communities. Siddiqui advocated the merits of Muslim laws. 'If we cut off the right hands of thieves in this country, we would be well off because there would be no burglary . . . Theft would disappear. A few people would lose their hands to begin with, but very soon we would be able to cut down the size of our police forces . . . We would save money all round.' A representative of the Islamic Party of Great Britain commented that Siddiqui's comments were 'ludicrous'. Thompson (1992) reported that amputating the hands of thieves is one of six specific punishments under Islamic law known as 'hadd'. They are in force in many Islamic countries. Others include death by stoning for extra-marital sexual relations and eighty lashes for an unproved accusation of unchastity and for drinking alcohol. Additionally, the law prescribes death — often by beheading — for apostasy and highway robbery.

Culture clash is further illustrated by a quotation from an earlier article entitled 'The Future for Multi-racial Britain': '. . . large segments of British cities such as London, Liverpool, Birmingham and Bradford seem to have been transformed into foreign enclaves and incipient casbahs.' Working-class families in such areas have been powerless 'as the neighbourhoods in which they have lived for years were taken over by hordes of alien people, often noisy, sometimes gaudy or garish, and not infrequently unkempt and unintelligible' (Mishan, 1988a). The same author subsequently wrote to the effect that it was largely the responsibility of the black community in Brixton that the housing stock had deteriorated and that the environment was bleak and demoralizing. The minority ethnic-group youngsters were represented as often alienated from mainstream society, aimless, cynical and all too frequently engaged in criminal activities including mugging and dope peddling (Mishan, 1988b).

On 12 December 1989, in a speech to the House of Commons, the MP for Northampton North made the following widely reported comment.

> We should debate the extent to which our multicultural experiment has succeeded before deciding whether it is prudent to extend it . . . Vast areas of our inner-cities have already been colonized by alien peoples with little commitment to our society or our way of life.

Such views reinforce the belief of the editors of this series that the development of harmonious race relations will be a continuing challenge to society and schools well into the next century.

The Chair of the Commission for Racial Equality said in 1992:

Legislation alone cannot create good relations and change attitudes. But it can set clear standards of acceptable behaviour and provide redress for people who have suffered injustice at the hands of others. Race Relations Acts were enacted by Parliament in this country when it was seen that exhortation and goodwill were not enough to present the countless individual acts of discrimination that arose from racial prejudice and hostility, or change the long established patterns of institutional behaviour which effectively denied equality of opportunity. (CRE, 1992)

In the United Kingdom legislation exists aimed at prohibiting both individual and institutional manifestations of racism. Despite this, the evidence of scapegoating, harassment and unfair discrimination of pupils and their families from minority ethnic groups is clearly documented.

We *all* have conscious and unconscious prejudices, namely beliefs founded on inadequate evidence. The argument that 'power plus prejudice equals racism' has considerable validity. However, the assumption that, because they control the sources of power, only members of the white majority can be racist, is suspect. Under the ERA, will majority ethnic groups fail to recognize and utilize the many, varied and valuable cultural and curricular contributions of minority ethnic groups? Will minority ethnic groups seek to distance themselves from the mainstream of society by, for example, pressing for separate schools? Will ethnic ghettos be established? Will the ERA result in cultural pluralism in primary schools being put firmly on an educational 'back boiler'? Almost certainly, the answer to this last question is a resounding 'No'. The answers to the previous three are much less clear. Whatever the answers, the creation and maintenance of educational 'Waste lands' must be avoided.

And I will show you something different from either
Your shadow at morning striding behind you
Or your shadow at evening rising to meet you;
I will show you fear in a handful of dust.
(Eliot: The Waste Lands)

And I will show you something different from either
Your shadow at morning striding before you
Or your shadow at evening falling behind you;
I will show you hope in a handful of dust.

Metaphorically, the 'dust' alluded to in the pastiche of Eliot's poem is that of chalk, although it could be silicon. Education can be anything from a powerful force for mutually benefical changes in society to an equally powerful one dedicated to the preservation of the status quo. In practice, tension between these two forces maintains a dynamic equilibrium. In determining the directions in which educational resources should be directed, a philosophy of education and the values underpinning it need to be made explicit. As representatives of the people, what are the government's 'Mission Statements' in respect of education in general and multicultural and antiracist education in particular? Can the gaps between the rhetoric of politicians and the reality of the curriculum in schools be bridged? Is the vision of an 'entitlement' curriculum in primary schools, based on nine foundation subjects and RE, cross-curricular elements and the additional components of a whole curriculum, one that inspires enthusiasm?

The pessimist sees the overwhelming problems presented by the growing ethnic, religious, linguistic and cultural diversity that characterizes the population of the UK and the tensions that are created. The extreme views represented by individuals such as Enoch Powell, Ray Honeyford, E.J. Mishan, and Kalim Siddiqui represent examples of the 'dynamite on the tongue' mentioned earlier. In contrast, the optimist sees the riches and promise inherent in diversity. The realist listens to both the extremes of pessimism and optimism, concludes that moderation has much to commend it and, like Voltaire's Candide, decides 'we must go and work in the garden.' Cultivating a multicultural and antiracist primary-school curriculum will require a great deal of goodwill and reciprocity from all parties to the venture. It also requires financial investment.

Education matters. In 1991, the UK invested the sum of 26,669,000,000 pounds in its education services. This represented 4.8 per cent of the country's Gross Domestic Product (DFE, 1993b). Schools matter. Making schools increasingly effective is a national concern. If schools are to carry out successfully the functions expected of them, curricular implications of the cultural diversity characteristic of the school population must be considered. The important cohesive educational and social effects of schools in a rapidly changing world are now acknowledged. The aims, objectives, curricula, methodologies and management of schools are nationally and locally debated. The formative and summative consequences of the education schools provide are increasingly under scrutiny. The accountability of all levels of the educational service to 'consumers', in the guise of parents who pay for the educational system as taxpayers, and to their children, the pupils, is now centre-stage. The introduction of LMS (Local Management of Schools) gives schools a high and increasing degree of autonomy in the management of their finances. Many decisions concerning educational priorities and resource allocations are dealt with at the school level by governors. Fortunately, a number of national responsibilities continue. Acknowledging and utilizing the resources represented by the cultural diversities within school and communities, is one of these.

The external and internal policies, provision, practices and processes that contribute to beneficial effects within primary schools are being made increasingly explicit (Mortimore *et al.*, 1988; Alexander *et al.*, 1991; Alexander, 1992).

Studies seeking to understand the nature of effective education and means of promoting 'good practice' are increasing. The 'International Congress for School Effectiveness' held its first meeting in London in 1988, underlining the importance of this field of research and practice (Reynolds, Creemers and Peters, 1989). Because of its concern with *all* pupils and schools, the growing professional interest in this field is both encouraging and promising (Reynolds, 1991).

In 1992, 31,075 full-time equivalent pupils attended nursery schools and 3,950,500 attended primary schools in England (DFE, 1993a). Because of other provision, including nursery classes attached to primary schools, in the UK 799,000 pupils under 5, representing approximately 53 per cent of the 3 and 4-year-old population received education in schools (DFE, 1993b). The cost per pupil per year of pupils attending nursery provision and primary schools was about 1,245 pounds in 1991. This represented an increase in real terms of 34 per cent since 1979–80 (Department of Education Analytical Services Branch, 1992). The pupil–teacher ratios in nursery and primary schools in 1992 were 19.1:1 and 22.2:1, respectively. Because such figures include teachers with full and part-time administrative responsibilities, class sizes are typically larger than the figures suggest. Is such provision adequate to ensure the delivery of a 'whole curriculum' and provide the first stage of formal education required for citizenship in a multicultural society? As a multicultural nation, do we value education and democracy sufficiently?

Education is but one plot (yes, the word was deliberately chosen) in the 'field' of society. It can be a crucial force for better or for worse. The multipurpose functions of education support the idea that the autonomous individual is the best support for the institutions and processes comprising a democratic society. Education for citizenship in a multicultural society represents the challenge of the 1990s (Lynch, 1992). Education for citizenship is largely based on modelling. The implications for the ethos and organization of a school are considerable (Gundara and Richardson, 1991). The tensions between primary schools that are caring and compassionate institutions and their existence within a much less caring and compassionate society, frequently leads to confusions by pupils about how they are expected to behave to each other. The balance between cooperation and competition between individuals and schools appears to have moved significantly towards the latter.

Friendships between pupils across ethnic and cultural groupings are common in multicultural primary schools. But what does a youngster who is a member of a minority ethnic group think when subjected to the name-calling by white peers? What does such a child think when his relatives are abused and attacked, the windows of his home smashed and individuals and families live in fear merely because they are members of minority ethnic groups? What lessons in citizenship are such a child and his family learning?

Who has the wealth and power?
Can we all have a fair share?
What 'freedoms' do we have?
What 'responsibilities' should we have?
Who cares?
(MEC, 1990a).

A survey of crime against schools in 1991 was carried out in relation to vandalism, theft and malicious fire. Concerning the costs involved, out of 109 LEAs, sixty-four replied. A separate questionnaire was sent to a nationally representative sample of 800 primary schools concerning details of the crimes and the security measures being taken (DFE, 1993c).

The total number of crime-related incidents in primary schools in 1991 was estimated at 95,800. This represented an average of five incidents per primary school and one incident for every forty-two pupils in primary schools. In primary schools, a third of all incidents caused disruption of education to some degree and one fifth of incidents resulted in major disruption. In the report, estimated costs involved were not disaggregated for primary and secondary schools. In all, some fifty-three million pounds were spent by LEAs and their maintained schools on these crime-related incidents. This represented an average cost of 2,300 pounds per school. What a *waste of scarce resources!*

It is not unlikely that a disproportionate number of these crimes occur in socially deprived areas characterized by ethnic, religious and cultural diversity. (The author is currently following up this point).

This alienation of a minority of individuals within society, against education and schools in general and against primary schools in particular, is a challenge both to the primary schools and to the communities of which they are members, *irrespective of the ethnic, religious or cultural composition of the community*. Education for Citizenship is one crucial curricular component (see Volumes 2 and 4). 'Education for All', the title and aspiration of the Swann report on the Education of Pupils from Minority Ethnic Groups, is unlikely to be achieved without it (Committee of Inquiry, 1985).

It is virtually certain that, under such circumstances, the effects of addressing the NCC requirements related to cultural diversity will have received relatively little attention. Indeed, the changes in funding arrangements under Section 11 of the Local Government Act 1966, as set out in Home Office Circular 78/1990, may represent a significant reduction in resources for special provisions consequent on the presence within local-authority areas of substantial number of immigrants from the Commonwealth whose language or customs differ from those of the community (see Appendix 3). Some workers engaged under Section 11 Funding have already lost their posts.

One example is presented to underline the gravity of the situation and its impact on pupils' education. Haringey LEA has a school population in which approximately 70 per cent of pupils are from minority ethnic group origins.

Section 11 Funding includes provision for additional teaching support for certain, but not all, ethnic-minority pupils. The Haringey multicultural curriculum support group has, since 1979, pioneered many initiatives aimed at developing equal opportunities and antiracist practices. At one time the group employed five staff and an inspector. It is reported that the group's demise started in 1992 when the Home Office announced that it was cutting the level of Section 11 Funding. The LEA was faced with the decision of either paying more from its already overstretched budget, or closing the service. The remaining staff are to be returned to classroom teaching. The groups had developed a library of some 12,000 books. This resource will remain in use through the LEA's bilingual service which has been retained by the injection of additional funds by an authority that is being forced to cut its overall budget by some thirteen million pounds this year.

Integration or Segregation in Education?

In March 1992, the Secretary of State for Education announced changes in the rules governing the state funding of religious schools. In line with the government's market economy philosophy, popular schools should be able to expand even if they are within LEAs having an overall surplus of places. Voluntary-aided religious schools are amongst the most popular. It is existing voluntary-aided schools that are eligible.

In 1992 there were 4,936 Anglican, 2,245 Roman Catholic, thirty-one Methodist and twenty-two Jewish voluntary-aided schools. They comprise 27.5 per cent of all state-funded schools. Although the Muslim Educational Trust supported the country's twenty-three private Islamic schools, and there is no law preventing Muslim schools applying for voluntary-aided status, as yet, there are no voluntary-aided Muslim schools. Members of Muslim communities are divided over the issue of segregation. Ibrahim Hewitt of the Muslim Educational Trust is reported as saying 'We are denied the choices open to other communities because they don't want us to join the state system'. 'Why are people so afraid of Muslim schools? We want our children to be both good British citizens and good Muslims. We want them to learn the full National Curriculum as well as the Islamic faith. We are not going to go away. I'd like to ask the Secretary of State this: how long is he intending to withhold choice from such a sizeable proportion of the taxpaying public?' In contrast, Hannana Siddiqui of the organization 'Women against Fundamentalism' considers that segregation of children into different religious groups hinders the development of communal and cultural cooperation and understanding. She has advocated the withdrawal of state funding from *all* religious schools (Pilkington, 1992).

Why are there such tensions? What can be done to address and resolve them during the minimum of six years spent by our nation's children in the primary school system? Can the National Curriculum be used to foster

Table 3.5: Education Reform Act: Nomenclature for the Years of Education

Chronological age	Description	Abbreviation	
Five or younger	Reception	R.	
5–7	Years 1 and 2	Y1–2	(Key Stage 1)
7–10	Years 3 to 6	Y3–6	(Key Stage 2)
11–14	Years 7 to 9	Y7–9	(Key Stage 3)
14–16	Years 10 and 11	Y10–11	(Key Stage 4)
16–18	Years 12 and 13	Y12–13	

interethnic understanding and social cohesion? If not, there is indeed something rotten in the state of both society and education. If so, how? Acknowledging the existence of a particular challenge, such as that represented by cultural diversity in a society, is a necessary but not sufficient condition for constructively addressing the challenges. It is important to recognize that all challenges present problems and opportunities. Pessimists tend to see only the former whereas optimists perceive the latter. Realists can accept both perspectives.

The current controversial debate concerning the Asylum Bill, in the context of moves towards integration under the umbrella of the European Economic Community, underlines the national and international importance of individual and national rights and responsibilities.

The Education Reform Act 1988 (hereafter ERA) aims to raise educational standards. With its 238 sections and thirteen schedules, the legislation is complex. Despite this, it is relatively easy to pass a law. Implementing one is much more demanding. Time and effort are required of already extremely busy teachers. The issues outlined earlier concerning cultural diversity in the population, pose challenges of the utmost importance.

Responses

A Common Curricular Language

One of the more valuable consequence of the ERA and the organizations it established is that a 'new' educational vocabulary has been created. Its merits are that a uniform terminology now exists in education having a national currency and the backing of law. Teachers in any state school are required to educate their pupils according to the requirements of the ERA. The parents of pupils are increasingly familiar with the terminology in use. As a consequence, communication between teachers, governors, parents, administrators and politicians should become more open, explicit and effective. Pupils should benefit from such improved channels of communication (NCC, 1989a; 1989b; 1989c).

Explicit links between the ages of pupils and their description in relation to the stages of the National Curriculum have resulted in a nationally adopted system. Key elements of this are presented in Table 3.5.

The major educational challenge of the 1990s in England and Wales is the effective implementation of the Education Reform Act 1988 in general and of the 'Whole Curriculum' in particular (Sweetman, 1992). The whole curriculum includes the basic curriculum and cross-curricular concerns. The basic curriculum comprises religious education and the National Curriculum. The National Curriculum consists of core and other foundation subjects, their associated Attainment Targets, Programmes of Study and assessment. Key definitions are presented in Table 3.6.

Whole Curriculum Overload

The NCC, SEAC and the DES/DFE can legitimately be criticized for 'publication hyperactivity' in which activity has been mistakenly confused with progress. Many forests have been unnecessarily sacrificed on this particular administrative altar dedicated to rapid change without adequate reflection and consultation (e.g. NCC, 1990). Before the author today (January, 1993) is a list of recent NCC, SEAC and DES/DFE publications spawned as a consequence of the ERA. To keep up with the reading alone would be a full-time occupation (see Appendix 2). To survive with sanity intact requires selectivity!

The primary school teacher is faced with heavy teaching and assessment loads. These are top priorities in the interests of the pupils in their care. Where is the time for reading, reflection and reorganization to be found? When and where can the implications of cultural diversity be considered? In such a pressurised situation, it is not surprising that avoidable problems are expensively created rather than efficiently resolved. The sad tale of the standard assessment tasks being developed for use at Key Stages 1 and 2 is but one example. It makes other earlier monumental governmental fiascos such as the North African Groundnuts Scheme pale into insignificance. The relative neglect of the contributions of minority ethnic groups to the effective delivery of the National Curriculum could prove to be even more expensive to the nation in the longer term.

Teachers fully appreciate that the current nine foundation subjects, plus RE, represented 'curriculum overload' for both them and their pupils, insofar as the thickets of NCC, DES, DFE, HMI, SEAC and OFSTED documentation are concerned. The paucity of resources in primary geography and history identified by HMI was seen as a reflection of the low priority accorded these NC subjects at that time. Primary-school teachers were presumably concentrating on other aspects of the NC that had been introduced earlier and had been deemed 'core subjects' (English, mathematics and science). These 'basics' were a focus of professional, parental, and political concern. In respect of these, national 'League Tables' have been produced for KS1 results. The massive press attention accorded to such matters may well have affected many teachers' opinions concerning the saliency of the core subjects. Primary-school science

Table 3.6: The Curriculum: Key Definitions

Whole curriculum: The full curriculum of a school incorporating the basic curriculum and all other provision.

National Curriculum: The core and other foundation subjects, their associated Programmes of Study, Attainment Targets and assessment arrangements.

Basic curriculum: This consists of the National Curriculum and religious education (RE).

Core subjects: English, mathematics and science.

Foundation subjects: English, mathematics, science, technology (including design), history, geography, music, art and physical education. At the secondary school stage, a modern foreign language is also included.

Programmes of Study: The matters, skills and processes that must be taught to pupils during each Key Stage in order to enable pupils meet the objectives specified in the Attainment Targets for each subject.

Cross-curricular elements: These comprise two dimensions, six skills and five themes. These elements help ensure that the curriculum extends beyond the traditional subject-based curriculum (see below).

Cross-curricular dimensions: Equal Opportunities and Multiculturalism represent two important statements of educational intent.

Cross-curricular skills: These are skills that are transferable, largely independent of content and capable of being applied and developed in different curricular contexts. The skills are: communication; numeracy; study skills; problem-solving; personal and social skills and information technology.

Cross-curricular themes: These refer to strands of provision running through the National Curriculum, RE and curricular provision additional to the basic curriculum. The themes are: Economic and Industrial Understanding; Careers Education and Guidance; Health Education; Education for Citizenship and Environmental Education (see Volumes 2 and 4).

Attainment Targets: The objectives for each of the foundation subjects, listing the knowledge, skills and understandings that pupils are expected to develop within that subject area. The Attainment Targets are further defined at each of ten levels of attainment through the use of Statement of Attainment.

Profile Components: Groups of Attainment Targets brought together for the purposes of assessments and reporting.

Statements of Attainment: These are more precise objectives than the Attainment Targets. They are related to one or more of the ten levels of attainment on a single continuous scale. This scale covers all four Key Stages including pupils from the beginning to the end of compulsory education.

Key Stages: These refer to the division of the period of compulsory education into four stages. Each is related to the chronological age of the majority of pupils in a typical teaching group. The stages are as follows:

- **KS1** From the beginning of compulsory education to the end of National Curriculum Year 2 (i.e. from the start to the end of infant school education).

- **KS2** From the beginning of National Curriculum Year 3 to the end of National Curriculum year 6 (i.e. from first to the final year of junior school education).

Table 3.6: (Cont.)

- **KS3** From the beginning of National Curriculum Year 7 to the end of National Curriculum Year 9 (i.e. from the first year of secondary-school education to the age of about 14 years).

- **KS4** From the beginning of National Curriculum year 10 to the end of National Curriculum year 11 (i.e. from age of about 14 years to the current end of compulsory education at about the age of 16 years).

Levels of attainment: The ten levels of achievement defined within each Attainment Target.

Assessment arrangements: Arrangements designed to demonstrate what pupils have achieved in relation to the Attainment Targets at the end of each Key Stage. These arrangements include both testing using standard assessment tasks and continuous assessment by teachers.

Standard Assessment Tasks: Externally prescribed assessments incorporating a variety of assessment techniques. These SATs are intended to complement teachers' assessments.

Records of Achievement: Cumulative records of pupils' work.

National Curriculum development plan: Each maintained school is required to develop a coherent plan which identifies changes in the curriculum organization, staffing arrangements and the allocation of non-teaching resources likely to be beneficial. Each school is also charged with producing an action plan to ensure that the changes specified take place, and with evaluating their effects.

and some aspects of primary English were seen by HMI as curricular areas in which improvements in teaching quality had taken place (ibid.).

Despite this, the introduction of the NC had highlighted the adverse consequences of under-resourcing certain activities in schools on teachers' ability to deliver the whole curriculum, as the government had intended. Financial restrictions were, and still are, forcing LEAs to reduce the numbers of advisory teachers and services. There are also clear signs that LEAs are unable to maintain the systems whereby dissemination of curriculum developments and the associated INSET training needs of teachers can be met. The opportunities for teachers to undertake full-time or part-time periods of seconded advanced study at institutions of higher education are now virtually nil. The entirely valid professional aspiration to sabbatical leave has disappeared. The policy of almost totally devolving responsibility to schools for its staff's 'Continuing Professional Development' (CPD) via In-Service Education of Teachers (INSET) has been severely criticized as locking some schools into a self-reinforcing cycle of inadequacy' (Alexander, 1992).

A major message to the teaching profession is that it considers, as a matter of urgency, whether the continuing professional development of teachers through the current INSET and GEST arrangements is adequate to the delivery of any multiculturally sensitive 'whole curriculum'. Then the profession should ensure that the third of the three cycles of professional development, so strongly advocated by a former Secretary of State for Education and subsequent Prime Minister, is prioritized and implemented.

Resources and Promising Practices

In their respective chapters, each of the contributors to this series provides information, comment and suggestions concerning the contexts, challenges and curricular responses to the questions raised by the multicultural requirements of the whole curriculum. The following resources and ideas complement their contributions.

Playing in Harmony Project (Save the Children Fund)

> Playing in Harmony Project,
> Playing in Harmony Pack,
> Save the Children Fund,
> Block 1, Unit C1,
> Templeton Business Centre,
> Templeton Street,
> GLASGOW, G40 1DA.

A large number of primary schools have integral nursery classes. Very young pre-school children are aware of cultural differences. Not infrequently, children as young as two and a half years can have developed and can hold negative opinions of other cultural groups. If 'prevention is better than cure', there is much to be said for pre-school programmes that foster positive views of cultural and ethnic diversity through antiracist and multicultural education. The 'Playing in Harmony Pack' is designed for use in nursery settings. It emphasizes the importance of nurseries having an antiracist policy addressing:

- religious education;
- respect for other languages;
- guidelines on the choice of materials;
- collaborative work with parents drawn from diverse minority ethnic groups;
- links with locally established minority ethnic groups; and
- a code of practice for staff on dealing with racist incidents.

Included in the pack are four multilingual posters dealing with colours, numbers and 'survival language' in Cantonese, Hakka, Punjabi and Urdu. Also included in the pack is information, together with suggestions on how to introduce different cultural backgrounds and religions to young children. The help of parents in the programme is advocated.

P.D. Pumfrey

Education for Peace Programme (Manchester Education Committee)
There is much to be said in being *for* something educationally positive (e.g., Peace education), rather than being solely concerned with being *anti* something negative (antiracism), although both sets of activities are clearly complementary. Expansion of the former may well be an effective strategy in minimizing the latter. Curricular 'weeds' find it more difficult to emerge and flourish in a full educational flower bed. Manchester City Council Education Committee has developed an 'Education for Peace' programme that has much to commend it. The work is published in two volumes (Manchester City Council Education Committee, 1990a; 1990b).

'There is also a widely recognized need to educate responsible citizens with a clear understanding of their own worth and potential, who are able to participate fully in the development of a democratic society. All these areas (of education) must embrace the need for easy access and equal opportunities if the requirements of everyone are to be met in any real measure' (MEC, 1990a, p. 1). The strength of these two publications is that they present a convincing case for 'Peace Education', have clearly defined objectives in terms of knowledge (N=12), attitudes (N=7), skills (N=10) and concepts (N=10). They consider the challenges of dealing with controversial issues. The characteristics of an educational establishment likely to make it receptive to the development of policy and practice in this field are also discussed. Appendix 2 lists thirty-one organizations and Appendix 3 provides 122 recommended resources categorized under the following heads:

- Resources for helping to develop skills and attitudes for creative conflict resolution.
- Tackling bias, stereotyping and prejudice.
- Cooperative games, simulations and drama.
- Teaching with a global perspective.
- War, peace and nuclear issues.
- Planning curriculum development and in-service work.
- Background reading and information.

The second volume comprises twenty case studies describing applications of the Peace Education programme. Of these, ten are from primary schools. Included are accounts of work on 'Cooperation and conflict' (NC Year 2); 'Using drama to help create a peaceful environment' (NC Year 1/2) and 'An approach to antiracist work' (NC Year 6). These accounts provide a valuable source of ideas that can be developed in primary schools (MEC, 1990b).

Working Group Against Racism in Children's Resources
The Working Group Against Racism in Children's Resources is a national consortium. It includes parents, professionals (e.g., childcare workers, social workers, librarians, teachers) and producers (e.g., publishers and toy manufacturers). They were interested in the prevalence of positive images of black

children in toys, books and packaging (Klein, 1992). In a nationwide survey of thirty-three high-street shops, including the nationally known chains such as Early Learning Centre, John Menzies, W.H. Smith and Woolworths, it is reported that they found 'very little in the high street toy and bookshops to indicate that black children and their communities are part of this society. The survey indicates that the toy industry discriminates against black children on a massive scale by ignoring their presence or presenting them with negative stereotypes of black people and their communities' (ibid.). The dangers of unconsciously or consciously transmitting racial stereotypes via the materials used in school texts and library books is a continuing concern. The above group has been active in countering this tendency for the past ten years. Verna Wilkins, who publishes and writes children's books, is a member of WGARCR. She is reported as saying 'My generation never saw themselves reflected in children's literature. We grew up with invisibility'. Recently (1993) WGARCR published a new guide devised to assist teachers and librarians select non-racist materials for primary school pupils. Details of about a hundred picture books are included. The organizations listed in Table 3.7 can provide information/ publications/toys that are of value in multicultural, antiracist and Peace Education programmes.

Table 3.7:   Sources of Information

Access to Information on Multicultural Education Resources (AIMER),
Faculty of Education and Community Studies,
The University of Reading,
Bulmershe Court,
Earley,
Reading, RG6 1HV.

Acorn (Percussion) Ltd.,
Unit 34,
Abbey Business Centre,
Ingate Place,
London, SW8 3NS.

African Video Centre,
7 Balls Pond Road,
London, N1 4AX.

Afro-Caribbean Education Resource (ACER),
Wyvil School,
Wyvil Road,
London, SW8 2TJ.

Centre for Research in Ethnic Relations,
Resources Centre Librarian,
University of Warwick,
Coventry, CV8 7AL.

Childsplay,
112 Tooting High Street,
London, SW17 ORR.

Table 3.7: (Cont.)

Close Links,
c/o Grimwade Street,
Ipswich, IP4 1LS.

Commonwealth Institute Resource Centre,
Kensington High Street,
London, W8 6NQ.

Folens Publishers,
Albert House,
Apex Business Centre,
Boscombe Road,
Dunstable, LU5 4RN.

Manchester City Council Education Committee,
Peace Education Project,
North Manchester Resources Centre,
Harpurhey,
Manchester.

Marigold Bentley and Tom Leimdorfer,
Education Advisory Programme,
Friends House,
Euston Road,
London, NW1 2BJ.

Heights Culture Shop,
13 Middle Row,
Stevenage Old Town,
Hertfordshire.

Humming Bird Book and Toy Services,
136 Grosvenor Road,
St. Pauls,
Bristol, BS28 1YA.

Kemet Educational Materials Consultancy,
111 Lakenheath,
London, N14 4RY.

Letterbox Library,
Leroy House,
436 Essex Road,
London, N1 3BR.

National Union of Teachers,
Education and Equal Opportunities Department,
Hamilton House,
Mabledon Place,
London, WC1H 9BD.

Star Apple Blossom,
13 Inman Road,
London, SW18 3BB.

Zuma Art Services,
Kings Place,
16 Stony Street,
Nottingham, NG1 1LH.

References

ALEXANDER, R. (1992) *Policy and Practice in Primary Education*, London, Routledge.

ALEXANDER, R., ROSE, J. and WOODHEAD, C. (1991) *Curriculum Organisation and Classroom Practice in Primary Schools*, London, HMSO.

BARBER, M. (1992) 'Rectify the religious anomaly', *Times Educational Supplement*, 25 September.

COHEN, L. (1989) 'Ignorance, not Hostility: Student Teachers' Perceptions of Ethnic Minorities in Britain', in VERMA, G.K. (Ed) *Education for All: A Landmark in Pluralism*, London, The Falmer Press.

COHN, T. (1988) 'Sambo — a study of name-calling', in KELLEY, E. and COHN, T. (Eds) 'Racism in Schools — New Research Evidence', unpublished paper, Department of Extra-mural Studies, University of Manchester.

COMMISSION FOR RACIAL EQUALITY (1992) *Race through the 90s*, London, CRE.

COMMITTEE OF INQUIRY INTO THE EDUCATION OF PUPILS FROM MINORITY ETHNIC GROUPS (1985) *Education for All* (Chairperson: Lord Swann), Cmnd., 9453, London, HMSO.

DEPARTMENT FOR EDUCATION (1993a) 'Pupil–teacher ratios for each Local Education Authority in England (including Grant-maintained schools) and information on the length of the taught week — January 1992', *Statistical Bulletin*, 1, 93, January, London, DFE.

DEPARTMENT FOR EDUCATION (1993b) 'Education Statistics for the United Kingdom 1992 edition', Statistical Bulletin, 2, 93, January, London, DFE.

DEPARTMENT FOR EDUCATION (1993c) 'Survey of Security in Schools', *Statistical Bulletin*, 4, 93, January, London, DFE.

DEPARTMENT OF EDUCATION (1992) *Education Observed: the implications of the curricular requirements of ERA, an overview by HM Inspectorate on the second year, 1990–91*, London, HMSO.

DEPARTMENT OF EDUCATION ANALYTICAL SERVICES BRANCH (1992) *Education Facts and Figures*, Darlington, DES Analytical Services Branch.

EVANS, E. (Ed) (1992) *Reading against Racism*, London, Routledge.

GUNDARA, J. and RICHARDSON, R. (1991) 'Citizenship is taught, not inherited' *Times Educational Supplement*, 3935, 29 November.

HASKEY, J. (1990) 'The ethnic minority populations of Great Britain: estimates by ethnic group and country of birth', *Population Trends*, 60, Summer, pp. 35–8.

HASKEY, J. (1991) 'The ethnic minority populations resident in private households — estimates by county and metropolitan district of England and Wales', *Population Trends*, 63, Spring, pp. 22–35.

HASKEY, J. (1992) 'The immigrant populations of different countries in Europe: their size and origins', *Population Trends*, Autumn, pp. 37–48.

KELLY, E. (1990) 'Use and Abuse of Racial Language in Secondary Schools', in PUMFREY, P.D. and VERMA, G.K. (Eds) *Race Relations and Urban Education*, London, The Falmer Press.

KLEIN, G. (1993) *Education towards Race Equality*, London, Cassell.

KLEIN, R. (1992) 'Toys aren't us', *Times Educational Supplement*, 4 December, p. 13.

KLOSS, D.M. (1990) 'The legal context of Race Relations in England and

Wales', in PUMFREY, P.D. and VERMA, G.K. (Eds) *Race Relations and Urban Education*, London, The Falmer Press.

LEE, K. (1990) 'Race Relations in Education in the UK: An Ethical Perspective', in PUMFREY, P.D. and VERMA, G.K. (Eds) *Race Relations and Urban Education*, London, The Falmer Press.

LEICESTER, M. and TAYLOR, M. (1992) *Ethics, Ethnicity and Education*, London, Kogan Page.

LYNCH, J. (1992) *Education for Citizenship in a Multicultural Society*, London, Cassell.

MAHON, B. (1992) '1991 census: the story so far', *Population Trends*, 68, Summer.

MANCHESTER CITY COUNCIL EDUCATION COMMITTEE (1990a) *Education for Peace in Manchester: Guidelines*, Manchester, North Manchester Education Committee.

MANCHESTER CITY COUNCIL EDUCATION COMMITTEE (1990b) *Education for Peace in Manchester: Case Studies*, Manchester, Manchester Education Committee.

MISHAN, E.J. (1988a) 'What future for multi-racial Britain? Part I, *The Salisbury Review*, 6, 3, pp. 18–27.

MISHAN, E.J. (1988b) 'What future for multi-racial Britain? Part II, *The Salisbury Review*, 6, 4, pp. 4–11.

MORTIMORE, P., SAMMONS, P., STOLL, L., LEWIS, D. and ECOB, R. (1988) *School Matters — The Junior Years*, Exeter, Open Books.

NATIONAL CURRICULUM COUNCIL (1989a) *A Framework for the Primary Curriculum,* York, NCC.

NATIONAL CURRICULUM COUNCIL (1989b) *An Introduction to the National Curriculum*, York, NCC, CCW and OU.

NATIONAL CURRICULUM COUNCIL (1989c) *From Policy to Practice*, York, NCC.

NATIONAL CURRICULUM COUNCIL (1989d) *Booklet 3: The Whole Curriculum*, London, NCC.

NATIONAL CURRICULUM COUNCIL (1992) *Starting out with the National Curriculum*, York, NCC.

NATIONAL CURRICULUM COUNCIL (1993) *The National Curriculum at Key Stages 1 and 2*, York, NCC.

NATIONAL UNION OF TEACHERS (1992) *Anti-Racist Curriculum Guidelines*, London, NUT.

OFFICE OF POPULATION CENSUSES AND SURVEYS (1992) 'In brief: Estimates of the ethnic minority populations of Great Britain, 1988–1990', *Population Trends*, 67, Spring, p. 1.

OFFICE FOR STANDARDS IN EDUCATION (1993) *Curriculum Organisation and Classroom Practice in Primary Schools*, London, OFSTED.

OWEN, D. (1992) *Ethnic Minorities in Great Britain: Settlement Patterns, 1991 Census Statistical Paper No 1*, University of Warwick Centre for Research in Ethnic Relations.

PILKINGTON, E. (1992) 'Islam opts out', *The Guardian*, 10 March.

PINSENT, P. (Ed) (1992) *Language, Culture and Young Children*, London, David Fulton.

PUMFREY, P.D., ELLIOTT, C.D. and TYLER, S. (1992) 'Objective Testing Insights or Illusions?', in PUMFREY, P.D. (Ed) *Reading Standards: Issues and Evidence*, Leicester, British Psychological Society, pp. 38–46.

PUMFREY, P.D. and VERMA, G.K. (Eds) (1990) *Race Relations and Urban Education: Contexts and Promising Practices*, London, The Falmer Press.

REYNOLDS, D., CREEMERS, A. and PETERS, T. (Eds) (1989) *School Effectiveness and Improvement*, Groningen, Rion Institute for Educational Research.

REYNOLDS, D. (1991) 'School effectiveness and School improvement in the 1990s', *Association for Child Psychology and Psychiatry*, 13, pp. 5–9.

SCOTT, R. (1971) *'A wedding man is nicer than cats, miss': A Teacher at work with immigrant children*, Newton Abbot, David and Charles.

SWEETMAN, J. (1992) *Curriculum Confidential Three: The Complete Guide to the National Curriculum*, Tamworth, Bracken Press.

THOMPSON, D. (1992) 'Chop off thieves' hands, says Muslim', *Daily Telegraph*, 1 September.

TROYNA, B. and HATCHER, R. (1991) *Racism in Children's Lives*, London, Routledge/National Children's Bureau.

VERMA, G.K. (Ed) (1990) *Education for All: A Landmark in Pluralism*, London, The Falmer Press.

WOLFENDALE, S. (1991) *A Bibliography and Resource-base on Anti-Racism and Multiculturalism: Foundations for a Categorised System*, London, Psychology Department, Polytechnic of East London (3rd version).

Part 2

Practice in Content Fields

Chapter 4

Religious Education

Philip Metcalf

Context

The 1988 Education Reform Act states that all new agreed syllabuses for religious education must

> . . . reflect the fact that the religious traditions in Great Britain are in the main Christian, whilst taking account of the teaching and prac- tices of the other principal religions represented in Great Britain.

In commenting on this statement, Hull observes:

> For the first time, therefore, the basic curriculum of children and young people in our schools will not be meeting the legal standards unless they are taught the teaching of the principal non-Christian religions in Great Britain. (Hull, 1989, p. 1)

In 1989, the Religious Education Council of England and Wales carried out a survey of agreed syllabuses produced between 1973–87. Appendix 1 analysed the results from twenty-three agreed syllabuses, showing that fifteen of the syllabuses specifically included the aim 'to appreciate Christianity and the Christian tradition', while thirteen have as an aim 'to explore world reli- gions and to understand living in a multi-faith society'.

It can be said with certainty that the population of Britain is increasingly characterized by cultural diversity, by both similarities and differences in values, expectations and opportunities linked to ethnic diversity. Religious education is well placed to address some of these crucial issues.

The demands of implementing the National Curriculum have put im- mense strains on primary-school time and resources. It seems that the govern- ment has been working on an adoption time-scale whereas the schools have been working on an implementation time-scale. The distinction is of peren- nial importance.

In practice, the desire of the agents of change to get started — not only because of internal and external pressures, but also because of the awareness, sometimes dim, that the road ahead will not be smooth — results in by-passing the different aspects of the time perspective problem, a by-pass that might have no immediate adverse consequences, but can be counted on to produce delayed, and sometimes fatal difficulties. (Sarason, 1971, p. 219)

The unrealistic time-lines imposed on schools are adding to the existing frustration amongst many teachers that too much is expected too quickly. The reforms are in danger of sinking under the weight of their own paperwork and religious education has suffered because of this. Perhaps many teachers have been pleased that religious education has not been given a high profile, because they realize that there is only so much that can be fitted into the school day, week and year.

To further complicate the matter, many teachers are uncertain how to deal with religious education in primary schools. Few schools have specialist teachers acting as curriculum consultants and, according to the Senior Chief Inspector of Schools, the religious education seen was poor in quality and superficially taught in almost two-thirds of English primary schools (HMI, 1990). Instead of cultural diversity adding to the richness of religious education, it may well be the case that teachers are so overwhelmed by the changes taking place within education in general, and religious education in particular, that opportunities are being lost to explore the benefits to the curriculum of such diversity.

The report of the Committee of Inquiry into the Education of Children from Minority Ethnic groups (1985) noted that:

We would probably all acknowledge that there have been few attempts to set out in any detail just what teachers require in the form of professional competence if they are to meet the challenge of cultural diversity. (*Education for All*, 1985, p. 233)

In March 1991, the then Department of Education and Science sent a letter to all Chief Education Officers in which the Secretary of State passed on the advice he had received concerning the interpretation of Section 8(3) of the 1988 Education Reform Act. This section stated that agreed syllabuses 'must reflect the fact that the religious traditions in Great Britain are in the main Christian whilst taking account of the teaching and practices of the other principal religions represented in Great Britain'. In his letter, he noted that an agreed syllabus 'cannot exclude from its teaching any of the principal religions represented in Great Britain' and 'cannot confine itself exclusively to religious education based on Christian traditions'. Further, the agreed syllabus must make clear what content should be covered. He goes on to say that the content must 'give sufficient guidance to the reader, and thus to the teacher, as to what Christian traditions, learning, teaching and festivals are going to be taught and what elements are going to be taught in respect of the other principal religions represented in Great Britain'.

Hull (1991) observes:

A syllabus which contained a great deal of attention paid to the teachings of the other principal religions but hardly any detail regarding Christianity would not be balanced, and the same would be true the other way. (Hull, 1991, p. 2)

In the light of this, not only will the agreed syllabus be locally determined, but each school will have to decide on the precise content to be covered in each age group. In this respect, religious education is no different from any other subject, except that the content is defined locally, not nationally.

Challenges

In examining HMI reports on primary religious education, several issues can be highlighted. They include:

- Schools appear to find it difficult to strike a satisfactory balance between implicit and explicit religious education.
- The most successful religious education seen was made relevant to the pupils' experience and linked with the general curriculum.
- Little use appears to have been made of visits to places of worship or visitors to the school.
- In most schools visited (60 per cent), the religious education seen was 'less than satisfactory' or 'poor'.

This is a bleak overview of the current state of religious education in primary schools. In its 'Religious Education: a Local Curriculum Framework' document, the National Curriculum Council (1991b) mentions the following areas to consider when devising an agreed syllabus:

- Content.
- Skills and concepts.
- Continuity and progression.
- Providing suitable activities.
- Providing learning experiences related to the age and level of attainment of pupils.

HMI (1989) made a number of observations in their review of the state of religious education in Welsh primary schools. They commented that most schools appeared to express concern about the nature and role of religious education in the curriculum. Whilst appreciating its importance, they seemed to find the aims of the subject, as found in the locally agreed syllabuses, difficult to achieve in practice. In most schools there was a failure to appreciate that the subject was like any other subject in that it involved pupils in a process of learning in which progress and growth should be evident. They further observed that religious education was not well organized. Most schemes of work failed to refer to a framework of skills, concepts, attitudes and values as a basis for selecting material that was appropriate for each age group. Most schools were inadequately resourced. Little systematic assessment occurred and no formal criteria existed to help identify objectives or to determine whether these had been achieved.

Many of these issues are not unique to religious education. However, it would seem that the observations made above by HMI and NCC could provide a useful framework for discussing the challenges facing the religious education curriculum in primary schools. If we consider the question of skills, knowledge, attitudes and values, it may be worth asking which of these attitudes or values are culturally determined. Ten years before the ERA, Warren (1978) observed:

> Our first task in approaching another people, another culture, another religion, is to take off our shoes, for the place we are approaching is holy. Else we may find ourselves treading on men's dreams. (Warren, 1978, p. 23)

And further, Norcross (1989) states:

> ... that children inevitably use their sub-conscious socio-cultural conditioning to fashion their perceptions of Jews, or Muslims, or Hindus or indeed Christians, when these groups are studied objectively. This can often result in the devaluing of other cultures and of the religious spirit. Awakening in children awareness of their own cultural conditioning, and of the relativity of all cultural expressions, of the nature of secularism, and of the primary value of a shared humanity is a necessary preparation for the study of any culture or religion. (Norcross, 1989, p. 87)

In the primary school, how can we teach practically the values of a shared humanity given the diverse cultural and religious backgrounds of so many of the children? What experiences are common to humanity in general and to children in particular? How can we make religious education relevant to each child's experience? As the Committee of Inquiry, Chaired by the late lord Swann, (1985) pointed out:

> A failure to broaden the perspectives represented to all pupils — particularly those from the ethnic majority community — through their

education not only leaves them inadequately prepared for adult life but also constitutes a fundamental mis-education, in failing to reflect the diversity which is now a fact of life in this country. (Committee of Inquiry, 1985, p. 233)

Hampshire Education Committee (1988) recognized in a policy document that multicultural education should be part of a process, not a one-off event and commented:

It ought to be apparent then that one can never *do* multicultural education, either in a subject sense or as part of a checklist that has been ticked off and completed. It is a task that, once started, can never be finished, for each generation presents a fresh challenge. What we can do is to develop within the service the thinking, values and practices which lie at the heart of multicultural education, that we can at least dispense with the label, and simply talk about good education for all and enhance our delivery of it. (Hampshire County Council, 1988, pp. 7–8)

So our schools should develop an ethos and a curriculum which, amongst other things, should:

... reflect and value cultural diversity and turn it to advantage in enriching pupils' and students' experience and understanding of the world in which they live. (ibid.)

Much of what has been said above about multicultural education can be equally applied to religious education. We should look at religious pluralism as a benefit which we, as teachers, can explore and develop for the richness it can give to the children's lives and to our own.

The document continues:

Let us recognise an irony. Multicultural education, which uses such concepts as 'prejudice', 'stereotype', and 'labelling', is itself a prime victim of these processes. The first task therefore is to create a climate in which we can all risk failure. This is after all an important part of the learning process, and we are all learners. To approach the task in an over-earnest and zealous way will, by creating anxiety, only block change. Multicultural education is not the preserve of the ideologically pure. We must develop skills in others, not disable them. That is why it is better to stress what we are for in education, not simply what we are against. (ibid.) (see Chapter 3 on Peace Education and Education for Citizenship).

According to the Education (Schools) Act 1992, one of the duties of inspectors is to report on the spiritual development of pupils. In a 1992 article

Table 4.1: *Summarizing Challenges: Religious Education*

CHALLENGES
* Finding a satisfactory balance between implicit and explicit religious education.
* Making religious education relevant to the pupils' experience.
* Making more use of visits and visitors.
* Implementing practically the aims of an agreed syllabus.
* Devising suitable skills, attitudes, knowledge and values to be taught.
* Resourcing the subject adequately.
* Drawing from a wide range of religious traditions in order to enrich children's experience and understanding.
* Addressing the issues of collective worship in schools.

in *The Tablet*, the Secretary of State for Education notes an important link between the spiritual and the religious. It is within RE and collective worship that he saw spiritual development largely but, fortunately, not exclusively, set. The concept of spirituality within a single religion is exceedingly complex. In an ethnically and religiously diverse community, its acknowledgment across religions could prove a powerful cohesive force dependent, in large measure, on the willingness of members of different religious groups to *live* the tolerance of others and the goodwill to mankind contained in their doctrines. The history of relationships between the Catholic and Protestant branches of Christianity in the UK suggests that such behaviour is not rapidly realized.

A new government White Paper reported in the *Times Educational Supplement* (1992) suggests legislation allowing councils twelve months to bring their agreed syllabuses in line with the requirements of the 1988 Education Reform Act. It has been estimated that as few as a third of local authorities have either adopted new agreed syllabuses or are in the process of reviewing them. It is one thing to adopt a new agreed syllabus; it is quite a different matter effectively to implement the agreed syllabuses in each school.

Although not the responsibility of the RE specialist or the primary-school class teacher, religious issues concerned with acts of collective worship in multicultural schools present challenges that merit mention. The Education Reform Act 1988 requires that 'All pupils in attendance at a maintained school shall on each school day take part in an act of collective worship' (part 1, section 6). In county schools, this act of worship, required under section 6 of the ERA, shall be wholly or mainly of a broadly Christian nature (DES, 1989). 'An act of worship which is "broadly Christian" need not contain only Christian material provided that, taken as a whole, it reflects the traditions of Christian belief. It is not necessary for every act of worship to be of this character, but within each school term the majority of acts must be so' (part IV, para. 34). In determining a school's policy and practice, consideration should be given to '. . . i. pupils' family backgrounds, for example, the faith of their family and ii. their ages and aptitudes (part IV, para. 35). Then comes the crucial issue: 'If the headteacher considers that the requirement of collective worship in paragraph 34 could conflict with what is required by paragraph 35 he or she can apply to the local Standing Advisory Council on Religious Education to lift or modify the requirements of paragraph 34' (part IV, para. 36).

Schools containing considerable numbers of children from faith communities other than Christianity, are providing, or wish to provide, combinations of multifaith and separate faith acts of collective worship. A survey of ninety-four LEAs revealed that twenty-four reported having more than 200 schools that had applied to opt out (Dean, Maxwell and McTaggart, 1992). In the case of Bradford, an LEA with a considerable proportion of pupils from minority ethnic groups, 25 per cent of schools are reported as having applied to be exempted from the requirements to provide a 'broadly Christian' act of worship. Of these schools, thirty-five are first schools, twenty-four middle schools, one upper school and one special school. It is anticipated that other schools will apply. In other areas containing considerable numbers of pupils from non-Christian faith communities, similar patterns appear. Twenty-eight applications have been received in Leicestershire for lifting or modifying the requirements of para. 34 and all but one application has been successful. Twenty-four of these applications are from primary schools.

In March, 1993, the chairman of the NCC told a London conference that religious education is too often marginalized in our schools. It has equal status with National Curriculum subjects and should have the same time devoted to it as, for example, history and geography. More than half of the content should be spent on Christianity because it is the main religious tradition in this country. Whilst accepting that an appreciation by pupils of the variety and breadth of religious beliefs was necessary, it was suggested that Christianity and two other religions should be studied in depth as some stage. Local religious education syllabuses allow flexibility for the inclusion of the beliefs of other religious communities. Seventy-four of the 112 locally agreed religious education syllabuses have not been reviewed since the changes introduced under the Education Reform Act 1988. It was also asserted that religious education in primary schools could, to advantage, be taught by specialist teachers to ensure rigour and adherence to the syllabus.

Responses

One practical response would be for each school to produce its own scheme of work for religious education based on the agreed syllabus. This would have several benefits:

Firstly, it would focus the attention of the school on religious education. This would enable the school to formulate its own philosophy of how to interpret the agreed syllabus. It would give teachers the opportunity to reflect on their current practice, and time to develop cooperatively a working document that can deliver the Attainment Targets and Programmes of Study not only for religious education, but for other areas of the curriculum as well. For example, if a visit to a local place of worship is envisaged, at least some of the following activities can be included:

- The opportunity for the children to sit in silence and think, leading to them expressing their feelings about the atmosphere, the architecture etc. Music can be played where appropriate.
- Exploring concepts common to different religious traditions e.g., prayer, worship, sacrifice, pilgrimage, family etc.
- Developing the use of explicitly religious language.
- Looking at symbols in the building.
- Exploring the use of colour and shape.
- Interviewing a range of people who are involved with the faith community.
- Allowing the children to share their experiences of visiting various faith communities.

The advantages of using a local place of worship include the following:

- It encourages links with the local community.
- It is suitable for any age group in the primary school.
- Continuity and progression can be built into the programme.
- Cost implications for most schools will be relatively small.
- First-hand experience will be given to the children.

Secondly, teachers would be given the opportunity to develop their own knowledge and understanding of developments in religious education over the past ten years or so. They may not be familiar with the phenomenological approach to religious education advocated by Smart and others twenty-five years ago. Smart (1968) suggested:

Religious education could be designed to give people the capacity to understand religious phenomena, to discuss sensitively religious claims, to see inter-relations between religion and society and so forth. (Smart, 1968, pp. 96–7)

And further:

Religious education can transcend the informative by being a sensitive induction into religious studies not with the aim of evangelising, but with the aim of creating the capacity to understand and think about religion. (ibid.)

This approach encourages the child to 'stand in someone else's shoes', by developing religious understanding and a spirit of openness. The assertion that these objectives be delayed until the secondary stage of education is rejected.

Perhaps some teachers are still being influenced unduly by the earlier research of Goldman (1964) and are uncertain as to how best to approach religious education. He related his study of children's interpretation of the religious ideas contained within particular Bible stories to the work of Piaget and suggested there was a sequence or pattern through which children appeared to pass which closely corresponded in religious thinking to Piaget's stages of development.

Goldman's conclusion was that the Bible was taught too much, too soon and he advocated religious education by means of 'life-themes'. These themes were so *implicit*, that it was difficult to find any *explicit* religious education at all. His work was also criticized for presupposing the validity of the Piagetian account of cognitive development and the application of Piagetian stage criteria to the promotion of religious thinking.

As in every other subject area, thinking in religious education has moved on. The in-service training requirement of the staff must include recent developments in religious education in order for the school staff to develop a scheme of work that reflects current good practice.

Thirdly, the impact of a new agreed syllabus in a local authority can have as beneficial an effect on the actual practice in schools as an HMI report (1989a) discovered. Some of the main findings included the importance of teachers' understanding of the aims of the agreed syllabus, the availability of support from advisers and advisory teachers and adequate provision of resources in the schools.

Whole-school approaches to the planning of the religious education curriculum enhanced the quality of the work seen and the report concludes:

> The implementation of an agreed syllabus needs an overall plan that sets out clearly defined roles for the LEA, advisory support, schools and the mandatory SACRE. It requires the proper provision of INSET courses and supporting resources. Without these, agreed syllabuses have less effect upon classroom practice than they deserve, and one of their main advantages, the development of a progressive, continuous and coherent provision of religious education for all pupils, is put at risk. (HMI, 1989a, p. 11)

Finally, the successful introduction of an agreed syllabus, or indeed any curriculum document, depends to a great extent on the quality of personal relationships in a school. Many of the issues faced in schools are, at root, relationship issues. Most of the major world religions stress the value of human relationships. At school level, the community becomes a microcosm of global issues and relationships, regardless of the religion or culture of the people in the school. It is equally important how the children treat the mid-day assistants as their relationship with the headteacher, caretaker or each other.

In relation to cultural and religious diversity and religious education, there are four areas to examine particularly if any school wants to respond effectively to some of the issues raised earlier. The first relates to the role of the headteacher. Many recent papers have confirmed the crucial importance of the headteacher in any primary school in the management of curriculum development (Mortimore *et al.*, 1988; Alexander, Rose and Woodhead, 1992). If the headteacher is not an active supporter of religious education and the positive benefits of cultural diversity, the rest of the school will be less likely to consider these aspects of the curriculum important.

The number of sensitive issues surrounding headteachers appears to be increasing. Leaving aside questions of who was right or wrong, the impact of Ray Honeyford on his Bradford school was considerable. It seems that the psychological and sociological problems of change confronting any headteacher are at least as great as those confronting teachers. It also appears to be the case that without a strong emphasis on supportive personal relationships, many headteachers will feel exactly as teachers, parents or children feel: other people simply do not seem to understand the problems they face. It is therefore the responsibility of the headteacher to model the kind of supportive behaviour that encourages individuals to feel accepted for who they are.

One central aim in a school's religious education curriculum document should be to create an ethos where children have respect for others, where they are encouraged, praised, find fairness, security, approval, acceptance and friendship and where every effort is made to cater for the individual needs of each child. This kind of aim impinges directly on the quality of religious education provided in a school. It can be achieved by example, but it should also reflect the positive attitudes towards cultural diversity shown by the headteacher in both formal and informal contacts with children, teaching and non-teaching staff and parents. Are different religious traditions treated with equal respect? Is there a balance between the religions explored in religious-education lessons? If the headteacher gives a positive lead in these areas, the rest of the school is more likely to follow. The role of the governors is also central (see Volume 4, Chapter 3).

The second issue is the quality of relationships between teachers and children. Children are acutely aware of being devalued or humiliated by teachers and are in a relatively weak position to do anything about it. Although its use by teachers is not unknown, sarcasm should never be used in response to a child. If a child feels humiliated, or not taken seriously by a teacher, almost invariably this will affect the child's self-image. Equally, the morale of staff is a crucial element in how they interact with the children. It is therefore disturbing to read the findings of a 1992 survey of more than 3,000 teachers by the Centre for Educational Research at the University of London's Institute for Education and the London School of Economics and Political Science. This showed that 28 per cent of teachers were 'not satisfied', 5 per cent 'not at all satisfied' with teaching and 19 per cent expected to have left the profession within five years. A demoralized profession is unlikely to model positive self-images, therefore the children are less likely to feel that their personal needs are being met. The growing disquiet with the complexities and time-demanding assessment requirements of the NC by the major teachers' organizations is not a good augury in education.

The third issue is how the children are encouraged to develop positive relationships with each other. The fact of racism is a serious flaw in many schools. As most schools now represent varying degrees of religious diversity, the children need positive encouragement to accept not only themselves but also one another. The earlier these issues are raised and discussed the better. They are too important to be left until attitudes have hardened and prejudices have been fuelled. Ground rules should be clearly laid down and consistently applied. Racism, name-calling, bullying etc., are unacceptable forms of behaviour. Whatever the immediate environment of the school, the school ethos can be accepting and supportive of all children, regardless of religion, disability, race or sex.

The fourth issue is the school's relationship with parents. Parents are rightly seen as partners with the school in which their children are educated. Increasingly, parents' views are being seen as an integral part of any successful change to be adopted by schools. Given the religious diversity of parents, it is important for the school to listen sensitively to questions and concerns about the curriculum in general and religious education in particular. Issues such as the type of food provided at lunchtime, the school policy on racism or the way the act of collective worship is arranged are all areas requiring tact and a listening ear on the part of the school. Good relationships with parents do not happen automatically. It is therefore vital to provide an open door for parents and for schools to be constantly looking for new creative ways of including parents in the life of the school.

One of the areas identified earlier by HMI as a weakness in primary religious education was the lack of visitors and visits to places of worship. Parents and adults from the local faith community can be invited into school in order to explain what their faith means to them in everyday terms. This approach helps particularly where no teacher feels competent to explain a faith they may not hold themselves. Care needs to be taken to ensure that the visitor does not proselytize.

The wide variety of celebrations held by different faith communities gives one helpful way into exploring religion phenomenologically. It can also build on the interests and experiences of the children from that faith community, while at the same time opening up new ways of looking at life by those children from a different faith community, or none.

We now turn to some sources from which information, and ideas relevant to RE in a multicultural society can be obtained.

Sources of Information and Materials

The response to the growing ethnic and religious diversity that characterizes the United Kingdom as a whole, has resulted in the development of six major

Table 4.2: National and Regional Religious Education Centres

BFSS RE Centre,
West London Institute of Higher Education,
Lancaster House,
Borough Road,
Isleworth, TW7 5DU.

Regional RE Centre (Midlands),
Westhill College,
Selly Oak,
Birmingham, B29 6LL.

Sacred Trinity Centre,
Chapel Street,
Salford,
Greater Manchester, M3 7AJ.

The York RE Centre,
The College,
Lord Mayor's Walk,
York, Y03 7EX.

The National Society's RE Development Centre,
23 Kensington Square,
London, W8 5HN.

Welsh National Centre for RE,
School of Education,
University College of North Wales,
Deiniol Road,
Bangor,
Gwynedd, LL57 2UW.

---

regional RE centres. These are listed in Table 4.2. These centres have loan collections of artefacts, books on a wide range of religions and on religious education and also provide in-service training. In addition to these six major regional RE centres, many LEAs provide additional RE resources.

At the Commonwealth Institute in Kensington High Street, London, the Commonwealth Resource Centre (CRC) has an extensive, valuable and relatively inexpensive loan system. Members are entitled to borrow up to four items, free of charge, on a monthly basis. The CRC also provides larger resource packs that include up to thirteen individual items. The selection of contents is determined by the requests made. Thus the resource pack can be constructed to suit any particular age group of pupils. The hire charges for these packs are on a sliding scale, dependent on the length of hire. Their thematic titles include Buddhist, Christian, Hindu, Jewish, Muslim, and Sikh festivals.

A valuable source of further information concerning particular faiths is the list of addresses of denominational organizations provided in the Longman Community Information Guides (1993). There is also a section on inter-denominational organizations. At a more local level, in most large towns and cities there exist specialist shops addressing the religious needs of various faith communities. Within the multicultural areas of the large conurbations, the most readily available resources are the local faith communities themselves. Schools situated in the 'White Highlands' of the UK may have to develop other strategies.

A vast range of religious symbols and objects are extremely potent for their respective faith communities. Such artifacts can provide avenues whereby pupils can be introduced to other religions. The intrinsic appeal of unfamiliar artefacts can be capitalized on by the primary-school teacher. The dangers of superficiality are avoidable, provided that the points made below concerning the teacher's preparation, are not neglected.

'A communion chalice, for example, is a piece of three-dimensional tactile shorthand which can lead into discussion of the importance that Christians place upon the Lord's Supper. A folding wooden holder for the Koran will promote discussion of holy books. A Jewish Tallith, or prayer shawl, can provide a focus for a lesson on prayer and its meaning'. (Haigh, 1992, p. 27)

The introduction of common religious themes found in different religions can be introduced via artefacts. Examples of such themes include prayer, sacred texts, festivals, ceremonies marking significant events in the lives of members of the faith community, the vestments worn by those officiating and those taking part in religious ceremonies and religious art. As mentioned earlier, preparation for a visit to the place of worship by a particular religion provides a further rich source of themes that can be related to the artefacts used by the particular faith community.

For the teacher who decides that the use of religious artefacts in the classroom is a line of multicultural curricular development in RE holding promise, there is a company that can help considerably. The company developed from a curricular materials-resource problem. Some years ago, whilst working as an RE advisory teacher in Manchester, Mrs Howard found she was not alone in having considerable difficulties in obtaining a collection of artefacts related to various non-Christian religions. Her solution to this problem was to gather such materials and advertize them to teachers. Mrs Howard, and her husband, who was an advisory headteacher in Manchester, subsequently established a company called 'Articles of Faith'. It provides religious artefacts and materials to schools throughout the UK. Its address is:

Articles of Faith,
Bury Business Centre,
Kay Street,
Bury,
Lancashire, BB9 6BU.

Additionally, the Howards provide exhibitions and in-service training for teachers. Mrs Howard continues working part-time as an RE teacher.

Consequently, the educational value of the variety of artefacts in relation to the requirements of the National Curriculum, is not overlooked. 'When she chooses artefacts, she applies her own test: 'I'll always ask what a teacher would do with it in the classroom' she says.

'The objects they sell are unfailingly fascinating. They have, for instance, the last Jewish prayer shawls to be made in this country — the old Salford man who used to make them has just retired at 85, and all future ones will come from Israel. Then there is the Koran stand, carved in India, complete with its hinge, from one piece of Shesham wood. The list seems endless — a colourful Christian cross from Salvador; a prayer wheel from Tibet; greeting cards from various faiths' (ibid.). The dangers of trivializing the profound must and can be avoided.

Sensitivity by the teacher to the religious significance of such symbols and objects requires an awareness of their religious contexts. If pupils are to learn to respect a range of religious symbols and objects, such sensitivity is an essential prerequisite. For example, the reverence shown to the Koran by Muslims requires that hands be washed before it is handled. Certain faith communities will show to groups of pupils, or even lend to teachers, religious robes. However, there may well be serious religious reservations concerning whether children should try them on. The guiding principle is that one must be sensitive to the beliefs and traditions of all faith communities. Using the expertise of members of the various faith communities within an area is one means of minimizing the possibility of misunderstandings. The fear of inadvertently failing to show due respect through ignorance should not deter the teacher from using artefacts in RE, provided that one is conscientious and, if necessary, willing to apologize for any mistakes.

One recently published book addresses such issues and also presents an illustrated catalogue showing the key artefacts of the six major world religions (Gateshill and Thomson, 1992). The Shropshire Religious Education Artefact Project has updated its series of five books on the role and relevance of artefacts used in Christianity, Sikhism, Islam, Hinduism and Judaism, respectively (Shropshire Education Committee, 1992). Longman has produced a valuable series of books 'Religions through Festivals'. Currently there are six titles covering: Islam; Buddhism; Judaism; Christianity; Sikhism and Hinduism (Brine, 1989; Connolly and Connolly, 1989; Lawton, 1990; Hughes, 1989; Babraa, 1990 and Jackson, 1989).

Understanding Religions is a series comprised of six books, each addressing major life events across religions. These events are *Death Customs, Birth Customs* (Rushton, 1992a; 1992b), *Marriage Customs* (Compton, 1992), *Pilgrimages and Journeys* (Prior, 1992), *Food and Fasting* (Burke, 1992) and *Initiation Rites* (Prior, 1992). These perennial themes provide another source of potentially cohesive concerns that can be sensitively approached through the beliefs and practices of different religions.

It is helpful to teachers if they have a calendar showing the major festivals of the various religious faiths. An attractive wall chart entitled 'The Festival

Table 4.3: Summarizing Responses: Religious Education

RESPONSES
- Producing a school scheme of work based on the agreed syllabus.
- Promoting good personal relationships throughout the school.
- Drawing on each child's experience when appropriate.
- Visiting local places of worship.
- Drawing on local expertise to enrich the religious education curriculum.
- Adequately resourcing the subject in terms of materials, budget and the appointment of a religious education coordinator.
- Addressing the issues raised by assemblies.

Year' presents the major religious and cultural festivals and provides additional information concerning them. The chart can be obtained from:

The Festival Shop, 56 Poplar Road, Kings Heath, Birmingham, B14 7AG.

The National Society's RE Development Centre (see Table 4.2) produces *The Shap Calendar of Religious Festivals*. It is accompanied by a very helpful explanatory booklet.

Devising assemblies for multiracial primary schools present teachers with many dilemmas. The importance of informing children about other people's religious beliefs and practices has to be achieved without attempting to convert. Suggestions for assemblies in multiracial primary schools, based on a child-centred approach, are available (Peirce, 1992). Her book contains a range of suggestions that can readily be adapted to suit any primary school. Peirce's latest book is a companion volume to *Activity Assemblies for Christian Collective Worship* (Peirce, 1991).

Coventry has recently published a new Agreed Syllabus for Religious Education based on the multifaith approach required by the Education Reform Act 1988. The Agreed Syllabus has been developed so that it is linked with other National Curriculum requirements. It is one of the first Religious Education syllabuses to provide such clear linkages. These are presented in a handbook entitled *Curriculum Guidelines* (Coventry LEA, 1992a). A Handbook for teachers is available that complements the guidelines (Coventry LEA, 1992b).

In conclusion, one of the aims mentioned in the Hampshire Agreed Syllabus, *Visions of Life* (1992) states:

Religious Education should offer insight into the religious dimension of life. Pupils need to meet, in action and dialogue, people who are believers, so as to become aware of reality, strength and consequences of religious convictions . . . They will thus become more familiar with the human dimensions of the world they live in, more respectful of some of the less immediately obvious values in the civilization to which they are heirs, and better able to play a responsible part in the generation of their own culture. (Hampshire County Council, 1992, p. 4)

If we can help our children to appreciate religious and cultural diversity by fostering good relationships at all levels, perhaps we could measure the success of our schools against Gandhi's observation that a civilization should be judged by how it treats its minorities.

References

ALEXANDER, R., ROSE, J. and WOODHEAD, C. (1992) *Curriculum Organization and Classroom Practice in Primary Schools*, London, HMSO.

ASSISTANT MASTERS AND MISTRESSES ASSOCIATION (1992) *Update*, 63, September.

BABRAA, D.K. (1990) *Sikhism*, London, Longman.

BASTIDE, D. (Ed) (1992) *Good Practice in Primary Religious Education*, Basingstoke, The Falmer Press.

BRINE, A. (1989) *Islam*, London, Longman.

BURKE, D. (1992) *Food and Fasting*, East Sussex, Wayland.

COMMITTEE OF INQUIRY INTO THE EDUCATION OF CHILDREN FROM MINORITY ETHNIC GROUPS (1985) *Education for All*, Cmnd., 9453, London, HMSO.

COMPTON, A. (1992) *Marriage Customs*, East Sussex, Wayland.

CONNOLLY, P. and H. (1989) *Buddhism*, London, Longman.

COVENTRY LOCAL EDUCATION AUTHORITY (1992a) *Curriculum Guidelines: Agreed Syllabus for Religious Education*, Coventry, Coventry LEA.

COVENTRY LOCAL EDUCATION AUTHORITY (1992b) *Handbook: Agreed Syllabus for Religious Education*, Coventry, Coventry LEA.

DEAN, C., MAXWELL, E. and McTAGGART, M. (1992) 'Government assembly policy: a survey', *Times Educational Supplement*, 3991, p. 4.

DEPARTMENT OF EDUCATION AND SCIENCE (1989) *The Education Reform Act 1988: Religious Education and Collective Worship*, Circ. 3/89 Section 20, London, HMSO.

FULLAN, M. (1982) *The Meaning of Educational Change*, New York, Teachers College Press.

GATESHILL, P. and THOMSON, J. (1992) *Religious Artifacts in the Classroom*, Sevenoaks, Hodder and Stoughton.

GOLDMAN, R. (1964) *Religious Thinking from Childhood to Adolescence*, London, Routledge and Kegan Paul.

HAIGH, G. (1992) 'Sacred Ground', *Times Educational Supplement*, 3990, 18 December.

HAMPSHIRE COUNTY COUNCIL (1988) *Education for a Multicultural Society*, Winchester, HCC.

HAMPSHIRE COUNTY COUNCIL (1992) *Visions of Life — Agreed Syllabus for Religious Education*, Winchester, HCC.

HER MAJESTY'S INSPECTORATE (1989a) *Agreed Syllabuses and Religious Education: the influence of the agreed syllabus on teaching and learning in religious education in three local education authorities*, London, DES.

HER MAJESTY'S INSPECTORATE (1989b) *Religious Education in the Primary Schools of Wales*, London, DES.

HER MAJESTY'S INSPECTORATE (1990) *Standards in Education, 1988–1989, The Annual Report of HM Senior Chief Inspector of Schools*, London, DES.

HUGHES, R.O. (1989) *Christianity*, London, Longman.

HULL, J.M. (1989) 'Agreed syllabuses since the 1988 Education Reform Act', *British Journal of Religious Education*, 12, 1.

HULL, J.M. (1991) 'Should agreed syllabuses be mainly Christian?, *British Journal of Religious Education*, 14, 1.

JACKSON, R. (1989) *Hinduism*, London, Longman.

LAWTON, C. (1992) *Judaism*, London, Longman.

LONGMAN COMMUNITY INFORMATION GUIDES (1993) *Education Year Book*, London, Longman.

MORTIMORE, P., SAMMONS, P., STOLL, L., LEWIS, D. and ECOB, R. (1988) *School Matters — The Junior Years*, Exeter, Open Books.

NATIONAL CURRICULUM COUNCIL (1991a) *Analysis of SACRE Reports 1991*, York, NCC.

NATIONAL CURRICULUM COUNCIL (1991b) *Religious Education —A Local Curriculum Framework*, York, NCC.

NORCROSS, P. (1989) 'The effects of cultural conditioning on multi-faith education in the mono-cultural primary school,' *British Journal of Religious Education*, 11, 2.

PEIRCE, E. (1991) *Activity Assemblies for Christian Collective Worship*, Basingstoke, The Falmer Press.

PEIRCE, E. (1992) *Activity Assemblies for Multi-racial Schools 5–11*, Basingstoke, The Falmer Press.

PRIOR, K. (1992a) *Pilgrimages and Journeys*, East Sussex, Wayland.

PRIOR, K. (1992b) *Initiation Rites*, East Sussex, Wayland.

RELIGIOUS EDUCATION COUNCIL OF ENGLAND AND WALES (1989) *Handbook for Agreed Syllabus Conferences, SACREs and Schools*, Lancaster, Religious Education Council for England and Wales.

RUSHTON, L. (1992a) *Birth Customs*, East Sussex, Wayland.

RUSHTON, L. (1992b) *Death Customs*, East Sussex, Wayland.

SARASON, S. (1971) *The Culture of the School and the Problem of Change*, Boston, Allyn and Bacon.

SHROPSHIRE EDUCATION COMMITTEE (1992) *Christianity; Sikhism; Islam; Hinduism; and Judaism*, SECRU, Radbrook Centre, Shrewsbury.

SMART, N. (1968) *Secular Education and the Logic of Religion*, London, Faber and Faber.

TIMES EDUCATIONAL SUPPLEMENT (1992) 'Enforced Conversion', 3971, 7 August.

WARREN, M. (1978) *World Faiths in Education*, in COLE, W.O. (Ed) London, Unwin.

WATSON, B. (Ed) (1992) *Priorities in Religious Education*, Basingstoke, The Falmer Press.

Chapter 5

Core Subject: English

Leslie S. Woodcock

Context

The purpose of the first part of this chapter is to provide a survey of cultural and linguistic diversity in the National Curriculum for English, and to furnish a context for the second and third parts about future challenges and possible responses to those challenges. This section will trace the development of diversity from the Kingman report (Department of Education and Science, 1988a) through to the present day, considering the Cox report (DES, 1989b) and briefly, on the way, the LINC (Language In the National Curriculum, 1991) materials and the National Writing and Oracy Projects, all three of which have fed fruitfully into the teaching of English during the last few years.

Three strands contributed to the general trend towards a specification of the English language curriculum, which culminated in the Kingman report (DES, 1988a). Callaghan's (1976) Ruskin College speech started the first strand, and his speech highlighted higher expectations from schools, and higher standards being demanded from their pupils than was formerly the case. This impetus led to documents being produced by Her Majesty's Inspectorate (HMI) and the Department of Education and Science (DES), starting in 1976 with a trickle which became a stream by 1988 and a torrent by 1993. All these had the intention either of exploring what was being taught in schools, or clarifying what was to be taught. These documents were clearly aimed at stating the curriculum to be followed.

A second strand focused on language. The Bullock report (DES, 1975) predated the calls for a National Curriculum, which this chapter considers as starting in 1976. One of the Report's legacies, however, following its recommendation, was the establishment in 1975 of the Assessment of Performance Unit (APU). This was created to explore new ways of assessing pupils' language performance and to see whether they were using language effectively for school use and in daily life. This language strand consisted mainly of reports from the APU, and concerned oracy, writing and reading, as well as general language performance. To these reports must be added 'English for

5–16' (DES, 1984), a much-criticized document, but a highly significant one in formulating the National Curriculum. In this booklet Sir Keith Joseph, then Secretary of State for Education and Science commented:

> We intend, subject to the outcome of the consultative process which the paper initiates, and in consultation with those concerned within and outside the education service, to move towards a statement of aims and objectives for English teaching in schools which can serve as a basis for policy at national and local level. (Joseph, 1984)

In all these documents, from 1979 onwards, little or no consideration was given to cultural or linguistic diversity in the curriculum.

A final strand, which added further pressure for a more detailed curriculum, consisted of public comments about the state of English language use in society, and English language teaching in schools. These often were the views of individuals (such as Marenbon, 1987), or small groups. Durham (1988), for example reported that celebrities, led by Frank Muir and Sir Michael Hordern, had petitioned the Education Secretary, urging him, in Durham's words 'to restore the teaching of compulsory, formal grammar, including parsing, into schools.' The implication of all these views usually was that a return to more formal teaching of grammar as had previously occurred in schools (though with debatable results) would help rectify matters.

The move towards clarifying the curriculum, then, the focus on language, and some public unease about English in school and society, all contributed towards the establishment of the Committee of Inquiry into the Teaching of English Language (DES, 1988a), chaired by Sir John Kingman. Although preceded by the documents mentioned earlier, the Kingman report can be regarded as the foundation of English in the National Curriculum, in a sense the grandparent, leading to the Cox reports (DES, 1988b and 1989b) and eventually to English in the National Curriculum (DES, 1989a and 1990). Figure 5.1 makes clear the relationship of these main elements and the time scale involved.

What did the report say about cultural diversity in English? As a general principle, it stated the importance of language in creating and expressing identity, and placing the individual in society as a member of various groups. In addition there were specific references to language in the home and community, and also to language variation.

About this variation, Kingman made two important points. Firstly, all languages are rule-governed and of equal linguistic importance, a fact which teachers and pupils should respect; English is not linguistically superior. Secondly, the child speaking another language on entering an English-speaking classroom has immense linguistic knowledge which can be used as a lively classroom resource.

In comments on language in the home and community there was acknowledgment, albeit briefly, of Britain's multicultural and multilingual character, although the emphasis was primarily on how incoming groups

Figure 5.1: *The Relationship of the Main Elements Comprising English in the National Curriculum and the Chronology Involved*

	DES	NCC	The National Curriculum
March 1988	The Kingman report		
November 1988	The Cox report 1 (5–11)		
March 1989		Consultation report 1 (5–11)	
May 1989 (Implemented Autumn 1989)			English in the National Curriculum KS1 (5–7)
June 1989	The Cox report 2 (5–16) (incorporated the Cox report 1)		
November 1989		Consultation report 2 (5–16)	
March 1990 (Implemented Autumn 1990)			English in the National Curriculum KS2 (7–11)

have enriched English. The significance of language, too, in ordering cultural and social experiences was acknowledged, the report endorsing the Bullock report's view that children's linguistic and cultural inheritance and facility in language should be encouraged, not suppressed (DES, 1975, para. 20.5). Pupils, the Kingman report stated, are members of 'at least three social groups', namely, the family, the peer group, and wider society. This means that different kinds of language, all legitimate, will be used within each group, and so pupils need this facility in language.

Despite these references to cultural diversity, there were adverse reactions to this aspect of the Kingman report. Many came soon after publication, but before the working group (the Cox committee) had reported. This group was charged with translating the proposals into workable form for schools (DES, 1989b). Before the Kingman committee reported, there was some hostility. Concern was expressed about the terms of reference (see Knight, 1987, for example) and its aims and composition (Kirkman, 1987). Surprisingly omitted from the committee, Rosen (1988) was critical, among other things, of the lack of representation of people with experience of multicultural education. It could be argued that the terms of reference did not specifically brief the committee to consider multicultural aspects and practice, although Brumfitt (1988) felt that the terms could easily have been changed 'to recognize the indivisibility of language acquisition in a multilingual society' (p. 9).

After publication, one comment was that the Kingman report viewed the pupil population simplistically, as homogeneous, 'whereas the reality for many teachers is a school population whose identities are shaped by considerations of race, class and gender' (N.A., 1988, p. 5). Perhaps partly because of this, the report was accused, again by Rosen (reported by Nash, 1988a), of greatly neglecting the role of linguistic diversity in the teaching of English, a point echoed by Brumfitt (1988) who wrote that both here and abroad English 'has a multi-lingual base and has irreversibly changed as a result' (p. 9).

The apparently low status accorded to minority languages in the Kingman report was highlighted by Masterman and Ashworth (1988), but much stronger comments came from Cameron and Bourne (1988). They thought that Figure 4 ('historical and geographical variation') of the Kingman model of the English language (which they called a 'territorial model') should have included variations based on class and ethnic groups — a highly significant omission, they thought, in Kingman's attempt 'to strengthen and protect the English language at the expense of other languages' (p. 59). Cameron and Bourne continued:

> If languages belong to geographical areas with unbroken continuity of use in those areas, then each has its own proper place within which speakers may have 'rights'. Punjabi in Birmingham becomes a historical accident and a territorial aberration, a temporary occupation of someone else's space. At best we can teach children to respect the languages their classmates bring to school, but the territorial model makes it clear that those languages to not 'belong' here in England. (Cameron and Bourne, 1988, p. 154)

In other words, reference to diversity was lip-service, they implied.

Despite this, the Kingman report could be regarded as a starting-point, the foundation for the later working group to build on, as we shall see below, and the range of further reading about the model showed that some consideration, however small and inadequate (and bearing in mind again the terms of reference), had been given to linguistic diversity (DES, 1988a, Appendix 7).

Or was this all make-believe, for Kingman omitted to mention the Swann report about the education of ethnic minority children (DES, 1985)? Was this because of the terms of reference mentioned earlier, or was there a feeling on the Kingman committee that it had said enough about diversity, without getting into deeper issues and implications? Whatever the reason, a major government report, with a chapter on 'Language and Language Education' (Chapter 7, pp. 385–464) and other parts throughout on language, was ignored by a subsequent committee dealing with the English language three years later.

Perhaps Kingman was simply putting the onus on the National Curriculum English Working Group, chaired by Professor C.B. Cox to take matters about diversity further. At first, apprehension about the results of this group's deliberations was felt by teachers and other educationalists concerned with linguistic and cultural diversity. Generally, there were two reasons for this unease.

Firstly, there was the appointment of Cox himself, a former Black Paper editor and writer, as Chair of the group, coupled with the absence of representatives from the National Association for the Teaching of English (NATE), perhaps the main professional association for English teaching. Would the limited treatment of cultural and linguistic diversity of the Kingman report be repeated, or reversed, in the Cox report?

Secondly, this anxiety was initially heightened by the terms of reference and supplementary guidance for the group (DES, 1989b, Appendices 2 and 3 respectively). These seemed to make little reference to diversity; if anything, they appeared to emphasize cultural and linguistic insularity and traditionalism.

Other comments in these appendices indicated scope for a broader perspective. The absence of detailed specification about literature, advice about consultation and what to consider, and the emphasis on teachers' enterprise and flexibility were all important. Equally significantly, the working group was asked to 'take account of the ethnic diversity of the school population and society at large'. On closer reading of the brief, it seemed that there were 'windows' which could be opened, if the group chose so to do.

To a large extent the Cox committee did take the opportunities presented, although some writers thought it should have gone much further on some issues. Generally, within education, the Cox report was met with some relief and some surprise. There was relief that there had been wide consultation, and that careful consideration had been given to produce a new 'consensus' about English teaching (Bayliss, 1988). There was also surprise about the amount of reference to cultural and linguistic diversity — no doubt due, in part, to the influence of a committee member, Professor Michael Stubbs, well-known for his writing on language diversity (Stubbs, 1980, 1982, 1986). The working group took advantage of its brief and commented at some length on cultural and linguistic diversity. Table 5.1 summarizes this diversity.

Of course, not everyone was satisfied. In fact the Secretary of State for Education and Science at the time, clearly was displeased (Nash, 1988b). Jones (1992) was critical of virtually the whole of the Cox report and its assumptions, whilst other comments ranged widely. The way 'to a firmly based but flexible and developing linguistic and cultural identity' (DES, 1989b, para. 2.12) was much more haphazard and lengthy than the Cox committee believed, wrote Gilliver (1989), whilst Carter (1988) commented on 'the lack of encouragement of personal growth through the nourishment of children's imagination and aesthetic lives' (p. 19). Texts from other cultures, too, were worthy of study in themselves, without being used simply to learn about the world, wrote Simons (1989).

But it was the report's treatment of bilingualism and mother-tongue issues which provoked the strongest feelings. Ambiguity between intention and practice was highlighted by Mines (1989), with bilingualism being *seen* positively, but *encouraged* very little, and only until facility with English was acquired (that is, bilingualism was seen as transitional[1]), a stance which Savva (1990) believed treated bilinguals only as learners of English as a second language. In short, the Cox report, she felt, was based on a deficit view of bilingualism. This view, argued Savva, was reinforced by the fact that resources reflecting linguistic diversity seemed to be needed only to give extra help to bilinguals and not as resources for all pupils to explore and develop diversity.

This concern about bilingualism was closely related to others about mother-tongue maintenance, although the two concepts are not synonymous. In short, mother-tongue maintenance implies a much more active approach to the mother tongue, involving time-tabled lessons in order to develop fluency, something the Swann report (DES, 1985) did not recommend. Whilst the Cox report had a chapter with seventeen paragraphs (Chapter 10) on bilingual children, it never mentioned maintaining the mother tongue. Stubbs (1989), writing after publication, felt that the committee had 'clearly failed on this topic', underestimating its importance and not thinking through the issues involved which, among other things, had 'to do with national heritage and unity' (p. 245). His strong comments about this were a sharp reminder of both the context of diversity in the National Curriculum for English and how practice should support intention:

> The Report was destined inevitably to be read against a background where linguistic and cultural homogeneity are offically valued, where an assimilationist policy is taken for granted, though never explicitly stated, where language diversity highlights social and cultural diversity which would rather be denied, and where discrimination against language diversity is all the more powerful because it is hidden (perhaps

Table 5.1: A Summary of Cultural and Linguistic Diversity in the Cox Report

THE MULTICULTURAL NATURE OF SOCIETY AND SCHOOL

2.8 • need for informed curricular discussion about multicultural society
• need for sensitivity to other languages and foreign languages
2.10 • need for citizens informed about language issues
10.3/ • about 5% of schools where a
10.4 significant proportion of pupils do not have English as mother tongue — a 'very great pool of linguistic competence'

STEREOTYPING AND RACISM

— see Section 2
7.4 • teachers need to give careful
11.6 introductions and support when using potentially offensive texts, and care in subject choice
11.7 • need for balanced selection of literature British/non-British, male/female etc.
11.8 • need for encouragement for all pupils to read variety of genres which challenge stereotypes etc.
11.13 • sensitivity to preferred language norms and knowledge of culture and conventions needed.

THE RICHNESS OF HOME LANGUAGES

2.8 — see Section 1
2.11 • large numbers of bilingual/biliterate children an enormous resource
6.10 • need to avoid underestimating complex competence in mother tongues
6.11 • need to start from pupils' own (often extensive) linguistic competence
10.3 — see Section 1
10.4 — see Section 1

RESPECT AND UNDERSTANDING

2.12 • school leavers should have acquired identity, understanding of languages and their roles, and cultural tolerance and adaptability
7.4 • pupils should understand how texts relate to interests and different groups

BASIC PRINCIPLES OF THE REPORT

2.5 the approach is 'enabling rather than restricting'
6.13 '... language in all its diversity can be approached in a non-prescriptive non-judgemental way ...'

LINGUISTIC AND CULTURAL IDENTITY

2.7 • endorsement of Bullock report para 20.5
2.12 — see Sections 2 and 3
11.5 • through language judgements are made about backgrounds, abilities and intelligence, and culture is often expressed through literature and other language media
11.6 — see Section 4
11.13 — see Section 4

MATERIALS/RESOURCES

6.15 • knowledge about language in the programmes of study should be based mostly on everyday resources which teachers and pupils should be alert to and knowledgeable about
7.4 — see section 2
7.5 • literature should be drawn from different countries. All pupils need this rich experience, and teachers should 'seek opportunities to exploit the multicultural aspects of literature'
8.7 • drama has especial value for learners of English as a second language
11.5 — see Section 7
11.6 — see Sections 4 and 7
11.7 — see Section 4

(Beddis and Mares, 1988)

SENSITIVITY TO LOCAL CIRCUMSTANCES
2.4 • need for LEA and school policies sensitive to local circumstances
2.12 — see Section 2
3.1 • teacher needs respect for, and interest in, learner's language, culture, thought and intentions etc.
6.14 • importance of relevant materials for understanding language diversity

BIAS, AND CARE NEEDED IN ASSESSMENTS
10.1 • all pupils need competence in English but consideration must be given to ethnic diversity of the school and society

10.7 • some exemptions are possible from assessment in English
11.2 • issues of gender, race, disability and religion etc. must be considered in the National Curriculum and its assessment
11.9 • need for care about gender and ethnicity when assessing pupils
11.10 • curricular/assessment arrangements should raise expectations and performance despite social/ethnic backgrounds
11.11 • possibility of bias in oracy because of interaction between oracy, personality and background

11.17 • need to minimise bias in assessment instruments/tasks and take care with comparisons
LINGUISTIC DIVERSITY
5.17 • for an understanding of linguistic diversity terms such as accent, received pronunciation, dialect, slang or style might be introduced . . . . .
5.36 • language variety arises because language changes according to topic, addressee, setting and task. It also changes over time in different areas and in different social groups. Language change is natural and inevitable
6.13 — see centre box
6.19 • the contents of courses involving knowledge about language are outlined

Note: This figure excludes mention within the Programmes of Study and Attainment Targets.
Source: DES, 1989b.

> even to the perpetrator) in an empty liberal rhetoric. (Stubbs, 1989,
> p. 245)

During the consultation period, following the publication of Cox report 2 (DES, 1989b), comments about cultural diversity were received by the NCC from interested parties, relating to the multicultural nature of society, to bilingualism and to the mention of literature in Cox's proposals (NCC, 1989a, 1989b). They did not, however, lead to changes relating to cultural and linguistic diversity in English in the National Curriculum, although other changes occurred as a result of comments received. The National Curriculum for English (DES, 1989a and 1990), then — both the early Key Stage 1 and later Key Stage 2 versions — was substantially the same as proposed in the Cox reports. The responses to the NCC consultation exercise did lead to a later circular (NCC, 1991) giving more detailed, and seemingly positive advice for teachers on how to use and develop diversity, and how to include the needs of bilingual pupils in school planning. Problems relating to this circular were pointed out by Parke (1991), however, who referred to 'conceptual confusion', the nature of bilingualism, which was undefined, and the kind of benefits (and for whom) of linguistic diversity. Parke concluded that the circular would be of little practical value to heads and teachers and little use for assessing bilingual pupils.

Shortly after publication of the first Cox report for ages 5–11 (DES, 1988b), and its NCC counterpart (NCC, 1989a), the LINC project started — a training programme for teachers and teacher educators based on the Kingman report and its model of the English language. Linguistic diversity permeated the LINC programme and materials, and in his introduction to the project Carter (1990) made it clear that linguistic variation was at its heart and a 'principle and underlying motivation' (p. 6). One assumption was the inter-relationship of language, culture and identity. Carter stressed how all pupils need 'to use as wide a range of language varieties as competently as possible' (p. 16) to prepare them for future life, and to strengthen them against those in society seeking to restrict individuals and groups.

In addition to these basic tenets, the final draft of the materials actively encouraged both cultural and linguistic diversity (LINC, 1991). This multi-cultural, multilingual approach also featured in much of the local LINC materials, certainly in Yorkshire. The 'cascade' model of LINC training was interpreted differently by LEAs. Some were very literal and used what might be called 'bottom-down' (i.e., imposed) systems, whilst others used 'bottom-up' approaches. The latter were usually more appreciated by teachers as successful and imaginative classroom practice influenced the training more (Carter, 1992a). To great consternation and protest, however, the government refused *both* publication of the materials, and *also* to waive Crown Copyright in order for them to be published commercially, although their use as training materials in both initial teacher-training and for in-service work was allowed, albeit reluctantly (Cook, 1991, Goddard, 1991, and Carter, 1992b). There were many protests, but one example will suffice. The British Association for Applied Linguistics asked the Minister to reconsider his action because 'the materials are now being limited to a narrow specialist group' (*The Times Higher Educational Supplement*, 1991). Among the reasons given by the government for refusing publication were that

> A number of fashionable secondary agendas have pushed into the foreground. An obvious example is the unit on 'Accents, Dialect and Standard English, most of which is in fact concerned with non-standard English . . . the end product would convey a number of wrong impressions — most dangerously that ungrammatical or badly presented work should be understood and condoned rather than corrected. (Eggar, 1991)

The LINC materials have generally proved very popular with teachers and there has been considerable demand for them from abroad.

Other materials beside the LINC ones have fed into English in the National Curriculum. The National Writing Project (September, 1985 to August, 1988) was almost complete when the Kingman report appeared in March 1988. Based as they were on classroom practice and teachers collaborating, the National Writing Project materials naturally reflected the cultural diversity of many of the classrooms. One volume of the published materials related to language diversity in writing (SCDC, 1990). It started with language use and moved through explorations in language to developing and supporting bilingual writers. Both during the project and since, the National Writing Project has proved an invaluable resource for teachers to draw on for the classroom. It has provided another example of the energy, imagination and enterprise of teachers in enriching the English curriculum.

The National Oracy Project is likewise influencing the English curriculum. Again, the evidence is that it reflects the diversity of cultures in the classroom and enriches the English curriculum (see, for example NCC, 1990, an issue devoted largely to language diversity, and also Norman, 1992), although, of course, oracy permeates the whole curriculum. Figure 5.2 shows how various language projects feed into the National Curriculum for English.

As well as these three major national ventures there have been many local initiatives to support the teaching of English in the National Curriculum, and these have often been undertaken by Local Education Authorities (LEAs) who have been mindful of the diversity of their school populations — a fact usually reflected in their materials.

What is the current position relating to cultural and linguistic diversity in the National Curriculum for English? By the end of the academic year 1992–3, most of the current English curriculum will have been implemented, and it appears to have been working well and liked by teachers generally. By the end of 1993–94, the whole curriculum for English should have been fully implemented. The government, however, proposed a revision of the English

Figure 5.2: The Chronology of the National Curriculum for English and the Various Projects which Feed into It (excluding 1993* Proposals)

	The National Writing Project	The National Oracy Project	Government Reports	The National Curriculum	Language in the National Curriculum (LINC)
1985	September				
1986					
1987					
1988	August	September	**March** The Kingman report **November** The Cox report 1 (5–11)		
1989			**June** The Cox report 2 (5–16)	**May** English in the National Curriculum KS1	**April**
1990				**March** English in the National Curriculum KS2	
1991					
1992					**March**
1993		**August**		**April** *Proposals: National Curriculum English (5–16)	

Order (NCC, 1992) before this full implementation, causing anxiety and incredulity within teaching. The English curriculum was claimed to be cumbersome and complicated and, in some areas, weak and lacking in clarity.

This review (NCC, 1993), or perhaps more correctly 're-write', has attracted much hostility. Called 'narrow and nostalgic' by Barrs *et al.*, (1993), the proposed new curriculum has been likened to a battlefield by some (*The Independent*, 1993, Hofkins, 1993). Marshall (1993) commented that:

> It returns to an arid curriculum which views language as something fixed and immutable and ignores the place of much modern literature. It is an attempt to return to a mythical consensus of a homogenous English culture and fails to address the rich diversity of modern Britain.

What do the proposals contain about cultural and linguistic diversity? The clear message is that linguistic diversity is to be *discouraged* and linguistic uniformity *encouraged*. Gone is the former acknowledgment of the value of pupils' cultural and linguistic backgrounds, both in their own right and as means to increased understanding about language and language use. Gone, too, are statements about encouraging respect for languages and dialects.

Former, specific references to cultural and linguistic diversity in the Programmes of Study and Attainment Targets are either absent or diluted. Remarks about cultural diversity related to stories for 5–7-year-olds, for example, are removed from speaking and listening. Throughout reading there is a new emphasis on 'texts of central importance to the literary heritage', although 'wide reading' is to be encouraged, including 'texts in English from other cultures and traditions'. No mention is made now of the value to reading of pupils' oral language experiences in the home, although parental reading support is acknowledged. Nor is there mention now of using literature which 'considers pupils' linguistic competencies and backgrounds'. The usefulness to early writing of seeing literacy in other languages at home is altered to the more generalized comment about 'existing linguistic knowledge' helping with the structure and meaning of writing. Finally, explorations of language, its use and diversity are removed from the Programmes of Study for 11-year-olds upwards.

The most controversial part of the proposals is the requirement that spoken Standard English (SE) be taught at Key Stage 1 (5–7-year-olds) rather than at Key Stage 3 (12–14-year-olds). By age 11, average pupils should have achieved 'proficiency' in spoken SE and be able 'to use *all* (my italics) its basic conventions', and testing attainment in SE is proposed for average 9 and 11-year-olds. Parinder (1993) calls this proposal 'the doctrinaire enforcement of spoken Standard English'. This earlier and more vigorous insistence on SE is likely to prove difficult both to teach and to assess (Cox, quoted in Dore, 1993), and it may well handicap pupils from homes where English is a second language or where strong dialect features exist. These changes, however, are, as yet, *proposals*, and as such are, in a sense, a footnote to the discussions in this chapter. These proposals apart, then, what are the challenges for the future?

Until now teachers have been able to choose and adapt methods and materials to their own, often multicultural circumstances, drawing on the imaginative national and local materials mentioned earlier, to enrich their work within the National Curriculum. It is probably true to say that linguistic diversity has been explored in many ways, in many parts of the country and by many teachers in manners that have surprised the Kingman and Cox committees. Considerable richness has been added to the English curriculum since 1988.

Challenges

At the beginning it must be said that all which follows, both here and in the later 'Responses', is predicated on the notion that developing cultural and linguistic diversity in English teaching is not only rewarding and enriching, but essential for *all* pupils and teachers, the school, community and society. Indeed, it could be argued that it is crucial at this stage in the country's development.

There are now two challenges for the future relating to cultural diversity in the English curriculum. One concerns developing diversity still further within the United Kingdom and the other with extending it to incorporate European or global aspects. In this first challenge — how to develop cultural and linguistic diversity still further — there are a number of issues to consider. One argument is that Britain has failed to produce coherent principles, policies and practices so that now there is a society which most people do not regard as multilingual — despite many people speaking languages different from English in their homes, and many pupils speaking and learning other languages, both in school and elsewhere (Mackinnon and Densham, 1989). The Linguistic Minorities Project (1985), for example, found that in five English LEAs 36,726 pupils were found to use a language other than English at home, with Haringey reporting eighty-seven 'identifiably distinct languages' (p. 330). Mackinnon and Densham (1989) quoted sources putting the number of children in Welsh primary schools having some tuition in Welsh as 169,000, and in Scotland over 10,000 were learning Gaelic. There are, however, primary schools where linguistic diversity is still minimally encouraged and where children's home cultures are largely neglected. There are also some 'all-white' schools, where diversity within the school is, to some extent, masked, and diversity in the community and nation acknowledged only a little. How, then, can teachers, whatever their circumstances, further develop linguistic diversity in English teaching?

A second challenge concerns diversity on a wider scale. Having established a substantial base for English teaching involving linguistic diversity

Table 5.2: Summary of challenges: English

---

1. How to develop acceptance and utilization of cultural and linguistic diversity *still further within Britain.*
2. How to extend explorations of diversity *to include Europe and the World.*

---

within Britain, perhaps the time is now appropriate to extend this, and explore diversity farther afield. With increasingly sophisticated communication methods, linguistic diversity can be explored, as is already happening to some extent, through intercultural contacts with Europe and the world. How can teachers respond? These considerable and demanding challenges are summarized in Table 5.2.

Responses

The first challenge was how to develop diversity still further within English teaching in Britain. Much to the distaste of some critics of present-day education, teachers have already considerably developed cultural and linguistic diversity within the English curriculum. Houlton has shown how multiculturalism and multilingualism can permeate the whole curriculum (Houlton, 1986, p. 112), and can infuse certain topics (Houlton, 1985, pp. 18–19); he has also described how diversity can be exploited in varied curriculum areas (Houlton, 1985, pp. 14–15). These are all highly effective and practical ways of highlighting diversity. Are they sufficient, however, to ensure that cultural and linguistic diversity is developed further, or is something more required? Here it is argued that more *is* required, and three areas will be considered, namely the creation of an appropriate policy, the management of topic work within school and the use of resources to support this work.

One recommendation of the Swann report (DES, 1985, para. 4.18) was that LEAs should ensure that schools develop policies relating to cultural diversity, and other sources have provided guidance and practical examples showing schools how this can be done (such as Houlton, 1986, Chapter 6). To develop diversity within English teaching, however, there is a need for more sharply focused policies; these would have as a clear aim the preparation of children for life in a linguistically-diverse society. Without coherent and systematic school policies relating to linguistic diversity in the English curriculum, the efforts of individual teachers, however committed or informed, are likely to be incidental or inappreciable. How can schools approach this task, and what should be considered for inclusion?

Corson (1991) thought that two key factors need to be considered: the linguistic and cultural backgrounds of the children, and the teachers' attitudes towards, and professional knowledge about, their school's languages and cultures. One way to start the process of making an appropriate language policy, Corson suggested, is to create databases in the two areas mentioned.

This involves small-scale, school-based research, and so some teacher expertise in this is needed. As input from the community is required (in the area of children's cultures and home languages), sensitivity to this information and its use is needed. Information collected about the children would include their cultural backgrounds and home languages (and facility in them). For teachers, information would be included on staff knowledge about language, dialect, mother-tongue issues and so on. From databases such as these, questions for discussion are formulated under various headings which eventually lead to clearer statements and the development of a policy. The task is complex, however, and many issues need to be resolved (Corson, 1991, pp. 10–16).

To complement an effective policy which exploits linguistic diversity, there needs to be clearly-planned topic management within the school. This involves thought being given to the strategic planning of topic work, by placing topics carefully within the short, medium and long-term development plans. Teaching and learning will then occur incrementally so that, by the time children leave primary schools at age 11, a clear and coherent programme has been followed.

But more than that, topic management involves giving prominence at certain appropriate times to topics which are clearly focused on linguistic diversity, such as writing systems, varieties of language, and multicultural stories. Primary schools can learn something from secondary school organization in this respect — certainly for older age groups in the primary school. Savva (1990), for example, gave a clear description of how a language-awareness course was designed for first year pupils in a comprehensive school, and aspects of this are clearly relevant to the primary school. These sharply-defined topics can occur either in the ordinary, careful sequence of topic work mentioned above, or they can run in parallel to it, perhaps using a half day a week; this has been an approach used by some schools in Bell's (1991) research. It may be that this way commends itself to schools unfamiliar with exploring diversity. It may also be more appropriate to explore European aspects first (as mentioned below) in very sensitive localities.

To support an effective policy in English and the careful management of topic work, thoughtful planning about resources is crucial. Three points can be made about resources. Firstly, they need to be available to support the development of cultural diversity in general, and this is a prerequisite to exploring linguistic diversity in the English curriculum. One way to develop diversity is by having focused, structured and portable resource packs about individual countries and cultures; such packs are common in some schools. Bell (1991) has reported the use of these packs in relation to European projects (see Bell, pp. 17–18), but the contents are highly appropriate for more widespread use. Packs contained: slides, large photos, posters, games, transparencies, maps/globes, and reading materials, dances, and songs. One starting point is by creating packs related to the backgrounds of children currently in school, followed by other countries in a priority order determined by the school. Countries involved would be from the:

- Asian subcontinent;
- Caribbean;
- EC; and
- other areas from which there are significant numbers of children in British schools — if not included above — namely: China, Cyprus, Italy, Poland, Ukraine and Vietnam (see Chapter 3 and Volume 4 Chapter 2).

In addition, resource packs can be created around multicultural themes such as alphabets, music etc.

Secondly, there are useful databases available for schools wishing to find resources for classroom use relating to cultural and linguistic diversity. One is the AIMER database (Access to Information on Multicultural Education Resources) operated by the University of Reading. Access to this is by postal enquiry and subscription, and materials are regularly updated. As well as multicultural materials generally, there are language-support materials available for learners of English at different stages, and materials in a variety of community languages. This AIMER database could also be accessed through the NERIS database (National Educational Resources Information Service) (See Chapter 1, Table 1.1 for addresses). Until recently, the latter was a large-scale database providing information on teaching and learning resources for teachers, other educationalists and librarians, although it was also used by pupils requiring information on topics. Material was available through subscription, using a computer, modem and telephone system or by using CD-ROM. Many descriptors were available, eight being listed under the National Curriculum dimensions of multiculturalism and multilingualism. The recent *Windows* and Macintosh versions are reported to have considerably improved NERIS (Kenny, 1992). Regrettably, the DFE has now withdrawn funding, although existing subscribers using CD-ROM will have the materials available until March, 1994.

Thirdly, schools need to be fully aware of, and to use to the maximum extent, materials from existing projects involving diversity. All schools need to have easily available the materials of the:

- LINC project;
- National Writing Project;
- National Oracy Project;
- Schools Council Mother Tongue Project (Houlton, 1985, 1986); and
- World Languages Project, (Garson, S. *et al.*, 1989).

These are invaluable classroom resources and would seem to form the core of materials in this area. Not only do the materials need to be *available* for staff use, but their use needs to be constantly *encouraged* by headteachers, senior staff, language-post holders and other teachers concerned with multicultural education.

Finally, how can explorations of diversity in English be extended to include Europe and the world? Here the holistic approach of much primary-school work is especially appropriate. Teaching and learning in any curriculum area in the primary school involves communication, whether through oracy, writing or reading (and exceptionally by other means). Work involving, or about, Europe or other world areas — as it by necessity involves language — is an excellent means of exploring cultural and linguistic diversity. An example of this was the BBC Television programme 'Primary Geography', where, in the year 1991–2, localities in India and Greece were examined (Scoffham, Jewson, and Bridge, 1991).

An exciting way of exploring diversity, both incidentally and intentionally, is by computer, through electronic mail (e-mail); this enables participants to send and receive messages and other documents world-wide. To do this requires a computer, appropriate software, a modem and access to a telephone. For newcomers to the area Wishart's (1988) and Mercer's (1989) articles offer an introduction, justification for e-mail's use, and practical comments on the logistics involved. Mercer's, too, gives a number of useful examples.

This approach can be particularly useful for smaller and more isolated schools where contacts can be limited. A small village primary school, for example, in South Yorkshire, near the Peak District moors, uses AppleLink and Apple Macintosh computers to communicate with a school in Massachusetts, USA, and also a tiny one on the Norwegian island of Røevaer (N.A., 1992)[2]. These contacts bring diversity into the classroom through the project work involved. A similar, but larger service is provided by Campus 2000,[3] a product of British Telecom and *The Times* newspaper. Primary projects are extensive in this system, and in addition to school links, computer conferencing, and access to databases and satellite images are all possible. Project Gemini is a recent addition which supports projects aiming to develop electronic communication still further (Holderness, 1992, Worsley, 1992).

A more simple and effective way to explore diversity is by using any personal contacts a class or school may have to twin with others elsewhere in the world. Children's parents originating from, say, Greece, may well be able to facilitate links with classes and schools in that country through relatives and friends there.

There are, however, more structured approaches for linking schools, and these often have the overt aim of developing intercultural understanding. In turn this leads to exploration of cultural, and, often, linguistic diversity. For those interested, there are primary-school projects which can be used as models for developing links between the UK and abroad. An important one was School Links International, a three-year programme to develop intercultural understanding through geography (Beddis and Mares, 1988). The project involved class-to-class linking, with pupils communicating readily with peers abroad and exchanging class work often and regularly. Schools in Avon were linked with others in Africa, North and South America, Australasia, the Far East and the Indian subcontinent, as well as Europe. Most pupils used their mother tongues when communicating, but there was much exploration of

Table 5.3: Summary of responses: English

1. To *develop* diversity still further within Britain the following *are needed:*
   - coherent and systematic language policies
   - careful topic management within a structured framework
   - specific topics to highlight diversity
   - the extensive use of well-planned resources
2. To *extend* explorations of diversity to include Europe and the world the following *are suggested:*
   - linking classrooms and schools by e-mail
   - personal contacts to establish informal links
   - structured approaches to establish formal links
   - using specialized agencies to help promote awareness and to develop projects

other languages. Clearly the pupils learnt much about one another's languages and cultures, and this project remains an important one to consider for anyone thinking of developing international links. Avon Education Department now has a leading role in promoting European awareness in education.

Specifically focused on learning about Europe was the action research project, 'Teaching about Europe in the Primary School' (Bell, 1991). This is an invaluable project to consult, and Bell produced a comprehensive and clear account of it, with detailed and practical examples. The work involved teacher-training institutions and primary schools in Italy, West Germany, Holland, Belgium, France and England. Both this project and the School Links International one mentioned above are examples of how careful research and planning beforehand lead to successful linking and, thence, to exploration of cultural and linguistic diversity.

Besides e-mail and projects such as these there are other ways of introducing study of diversity into the language curriculum. One example is the use of the Central Bureau for Educational Visits and Exchanges.[4] This is very active in promoting European awareness and sponsoring development projects in primary education and its work goes far beyond what its title may suggest. The Schools' Unit offers very useful information to those teachers seeking to introduce European aspects into the curriculum, and it can assist with school and class links. There is also a free 'Penfriend Service'.

After tracing the development of the National Curriculum for English and the treatment of diversity within it, challenges for the future and possible responses to them have been presented. The challenges appear simple, but the responses to them are complex. These responses are summarized in Table 5.3.

The English curriculum in the last decade of the twentieth century needs to move forwards, not backwards as some critics seem to wish. More than ever before, committed and imaginative teachers are needed, and they have to defend and articulate their practices in order to retain control of the English curriculum. If they use some of the responses outlined here to develop and extend cultural and linguistic diversity, then this curriculum will be a rich, varied and effective one for all pupils.

Notes

1 'Transitional bilingualism', according to Fishman (1976), is where, in this country, the mother tongue is used until some facility in English is developed. At this point bilingualism stops as the goal is not dual fluency. It can be regarded as the first of four stages, with the last being full (biliterate) bilingualism.
2 For information about AppleLink contact:
   AppleLink Services, 6 Roundwood Avenue, Stockley Park, Uxbridge, UB11 1BB (Tel. 081–569–1199).
   After a registration fee (which includes software) the subsequent cost depends on how much the system is used, the speed desired to connect with others, and the cost of a phone call to an access point, often locally.
3 For information about Campus 2000 contact:
   Campus 2000, Priory House, St. John's Lane, London, EC1M 4HD (Tel. 071–782–7104/7401).
   There are varied levels of annual subscription and also premium services, and software is available for most of the major computer systems.
4 Central Bureau for Educational Visits and Exchanges, Seymour Mews House, Seymour Mews, London, W1H 9PE (Tel. 071–486–5101).
   The Bureau is also the UK Centre for European Education; these centres exist in all EC countries.

References

BARRS, M., DOMBEY, H., FRATER, G. and JOHNSON, J. (1993) 'A love of nostalgia', *The Times Educational Supplement*, May, p. 3.

BAYLISS, S. (1988) 'Cox committee spells out a new consensus', *The Times Educational Supplement*, 18 November, p. 8.

BEDDIS, R. and MARES, C. (1988) *School Links International: A New Approach to Primary School Linking Around the World*, Avon, Avon County Council Education Department/Tidy Britain Group Schools' Research Project.

BELL, G.H. (1991) *Developing a European Dimension in Primary Schools*, London, David Fulton.

BRUMFITT, C. (1988) in 'Responses to Kingman: A Symposium', *English in Education*, 22, 3, pp. 4–13.

CALLAGHAN, J. (1976) 'Towards a national debate', *Education*, 22 October, pp. 332–3.

CAMERON, D. and BOURNE, J. (1988) 'No common ground: Kingman, grammar and the nation. A Linguistic and Historical Perspective on the Kingman Report', *Language and Education*, 2, 3, pp. 147–59.

CARTER, D. (1988) 'A depressing utilitarian ring', *The Times Educational Supplement*, 9 December, p. 19.

CARTER, R. (1990) Introduction, CARTER, R. (Ed) *Knowledge About Language and the Curriculum: The LINC Reader*, London, Hodder and Stoughton, pp. 1–20.

CARTER, R. (1992a) Personal communication to the author, 5 November.

CARTER, R. (1992b) 'The LINC Project: The Final Chapter', *NATE News*, July, pp. 12–14.

COOK, M. (1991) 'Paying the piper', *Education*, 12 July, p. 33.

CORSON, D.J. (1991) 'Realities of teaching in a multiethnic school', *International Review of Education*, 37, 1, pp. 7–31.

DEPARTMENT OF EDUCATION AND SCIENCE (1975) *A language for life* (The Bullock Report), London, HMSO.

DEPARTMENT OF EDUCATION AND SCIENCE (1984) *English from 5 to 16, Curriculum Matters 1: An HMI Series*, London, HMSO.

DEPARTMENT OF EDUCATION AND SCIENCE (1985) *Education For All: The Report of the Committee of Inquiry into the Education of Children from Ethnic Minority Groups* (The Swann Report), London, HMSO.

DEPARTMENT OF EDUCATION AND SCIENCE (1988a) *Report of the Committee of Inquiry into the Teaching of English Language* (The Kingman Report), London, HMSO.

DEPARTMENT OF EDUCATION AND SCIENCE (1988b) *English for ages 5–11* (The Cox Report 1), London, HMSO.

DEPARTMENT OF EDUCATION AND SCIENCE (1989a) *English in the National Curriculum* (Key Stage 1), London, HMSO.

DEPARTMENT OF EDUCATION AND SCIENCE (1989b) *English for ages 5–16* (The Cox Report 2), London, HMSO.

DEPARTMENT OF EDUCATION AND SCIENCE (1990) *English in the National Curriculum* (Key Stages 2 and 3), London, HMSO.

DORE, A. (1993) 'Critics rude about rise of mechanics', *The Times Educational Supplement*, 5 April, p. 4.

DURHAM, M. (1988) 'Not just a parsing fancy for grammar', *The Daily Telegraph*, 15 February, p. 14.

EGGAR, T. (1991) 'Correct use of English is essential', *The Times Educational Supplement*, 28 June, p. 14.

FISHMAN, J.A. (1976) *Bilingual Education: An International Sociological Perspective*, Rowley, Massachusetts, Newbury House.

GARSON, S. *et al.*, (1989) *World Languages Project*, London, Hodder and Stoughton.

GILLIVER, J. (1989) 'The National Curriculum: English for Ages 5–11', *The Use of English*, 40, 3, pp. 1–11.

GODDARD, R. (1991) 'Why LINC Matters', *English in Education*, 23, 3, pp. 32–9.

HOFKINS, D. (1993) 'England rejects the prints of Wales', *The Times Educational Supplement*, 23 April, p. 14.

HOLDERNESS, M. (1992) 'Dial direct', *The Times Educational Supplement*, 13 November, p. 18.

HOULTON, D. (1985) *All Our Languages: A Handbook for the Multilingual Classroom*, London, Edward Arnold.

HOULTON, D. (1986) *Cultural Diversity in the Primary School*, London, Batsford.

JONES, K. (1992) 'The Cox Report: Working for Hegemony', in JONES, K. (Ed) *English and the National Curriculum*, London, Kogan Page, pp. 1–31.

JOSEPH, K. Sir (1984) *English from 5–16* (Statement by the Secretary of State for Education and Science), 2 October, London, DES.

KENNY, J. (1992) 'Nips and tucks', *The Times Educational Supplement*, 20 November, p. 17.

KIRKMAN, S. (1987) 'Attack on composition and aims of Kingman Inquiry', *The Times Educational Supplement*, 1 May, p. 15.

KNIGHT, R. (1987) 'English as it is written — and as it should be taught', *The Guardian*, 2 June, p. 15.

LANGUAGE IN THE NATIONAL CURRICULUM (1991) *Materials for Professional Development*, Final Draft, 12 June, Nottingham, Department of English Studies, University of Nottingham.

LINGUISTIC MINORITIES PROJECT (1985) *The Other Languages of England*, London, Routledge and Kegan Paul.

MACKINNON, K. and DENSHAM, J. (1989) 'Ethnolinguistic diversity in Britain: Policies and practice in school and society', *Language, Culture and Curriculum*, 2, 2, pp. 75–89.

MARENBON, J. (1987) *English, Our English: The New Orthodoxy Examined*, London, Centre for Policy Studies.

MARSHALL, B. (1993) 'Simple argument off the spectrum', *Guardian Education*, 13 April, p. 3.

MASTERMAN, L. and ASHWORTH, E. (Eds) (1988) *Responding to Kingman*, Nottingham, School of Education, University of Nottingham.

MERCER, J. (1989) 'Electronic Mail in Curricular Development', *Primary Teaching Studies*, 4, 2, pp. 166–71.

MINES, H. (1989) 'A review: English 5–11', *Issues in Race and Education*, 56, pp. 8–9.

N.A. (1988) 'The Kingman Report', *The English Magazine*, 20, pp. 4–5.

N.A. (1992) 'Starting with Macintosh', *Fact File 100 Series* (Imagination Technology, Oven House, Water Lane, Eyam, S30 1RG).

NASH, I. (1988a) 'Report's omissions a scandal', *The Times Educational Supplement*, 24 June, p. 8.

NASH, I. (1988b) 'Ministers hanker for traditional English', *The Times Educational Supplement*, 11 November, p. 1.

NATIONAL CURRICULUM COUNCIL (1989a) *English in the National Curriculum: Consultation Report* (Key Stage 1), York, NCC.

NATIONAL CURRICULUM COUNCIL (1989b) *English in the National Curriculum: Consultation Report* (Key Stages 2, 3 and 4), York, NCC.

NATIONAL CURRICULUM COUNCIL (1990) *Talk: The Journal of the National Oracy Project*, 3, Summer, York, NCC.

NATIONAL CURRICULUM COUNCIL (1991) *Circular No. 11: Linguistic Diversity and the National Curriculum*, York, NCC.

NATIONAL CURRICULUM COUNCIL (1992) *National Curriculum English: The case for Revising the English Order*, York, NCC.

NATIONAL CURRICULUM COUNCIL (1993) *English for ages 5–16*, York, NCC.

NORMAN, K. (Ed) *Thinking Voices: the work of the National Oracy Project*, London, Hodder and Stoughton.

PARINDER, P. (1993) 'War of the words', *The Times Higher Educational Supplement*, 16 April, p. 19.

PARKE, T. (1991) 'Diversity or Disadvantage: A commentary on National Curriculum Circular No. 11', *Education 3–13*, 3, pp. 37–40.

ROSEN, H. (1988) 'Struck by a particular gap', in JONES, M. and WEST, A. (Eds) *Learning me your language: perspectives on the teaching of English*, London, Mary Glasgow, pp. 1–14.

SCHOOL CURRICULUM DEVELOPMENT COMMITTEE (1990) *A rich resource: Writing and language diversity*, Walton-on-Thames, Nelson.

SAVVA, H. (1990) 'The Multilingual Classroom', in HARRIS, J. and WILKINSON, J. (Eds) *A Guide to English Language in the National Curriculum*, Cheltenham, Stanley Thornes, pp. 28–44.

SCOFFHAM, S., JEWSON, T. and BRIDGE, C. (1991) *BBC Education Teaching Today: Primary Geography*, London, BBC Publications.

SIMONS, M. (1989) 'Things Fall Apart', *The English Magazine*, 22, pp. 2–4.

STUBBS, M. (1980) *Language and Literacy: The sociolinguistics of reading and writing*, London, Routledge and Kegan Paul.

STUBBS, M. (1982) 'What is English? — Modern English language in the curriculum', in CARTER, R. (Ed) *Linguistics and the Teacher*, London, Routledge and Kegan Paul, pp. 137–55.

STUBBS, M. (1986) *Educational Linguistics*, Oxford, Blackwell.

STUBBS, M. (1989) 'The state of English in the English state: reflections on the Cox Report', *Language and Education*, 3, 4, pp. 235–50.

STUBBS, M. (1993) 'English as it is taught', *The Independent*, 16 April, p. 19.

THE TIMES HIGHER EDUCATIONAL SUPPLEMENT (1991) 'Linguists [sic] plea to Clarke', 25 October, p. 8.

WISHART, E. (1988) 'Using a TTNS Electronic Mailbox in a Junior Class: A Case Study', *Reading*, 22, 3, pp. 144–51.

WORSLEY, R. (1992) 'Project Gemini launched', *Campus World 1992*, p. 79.

Chapter 6

Core Subject: Mathematics

Michael McLachlan

Context

The Secretary of State's decision to initiate discussions on a National Curriculum for mathematics followed from the debate started by the Cockcroft report (DES, 1982) some seven years earlier and contributed to by subsequent HMI papers (DES, 1988). The outcome of these deliberations, as described in the orders for mathematics, now defines for schools the content of mathematics to be taught. The documents clearly state that the methodology is in the hands of individual teachers.

Parallel to these developments have been discussions on the approaches to the delivery of the curriculum in the primary classroom from the notable Plowden report (DES, 1967) through to the most recent pronouncements in the report of the 'three wise men' on curriculum organization and practice (DES, 1992; Alexander, Rose, Woodhead, 1992).

The focus for this chapter is to explore how these two elements, a National Curriculum and a rationale for curriculum delivery, can meet in a multicultural context. The intention of this chapter is to:

- describe the requirements of the National Curriculum for mathematics;
- examine current models of curriculum delivery;
- define what is understood by the author to be the scope and purpose of a multicultural approach to mathematics teaching; and
- present a model for curriculum planning which recognizes the value of a multicultural approach to curriculum delivery and provide examples and resources to support this approach.

The National Curriculum Requirements for Mathematics

The National Curriculum for mathematics is statutorily defined in orders published by the Department of Education and Science (DES, 1989; 1991b) (now the Department for Education: DFE).

The current order outlines five interrelated subdivisions to the National Curriculum for mathematics. These are defined as Attainment Targets (ATs) and consist of a collection of Statements of Attainment (SoAs) collated in ten ascending levels (implying a hierarchical approach to learning). The five areas are identified as 'Using and applying mathematics' (Ma1), 'Number' (Ma2), 'Algebra' (Ma3), 'Shape and space' (Ma4) and 'Handling data' (Ma5).

The Statements of Attainment describe what is to be statutorily assessed at the end of each Key Stage, however the detail of what is to be taught is outlined in associated Programmes of Study (PoS). The Programmes of Study, which are also statutory, put flesh on the bones of the Statements of Attainment. The orders also contain non-statutory examples to illustrate appropriate mathematical tasks, skills or content associated to SoAs and the PoS.

Ma1 is different from the other four Attainment Targets in that it describes behaviours and processes whereas the other ATs are concerned with the knowledge, skills and content of mathematics.

It is generally agreed that most primary teachers are able to make connections between what used to be taught and what is now required in Attainment Targets Ma2–5. Teachers appear to be facing some problems with the delivery of the content of the higher levels. The interpretation and delivery of Ma1 has also been problematical to teachers in secondary as well as primary schools (DES, 1991; DES, 1992).

Some examples of SoAs from Attainment Targets Ma1 and Ma2 might clarify these assertions

Ma1 Level 1   a)   use mathematics as an integral part of practical classroom tasks.
                       b)   talk about their own work and respond to questions.
                       c)   make predictions based on experience.

Ma1 Level 4   a)   identify and obtain sufficient information necessary to solve problems.
                       b)   interpret situations mathematically using appropriate symbols or diagrams.
                       c)   give some justification for their solution to problems.
                       d)   make generalizations.

Ma2 Level 1   a)   use numbers in the context of the classroom or school.
                       b)   add and subtract numbers using a small number of objects.

Ma2 Level 4   a)   solve problems without the aid of a calculator considering the reasonableness of the answer.

b) demonstrate an understanding of the relationship between place values in whole numbers.

c) use fractions, decimals or percentages as appropriate to describe situations.

d) solve number problems with the aid of a calculator, interpreting the display.

e) make sensible estimates of a range of measures in relationship to every-day objects.

Recent National Curriculum Council in-service training material (NCC, 1992a,b) and the identification of the three strands within Ma1 of application, mathematical communication and reason, logic and proof in the latest orders for mathematics are beginning to clarify this position. However, a common understanding by teachers of Ma1 within and across schools is still in its infancy.

The issue of the interpretation of SoAs within Ma1 is matched by concerns over progression within and through this Attainment Target. For example, the SoA at level 1, 'use numbers within the context of the classroom . . .', could equally apply at level 10.

Current NCC advice not only intertwines Ma1 with similar levels within the other ATs but also relates progression within Ma1 to progression in some or all of the following four dimensions (NCC, 1992b).

Figure 6.1: Dimensions

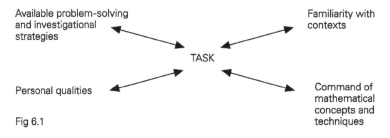

Fig 6.1

It will be argued later in this chapter that a multicultural approach to the delivery of mathematics teaching and learning will provide rich opportunities to develop the above dimensions for all pupils, irrespective of ethnic and cultural backgrounds.

Approaches to Curriculum Delivery in the Primary School

The recent debates over classroom practice in the primary school find a sharp focus in the way mathematics is often delivered in the primary classroom (Alexander, Rose and Woodhead, 1992).

While the following picture may not represent reality in all schools, it is true to say that a significant number of pupils receive their mathematics education largely by working through published schemes. These schemes, for the most part, provide a comprehensive set of worksheets, workbooks and textbooks. Children are allocated to a level within the scheme and then progress page by page, workcard by workcard, workbook by workbook through the scheme. The pupil's experience is often a solitary journey through the material and the teacher's role is to react to the individual's problems as they arise.

This model has its critics (DES, 1987; DES, 1992; Alexander, Rose and Woodhead, 1992). Teachers are exhorted to return to a mixed mode of delivery which values not only pupils' research and individual and group learning but also recognizes the key role that teachers have, through their subject knowledge, appreciation of child development and skills of dissemination, in developing children's understanding and growth of knowledge. The Alexander report's heavy emphasis on teacher direction is balanced by the wider view which recommended exposition by the teacher alongside practical, problem-solving, investigative work, teacher–pupil, pupil–pupil interactions and consolidation (DES, 1982, para. 243).

Much of what pupils are now expected to experience through Ma1 is not easily instigated and developed through the written word. Pupils can be exhorted by the text to discuss a problem, to work in a team or to develop their own line of enquiry but only a teacher can systematically monitor, develop and extend such discussions.

In stark contrast to this approach to the teaching of mathematics, many of the other curriculum areas are delivered through a cross-curricular or topic-based approach in which pupils are expected to act as researcher and developer whilst the teacher functions as a key resource. If mathematics is identified within a topic, it is often at best incidental to the main focus of the topic and at worst a 'service' subject contrived to fit into the theme.

Afzal Ahmend suggests that

> If pupils of all abilities are to experience both the richness of individual subjects and gain an overview of the subtle interrelationships and interactions that exist amongst the disciplines it is essential to maintain both the links and the separation between subjects. (DES, 1987, p. 57)

A multicultural approach to mathematics teaching provides a number of opportunities to the teacher in the primary school. The first is to act as a leader within the field of mathematics. The second is to examine and correct any cultural bias within textbooks and other resource materials. And the third is to provide a wealth of pedagogic contexts which link curriculum areas through the study of mathematical developments alongside other curriculum spheres.

The Scope and Purpose of a Multicultural Approach to Mathematics Teaching

It is sometimes argued that the historical and cultural origins of mathematics are unimportant. It is asserted that what matters in education and life is the extent to which the individual can do, understand and use mathematics in problem-solving. In this context, mathematics is often described as culturally free. Exploring the National Curriculum orders to discover a route into multicultural education is infertile ground. There is scant reference in the document to any cultural or historical context (only Pythagoras is mentioned by name) and therefore the culturally free view is reinforced. An examination of the non-European roots of mathematics clearly demonstrates the extremely important contributions made by other cultures (Joseph, 1991).

Sharan-Jeet Shan and Bailey (1991) in their excellent book on this subject *Multiple factors: Classroom mathematics for equality and justice* argue that this cultural neutrality is a myth which has developed through two independent notions. Firstly, that mathematics is the prerogative of a selected few and therefore a mystique is accorded to the study of mathematics in all civilizations; and secondly that the European dominance of the past 400 years has, according to Gooneatilake (1984):

> suppressed the high achievements in mathematics and science of pre-colonial times in all countries colonized. (Sharan-Jeet Shan and Bailey, 1991, p. 2)

Additionally, the value of the educational outcomes of those who, in the past, have attempted to use a multicultural dimension within their teaching, have been questioned (Cotton, 1989; DES, 1988). The working party which drafted the original mathematics National Curriculum document stated:

> Many of those who argue for a multicultural approach to the mathematics curriculum do so on the basis that such an approach is necessary to raise the self esteem of the ethnic minority cultures and to improve mutual understanding and respect between races. We believe this attitude is misconceived and patronising! (DES, 1988, para. 10.22, p. 87)

Challenges

How then are teachers to avoid this trap of patronizing pupils? The key lies in the rationale behind a multicultural approach to teaching mathematics. Joseph (1990) suggests two purposes:

> First . . . the need for examplars from cultures and traditions that have been ignored or devalued for so long. Second . . . a multicultural

approach to mathematics is seen as part of a general strategy of making mathematics more accessible and less anxiety arousing among a wider public'. (Joseph, 1990, p. 32)

The purpose of multicultural approach is not simply about raising the self-esteem of minority cultures but is about

challenging the overall content and pedagogy of the standard curriculum in its singular failure to make mathematics more accessible to working class, female and black students. It counters the view that mathematics is a sequence of unconnected skills taught in isolation from the real world or applications. (ibid., p. 32)

A distinction must also be made between the mathematics education of pupils which recognize the many cultural influences which shaped the discipline and educating pupils, through using mathematics, to enable them to take their place within a society which is multicultural. The former should be part of good teaching and learning and the latter is enshrined in The Education Reform Act 1988 which states:

The curriculum for a maintained school satisfies the requirements . . . if it is a balanced and broadly based curriculum which
a) promotes the spiritual, moral, cultural, mental and physical developments of pupils at the school and of society; and
b) prepares such pupils for the opportunities and responsibilities and experiences of adult life.

NCC (1989) advice to primary schools suggests that teachers should 'set the basic curriculum subjects in the context of the whole curriculum of the school by examining current policies or initiating new policies to include: . . . multicultural education.'

Sharan-Jeet Shan and Bailey (op. cit.) suggest that

A multicultural approach should not be trivial . . . the cultural aspects of the work should be interwoven into the courses so that they do not appear as optional extras but as important aspects of an integrated whole . . .
The approach is cross curricular and should help the school to be more coherent . . .
The universal activities of learning the key concepts in mathematics and how these apply to real life problems are the basis of a multicultural approach. (Sharan-Jeet Shan and Bailey, 1991, p. 62)

Table 6.1: Summary of Challenges: Mathematics

In summary the challenges are that multicultural mathematics teaching within the primary school should;

- be non-trivial;
- be integrated into the whole curriculum;
- reflect good teaching practice;
- show the universality of mathematics;
- develop positive images of students from all cultures;
- create enthusiasm for mathematics through drawing on the experience of students;
- reflect the content of the National Curriculum;
- provide real contexts for pupils' achievements in Attainment Target Ma1;
- provide opportunities for mathematics teaching in genuine cross-curricular activities;
- and recognize and counter examples of gender and cultural bias in published or home produced schemes.

Responses

Earlier examples of multicultural approaches to mathematics teaching have often concentrated on Rangoli patterns, Islamic art and number systems of other countries. However, as outlined earlier, the National Curriculum recognizes and values a wider range of mathematical concepts, knowledge and skills. The following examples serve to illustrate a number of activities from different cultural backgrounds which may be used as for exploration within mathematics itself or be included within a thematic approach.

They have been grouped under each of the four content Attainment Targets although many of the activities address other Attainment Targets. The scope of this chapter only allows for a limited number of examples and many more can be found in the books listed in the references. An ideal starting point is the work of Sharan-Jeet Shan and Bailey (1991) which includes a large number of examples and ideas for extended project work. Many of the following activities are expanded in their book.

In order to address the challenges outlined earlier, it is essential that due consideration is given to the strands and dimensions relating to Attainment Target Ma1 when adapting the examples for use in the classroom.

Attainment Target Ma2: Number

Skills in non-calculator methods for number crunching have often been seen as a measure of success. However the common western algorithms for multiplication and division have often taxed pupils and their understanding of place value has often been wéak. NCC advice in the Non-Statutory Guidance issued with the original mathematics orders stressed the need for mental approaches to arithmetic as the first resort followed by use of a calculator or a pupil's own pencil and paper methods (NCC, 1988). The following section offers some different approaches to multiplication and the study of number.

VEDIC Mathematics

The Vedas are the most ancient Indian scriptures and Holy Books of the Hindu religion. They are written in Sanskrit and are said to contain complete instructions on all mathematics. In the Vedic language, simple maths formulae are known as *sutra*. They are precise statements which reduce seemingly complicated problems to a few simple steps requiring a fraction of the time taken by traditional methods. They offer opportunities for practising mental mathematics and developing non-calculator methods for many of the arithmetical operations such as generating tables, long multiplication, squaring numbers and pattern spotting. Justifying why the *sutra* works through the use of algebra, offers access to higher levels of Ma1.

Tables

Nikhilam sutra: this provides a quick method for generating multiplication tables.

Example: 17 times table

$17 = 20 - 3 = 2 \times 10$ and -3×1 and this defines two operators, $+2$ for the tens column and -3 for the units. These values are used to increment the tens and units column

1	7	×1	
+2	−3		
3	4	×2	
+2	−3		
5	1	×3 →	To take away the next 3 we need to convert
+1	(11–3)		1 ten to units so only add 1 to the tens column.
6	8	×4	
+2	−3		
8	5	×5	and so on.

Example: 37 times table

$37 = 30 + 7 = 3 \times 10$ and 7×1 gives the two operators $+3$ and $+7$

	3	7	×1	
	+3+1	+7		7 + 7 is 14, the 1 ten is carried into the next column
	7	4	×2	
	+3+1	+7		
1	1	1	×3	
	+3	+7		
1	4	8	×4	
	+3+1	+7		
1	8	5	×5	

Multiplication
Nikhilam sutra (all from 9 and last from 10) : There are many different variations on the Nikhilam *sutras* depending on the type of sum involved.

Example: $8 \times 7 = 56$

```
 8(–2)      –2 an–3 are known as the 'deficiencies' of 8 and 7 i.e.,
×7(–3)      the difference from base 10
 5  6
```

The right-hand side of the answer (units) is given by multiplying the 'deficiencies'. The left-hand number (5) (tens) is given by 'cross- subtraction' i.e., $8 - 3 = 5$ or $7 - 2 = 5$

Example: $89 \times 95 = 8455$

The nearest base is 100 so deficiencies are–11 and–5

```
89(–11)
95(– 5)
84   55
```

right-hand side is given by multiplying $-11 \times -5 = 55$
left-hand side is given by $89 - 5$ or $95 - 11$ which equals 84

Example: $112 \times 97 = 10864$

The neárest base is 100 so deficiencies are +12 and –3

```
112(+12)     12 × –3 = –36
 97(– 3)     112 – 3 = 109
109 –36      97 + 12 = 109
108  64
```

Because the right-hand side is negative it is subtracted from 10900 giving $10900 - 36 = 10864$

The *Anurupyena sutra* (proportionality): this is used for number whose deficiencies are large numbers e.g., 47 squared.

Example: $47 \times 47 = 2209$

```
 47     (–3)     Use 50 as a working base
×47     (–3)
 44      09      Left-hand side divided by 2 as 50 is 100÷2.
 22      09
```

Urdhvatiryagbhyam sutra (vertically and crosswise): this is an alternative method for multiplication.

Example: $57 \times 36 = 2052$

5	7	Vertical product on the right $6 \times 7 = 42$
		Vertical product on the left $3 \times 5 = 15$
×3	6	Crosswise $(5 \times 6) + (3 \times 7) = 51$

$$
\begin{array}{r}
1\;5\;4\;2 \\
5\;1(0) \\
\hline
2\;0\;5\;2
\end{array}
$$

Square Numbers

Urdahav Tiryak sutra: This is corollory of the *Nikhilam Sutra*. It enables large numbers to be squared. The square of a number is given by using 'deficiencies' from the nearest base of 10, 100 etc. The deficiency squared gives the last digits and the number plus the deficiency gives the leading digits.

Example: 14^2 'deficiency' is 4 from 10

$$14^2 = (14 + 4) \quad 4 \times 4$$

$$
\begin{array}{r}
18 \\
16 \\
\hline
196
\end{array}
$$

Example: 987^2 'deficiency, is -13 from 1000

$$987^2 = (987 - 13) \quad -13 \times -13$$
$$= 974169$$

The above examples show the power of different approaches to arithmetic and could be combined with other methods of calculation such as the Italian *Gelosia* and Russian or Chinese methods of multiplication as a means of exploring place value (Doderidge, 1985).

Historical Approaches to the Teaching of Mathematics

The history NC orders suggest that primary schools should study ancient civilizations and examples given include the Mayan and Egyptian cultures. An exploration of the mathematical developments within these cultures would provide a valuable focus and reinforce the universality of mathematics. A study of historical developments of mathematics also provides an opportunity to counter the Eurocentric view of mathematics outlined earlier. Joseph traces the major worldwide mathematical developments which took place during the European 'Dark Ages' (Joseph, 1990; 1991). He outlines the transfer of knowledge between China and India and on through Jundishapur, Baghdad, Cairo, Cordoba, and Toledo to western Europe.

Similarly significant mathematical developments occurred in Mesopotamia, Egypt, South America, India, China and the Arab world. Such understandings predate many European 'discoveries'. For example, the earliest known demonstrations of Pythagoras' Theorem can be found in a Chinese text, *Choui Pei*, written in the latter half of the first 1000 years BC and also in Indian works written c800-600BC. European developments are only a part of this rich tapestry. Studies of this development provided context for mathematical and cross-curricular themes within the primary classroom.

Further examples for classroom use include work on the comparison of number systems, numbers in other languages and the historical development of particular concepts such as time, the idea of place value and the 'invention' of zero.

Number systems and symbols can be used to show similarities and irregularities of different languages in their interpretations of counting. For example English irregularities include 11 (one left of ten fingers) and 12 (two left) and numbers in the 'teens' which start with the units and follow with the tens. An examination of irregularities reinforces the understanding of the underlying structure and power of a number system which uses place value to hold large numbers. This can be strengthened by attempting calculations using non-place value systems such as Roman numerals.

A study of calculating aids such as the abacus, soroban, Napier's Bones or a range of algorithms, such as *Gelosia* or Vedic methods of calculations, reinforces place value as does a study of other ancient number systems. For example, the Mayan systems from around 3000BC worked to a base of 20 by using a combination of dots and horizontal lines. With the advent of the decimal system for weights and measures there is scope to make historical comparisons within our own families' lifetimes. Roods, poles, pecks, nipperkins etc are part of a rich mathematical and cultural heritage which could usefully be considered in comparison to other cultures within the history 'topic'. Their contrasting mathematical bases are of considerable interest and utility in understanding number structures.

Approaches to fractions also provided multicultural opportunities. Early Egyptian texts show fractions with 1 as the numerator so that $^7/_8$ would be shown as $^1/_2 + {}^1/_4 + {}^1/_8$. The Babylonians used 60 as the denominator and the Romans used 12. Exploring the advantages and disadvantages of such approaches would provide opportunities for access to Attainment Targets Ma1 and 2.

Finally, working with unfamiliar number systems and languages also strengthens understanding of how children face coping with learning in unfamiliar surroundings. Used sensitively, it can help develop understanding and tolerance between pupils.

Attainment Target Ma3: Algebra

Access to this Attainment Target is often seen as problematical in the primary school. Fortunately, algebra has its early roots in pupils' spotting pattern and structure and then being able to find words to describe the pattern. Algebraic symbols are then simply the shorthand for those verbal or written descriptions.

A study of games from different cultures often provides the context within which pupils find ready access to finding words to describe pattern. Explaining and understanding rules provide a rich experience in language and mathematical development. The following examples provide a starting point and further examples can easily be found (Dodd, UDa, UDb; Bell and Cornelius, 1988; Ball, 1989; Sharan-Jeet Shan and Bailey, 1991).

The 'Tower of Hanoi' or 'Tower of Brahma' is an interesting problem based on a legend. This states that priests in holy temples on the edge of the Ganges were set a task by Brahma, the creator of the world. On completion of the task, the world would end. Brahma had built a tower of sixty-four stones which were arranged from largest to smallest, but it had been built in the wrong place.

The priests had to move the tower according to the following conditions; only one stone could be moved at a time; there were to be no more than three piles of stones at any one time and only small stones could be placed on large stones. This problem can be imitated by using coins which provide convenient concentric decreasing-size objects. The general solution involves powers of two.

Chess (India, Persia and Arabia), Go (China), Nerenchi (Sri Lanka) — a 2000-year-old game similar to 9 Men's Morris, all provide opportunities for pattern spotting and generalization. Describing the origins and developments of these games and puzzles provides valuable contextual and multicultural dimensions. They can also be extremely enjoyable.

Attainment Target Ma4: Shape and Space

This Attainment Target, which addresses concepts of symmetry, transformation, measuring, designing and model-making provides a natural link between the teaching of mathematics and art (Jones, UD) This has been recognized as a valuable approach to exploring jointly the contribution of many cultures. Islamic art and architecture (El-Said and Parman, 1976), Rangoli patterns, calligraphy, Egyptian hieroglyphics and decorative repeating patterns provide valuable resources.

Rangoli patterns, which are popular amongst Gujeratis, are made during *Holi*, the festival associated with spring. The patterns are created on a grid made by placing pegboards over a surface and sprinkling coloured chalk

Figure 6.2: Decorative Patterns Involving Mathematics.

Source: Sharan-Jeet Shan and Bailey (1991) (With permission).

Figure 6.2: *(Cont.)*

4.

5.

6.

1. *Islamic: Filigree window pattern*
2. *Medieval Rome: Mosaic pattern*
3. *Mexico: Manuscript drawing*
4. *China: Lattice pattern*
5. *Inca: Puma and Bird pattern*
6. *Russia: Gold sculpture work*

Figure 6.3: Rangoli Patterns

Source: Sharan-Jeet Shan and Bailey (1991) (With permission)

through the holes to create patterns which can be reflected in the lines of symmetry.

These patterns can be permanently produced in the classroom by blocking off some holes in a pegboard to create the Rangoli pattern of holes. Sprinkling sand or powdered chalk through the open holes onto paper covered in adhesive and rotating the board would produce symmetrical patterns.

Origami provides a rich source of geometrical investigation in both two and three dimensions. The Chinese 'Water Bomb' was originally a vessel for holding rice to throw at weddings and is now used to hold water for throwing in the playground following the lesson! Variations on the theme such as the pyramid shown in Figure 6.4 provide an excellent investigative way into properties of plane and solid figures (McLachlan, 1988).

Attainment Target Ma5: Data Handling

The National Curriculum requires, through Attainment Target Ma5, that primary-school pupils not only learn statistical techniques but also have opportunities to interpret and draw conclusions from the data. Developing the data from pupils' own experiences within a multicultural classroom or using data from a multicultural perspective in a monocultural class provides significant opportunities for developing shared understanding of the world. The statistics, if well chosen, can offer young pupils a variety of contexts to address social, economic and cultural issues. They also provide significant opportunities for developing mathematics in real contexts.

Jeet-Shan and Bailey (1991) also provide a wealth of examples for project work based on world statistics which draw contrasts between the advantages and struggles of different cultures. The University of York, World Studies

Figure 6.4: Origami Pyramid

You will need: A4 (or larger) paper, coloured crayons or felt tip pens, geometric instruments

Make a square from your paper $----$ means valley fold $\vee$
$\underline{\qquad\qquad}$ means mountain fold $\wedge$

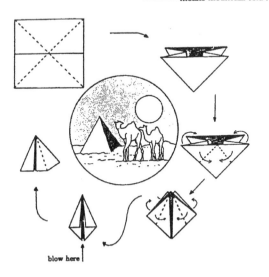

blow here

Source: McLachlan, 1988

Teacher Training Centre (WTTC) involved a number of seconded teachers in developing support material in 1984–5. Hudson (1987) offers a number of activities to develop global perspectives using the 'Quest' computer database. This database contains statistics on 127 counties including life expectancy, number of doctors, teachers, military personnel and so on. Whilst the original data are now out of date, they offer the added advantage of providing data for comparison with the figures for today.

Weeden (1987), working on the same project, suggested a number of activities which are particularly useful in the primary school. The first involves simplifying world statistics so that they match the numbers in a class or school or using a base value of 100. He suggests we pose the question 'suppose the world was a village of exactly 100 people, how many would be American or English, or African, Chinese or Indian? How many would be suffering from malnutrition or overcrowding? How many would live in the northern hemisphere?' and so on.

It is suggested that the children could then group themselves according to their answers. An extension could involve a simplification of land-mass area where one desk equals the area of western Europe (about 3 per cent of

Table 6.2: A Simplification of World Statistics

	100 PEOPLE (1980)	100 BANKNOTES (1976)	LAND%	FOOD
Western Europe	8	27	3	10
South West Asia	32	6	12	27
East Asia	26	14	9	25
USSR E. Europe	9	15	17	12
Africa	11	2	2	9
N. America	6	29	14	8
Latin America	8	5	17	8
Oceania	1	2	6	1

total land mass) On this scale North America is 14 per cent, Africa 22 per cent, Latin America 17 per cent etc.. A study of population would involve using the appropriate number of children to occupy the available space. The world total of available food, it is suggested, could be represented by 100 sweets. Table 6.2 summarizes this information. Other models could be used where a tube of sweets represents the world total of available food grown, exported or imported into each region.

Summary of Responses

The examples provided represent but a small selection of currently available material. Sadly it is difficult to find many of these examples within the major published work schemes. The solution to the challenges identified in the previous section must therefore involve teachers and pupils in researching and then creating a range of activities reflected through Ma1. The rationale for this is not only that socially and morally we should be taking a multicultural stance but also that such an approach makes for quality mathematics teaching.

Quality teaching and learning of mathematics depend on teachers creating enthusiasm for mathematics through drawing on the experience of students. This good practice should show how mathematics is integrated into the whole curriculum and therefore show the universality of mathematics.

A multicultural approach to the teaching of mathematics will develop positive images of students from all cultures and provide real contexts for pupils achievements in Attainment Target Ma1. Above all, it will provide natural opportunities for mathematics teaching within cross-curricular activities in the primary school.

As always, each set of solutions creates new challenges and the ultimate challenge that faces primary education is to embed such approaches into its core values, not simply to introduce some new topics into the school mathematics scheme.

References

ALEXANDER, R., ROSE, J. and WOODHEAD, C. (1992) *Curriculum Organisation and Classroom Practice in Primary Schools,* London, HMSO.

BALL, J. (1989) *Games from around the World* (published to support the Pop Maths Roadshow), London, Royal Society.

BELL, R. and CORNELIUS, M. (1988) *Board games around the world,* Cambridge, Cambridge University Press.

COTTON, A. (Ed) (1989) 'Anti-Racist Education in the National Curriculum' a draft paper unpublished summary of working group from conference 'Developing an Anti-Racist National Curriculum', Manchester, Manchester Polytechnic.

DEPARTMENT OF EDUCATION AND SCIENCE (1967) *Children and Their Primary Schools: Plowden Report,* London, HMSO.

DEPARTMENT OF EDUCATION AND SCIENCE (1982) *Mathematics Counts: Cockcroft Report,* London, HMSO.

DEPARTMENT OF EDUCATION AND SCIENCE (1987) *Better mathematics,* London, HMSO.

DEPARTMENT OF EDUCATION AND SCIENCE (1988) *Mathematics from 5–16,* London, HMSO.

DEPARTMENT OF EDUCATION AND SCIENCE (1988) *Education Reform Act,* London, HMSO.

DEPARTMENT OF EDUCATION AND SCIENCE (1989) *Mathematics Statutory Order,* London, HMSO.

DEPARTMENT OF EDUCATION AND SCIENCE (1991a) *Mathematics in Key Stages 1 and 3: A Report by HMI on the first year, 1989–1990,* London, HMSO.

DEPARTMENT OF EDUCATION AND SCIENCE (1991b) *Mathematics in the National Curriculum (revised) Order and Circular,* London, HMSO.

DEPARTMENT OF EDUCATION AND SCIENCE (1992) *Mathematics in Key Stage 1, 2 and 3: A Report by HMI on the second year, 1990–1991,* London, HMSO.

DODD, P. (UDa) *Mathematics from around the world: a multicultural resource book,* 73 Beech Grove, Whitley Bay, Tyne and Wear.

DODD, P. (UDb) *Puzzles; a mathematical resource book,* 73 Beech Grove, Whitley Bay, Tyne and Wear.

DODERIDGE, J. (1985), *The Venerable Bede, an approach to calculators in the classroom,* Chester, Cheshire County Council.

HUDSON, B. (1987) *Global Perspectives in the Mathematics Classroom,* World Studies Teacher Training Centre, York, University of York.

EL-SAID, I. and PARMAN, A. (1976) *Geometry concepts in Islamic art,* World of Islam Festival trust and Scorpian Publishing Ltd., Colchester, Jonathan Press.

GOONEATILAKE, S. (1984) *Aborted Discovery-science and creativity in the Third World,* Zed.

JONES, L. (Ed) (UD) *Teaching mathematics and art,* Cheltenham, Stanley Thornes.

JOSEPH, G.G. (1990) 'The politics of Anti-Racist Mathematics' in *Multicultural Teaching 9.1,* Stoke on Trent, Trentham Books.

JOSEPH, G.G. (1991) *The Creast of the Peacock: non-European Roots of mathematics,* London, Tauris.

JOSEPH, G.G., NELSON, R.D. and WILLIAMS, J.S. (1992) *Multicultural Mathematics*, Oxford, Oxford University Press.

MCLACHLAN, M.J. (1988) *The What If? pack :Mathematics assignments*, Ormskirk, Causeway Press.

NATIONAL CURRICULUM COUNCIL (1988) *Non Statutory Guidance*, York, NCC.

NATIONAL CURRICULUM COUNCIL (1990) *Curriculum Guidance 1: a framework for primary schools*, York, NCC.

NATIONAL CURRICULUM COUNCIL (1992a) *Inset for Key Stages 1 and 2*, York, NCC.

NATIONAL CURRICULUM COUNCIL (1992b) *Using and Applying Mathematics INSET Book A and B*, York, NCC.

ROCKPORT PUBLISHERS (1988) *Visual elements — World Traditional Folk Patterns*, Rockport, Massachusetts, Rockport Publishers.

SHARAN-JEET SHAN and BAILEY, P. (1991) *Multiple factors: Classroom mathematics for equality and justice*, Stoke on Trent, Trentham Books.

WEEDEN, P. (1987) *Numbers in an Unequal World*, World Studies Teacher Training Centre, York, University of York.

Chapter 7

Core Subject: Science

Alan Cross and Gillian Pearce

Context

Science education must take account of the ethnic and cultural diversity that the school population and society at large offers. Although
the skills of observation, prediction, analysis and experimentation
characterise the view of Science and science education which we have
taken, we recognise that interpretation of the nature of Science may
vary from culture to culture. It is in the implementation of science
that account needs to be taken of the special needs of ethnic minority
children. (DES, 1988 para. 7.12)

It is essential that this curriculum be implemented in a way that is
sensitive to the special needs of individual pupils of different cultural
and linguistic backgrounds and cultural diversity of modern English
and Welsh society. (ibid. para. 7.17)

All primary-school teachers have to be knowledgable about, and sensitive to,
the nature and limitations of the developing child's thinking in various contexts and modalities. Indeed, teachers' initial training, continuing professional
development and everyday practice provide ongoing opportunities for extending such professional competencies. Primary-school teachers would be
well advised to capitalize on their many existing professional strengths when
the task of teaching the science curriculum is undertaken. Primary-school
teachers know a great deal about how young children learn and the variety of
educational approaches that can facilitate or impede children's intellectual
development. The pedagogic 'wheel' does not have to be reinvented by
primary-school teachers in order to 'deliver' a sound education.

In relation to science in the National Curriculum, primary-school teachers'
'Achilles' Heel' is often their own perceived limited knowledge of science as
subjects and methods. The current programme of twenty-day INSET courses
is one means of addressing this. The cultural diversity characteristic of schools

and society compounds the educational issues in relation to science as a 'core subject' in the National Curriculum.

With reference to science in the primary school, how, for example, do children come to understand a concept of central scientific and everyday importance such as 'causality'? Piaget was a pioneer in this field. In his early work, he described some seventeen distinct types of explanation, characteristic of different stages in the development of causal thinking in young children (Piaget, 1930). Challenges to his findings led to considerable research in the USA and to some in the UK. The late Susan Isaacs was a particularly influential critic. The major focus was on explicating the thinking that young children brought to bear when trying to make sense of scientific phenomena, not primarily on the teaching of aspects of science. A rising groundswell of interest in the learning, teaching and understanding of scientific phenomena by pupils developed. In particular, this was fostered by institutions and individuals involved in initial teacher training and INSET.

The methodologies of effective science teaching aroused, and continues to arouse, interest amongst secondary-school teachers. This interest has been less marked amongst their colleagues in primary schools. One instance of the 'groundswell' indicated earlier concerned primary-school pupils. It involved an application of a scientific and empirical approach to identifying effective methodology in the top two forms of a junior school (Pumfrey, 1960). It investigated the effects of using an heuristic approach to science teaching on pupils' understanding of causality. The study was undertaken by a practising primary-school teacher. The results were subsequently read by members of the Inspectorate at the then Ministry of Education and published in a journal (Pumfrey, 1962). Increasing interest in extending science into the primary-school curriculum has developed at local and national levels. In 1988, science was included in the National Curriculum. The field was one in which primary school teachers required a considerable INSET provision to prepare them to teach and assess the Programme of Study.

As we move towards the turn of the century we are at a time of great change in primary education. The teaching of science in primary schools has been, and remains, at the forefront of that change and in many ways symbolizes the move towards a more balanced curriculum with its base in the notion of entitlement. Science can be seen to be part of everyone's life, essential to all individuals whatever role they occupy. Taking account of cultural diversity in our teaching of science presents teachers with significant challenges as many are still coming to terms with science in the classroom. Feelings of inadequacy may be compounded if the science then has to encompass a cultural breadth with which the teacher also lacks familiarity. Acknowledging a problem is a first step in addressing it. Whilst this is a necessary condition for resolving this educational issue, by itself it is not sufficient.

Whilst there is some writing in the area of culturally diverse science as part of primary education, it remains somewhat misunderstood amongst teachers. A major contribution to the confusion is terminology. Terms such as race, culture and ethnicity have a history of misuse and this continues (see Chapter 2 and Thorp, 1991).

In state schools, science is compulsory in the UK. In England and Wales science is listed amongst the nine foundation subjects (plus RE) taught as such in the primary school curriculum. Along with English and mathematics, it is deemed a 'core' subject. If we are to meet these curricular requirements and give equality of opportunity in the science curriculum to all children, we must ensure through our teaching that we do not give a culturally biased account of science but that we provide a valid reflection of the contributions made to science by all cultures. 'Children need to be taught the fact that science and technology are not exclusively white, European and male phenomena' (Siraj-Blatchford, I. and Siraj-Blatchford, J., 1991).

A View of Science

It is worth considering our own and society's popular perspectives concerning science. How many female scientists can we name (apart from M. Curie)? How many black scientists can we identify? These two questions are usually enough to convince people of the existence of a Eurocentic view of science in this country.

Eurocentricism becomes more obvious when we note the following:

- non-white cultures have frequently been the subject of scientific study (numerous anthropological studies this century);
- science tends to value a European view of science, whereas science teaching should reflect an international perspective (Department of Education and Science, 1989);
- there is an ideology which devalues non-European science, the science from other cultures often being 'demoted' to technology (Dennick, 1992);
- science is language based; words are used specifically; if you do not have the word, the concept may be difficult to develop and articulate (Reid and Hodson, 1987);
- notions about high and low technology reinforce ideas that the science and technology of some cultures is better than that of others (Jenkins, 1991); and
- science is also bound up with economic development, considerable efforts are being made in African countries to develop science in their primary schools (Peacock, 1992).

Fortunately, there are important communalities between peoples of all cultures. Human beings regularly ask relatively straightforward questions such as 'Can I open this cupboard?' 'Will this float on water?'

They also ask much more difficult and, at times, unanswerable questions. To address such questions, and the myriad others that arise in the everyday life of all individuals in *all cultures*, requires more than 'trial and error' behaviour. Irrespective of how elementary it may be, thought is required. To hypothesize, to predict, to test the prediction and to learn from the outcome of the experiment, represent a sequence characterizing the learning of all. The formal elaboration of this sequence into an explicit scientific method with its specialized vocabulary, equipment and techniques, can make teachers forget that, in essence, all of us are scientists (Kelly, 1955).

Science allows humans to enquire in particular ways. It is an integral part of everyone's life but we are working against a considerable pressure which tells many youngsters that science is not for them. The excitement of discovery that exemplifies science can all too easily be neglected. Science has never been a body of absolute knowledge; it is continually growing and changing. Ideas which were taught to us in school have been, and will continue to be challenged, e.g., the beginning and future of the universe (Hawking, 1988). Many presently cherished theories held up as valid will be replaced and dismissed. We are all operating in the world with numerous misconceptions or alternative non-scientific understandings. Science itself develops by speculating, testing, reflecting rejecting, not rejecting and modifying ideas.

Commonly when adults and children are asked, 'what is heat?' heads are scratched, ideas expressed and experiences related. Rarely is a precise scientific definition given. Yet we all keep warm. We all know how to cool off, if required. Our personal ideas about science are typically sufficient for everyday life. Of course, the time comes when our limited understanding is revealed and we start asking questions. For example, when, on a very cold morning, salt will not 'melt' ice, we are finally challenged to be scientific, if we wish to 'understand' this particular phenomenon more adequately than at a descriptive level. 'Why?' raises its beautiful head.

Where children come from a variety of cultural backgrounds, the necessity to account for their alternative understandings surely becomes greater (Driver, 1983; DES, 1989). Perhaps it is more appropriate to celebrate this diversity in understandings about a concept (where does water go during evaporation) and subsequent investigation?

Practical investigation by all pupils is well established in the Programme of Study for science in the National Curriculum:

Key Stage 1 (ages 5–7 years)
Pupils should be encouraged to develop investigative skills and understanding of science in the context of explorations and investigations largely of the 'Do . . .', 'Describe which . . .', and 'Find a way to . . .' type, involving problems with obvious key variables which are within their everyday experience. (DES, 1991)

Challenges

Developing an Approach

Addressing cultural diversity is a whole-school issue and should receive attention at that level. The school must move towards a clear policy which is implemented throughout the school. By its nature, and as a core subject, science will be an important component in this policy. A key question for a primary school which should be discussed as part of a school-development plan is: 'In National Curriculum Science how will we ensure that content, pedagogy and assessment contribute towards antiracist science education and multicultural science education?'

A distinction exists between a policy where one actively tackles racism, does all one can to empower both Blacks and Whites (antiracist education), and one which celebrates aspects of different cultures (multicultural education) (Dennick, 1992). These approaches are, of course, not mutually exclusive. Dennick recognizes that the former may be seen as challenging and a little radical; the latter might be perceived as lip service and liberal minded good-will which might do little to provide the entitlement of science for all.

Awareness is more than recognizing the issue! Children need to be able to identify, recognize and reflect upon their own experience and lifestyles within science. They must appreciate that what they are learning is important for them. Planning should ensure that all children feel valued and that there is nothing offensive or discriminatory and, as such, likely to affect adversely their self-esteem. To achieve this we need to guard against the view that one's values or one's cultural group are either superior or inferior to others, and against judging others by our own standards. We cannot assume that all groups in society do things in the way in which we ourselves would do them.

A Muslim teacher recounted how, on one occasion when she was a student teacher, she observed another teacher talking to a group of Muslim children about bubbles. The teacher described bubbles to the children as the things we get when we put bubble mixture in the bath. The children had no idea what the teacher was talking about. The teacher was not aware that the Islamic religion requires that people wash under running water and not sit in bathwater in the way that other people might. None of those children had seen a bubble bath. For a related reason some children may not like to put their hands in water that has been soiled by others.

The Association for Science Education makes the point that there are insufficient science specialists available for the subject to be taught as such in primary schools. Despite the appointment of, and INSET work with, science coordinators, problems remain. Only a small percentage of primary-school teachers have science qualifications. Reductions in INSET and the number of advisory teams augur badly for the future. Although not all aspects of the science curriculum lend themselves to the approach, the importance of topic work through which overlap between subjects encourages understanding, is

Table 7.1:   Summary of Challenges: Science

As you move towards determining your action you must consider whether your school has considered:

- a challenge to possible racism amongst teaching and non-teaching staff;
- a clear and common understanding of the terminology e.g., antiracism, cultural, ethnic;
- a science policy which embraces not only notions of antiracism and cultural diversity but which also contains positive statements to assist teachers implement that policy;
- awareness of culturally relevant information e.g., that Islamic culture has developed and use superbly complex geometrical patterns in decoration but that Islamic law forbids individuals to draw representations of living things (though some individuals choose to ignore this ruling);
- an agreed approach to the needs of bilingual learners;
- an agreed approach to the needs of children for whom English is a second language;
- agreement about approaches to science which celebrate cultural diversity;
- the place and use of scientific language;
- the role of parents and the community; and
- the potential conflicts between scientific and non-scientific positions concerning the ideas in the NC science PoS.

commended. (Association for Science Education, 1993). Interestingly, primary science is one of the NC subjects that HMI sees as having made considerable progress during the first two years of the NC (DES, 1992). Nonetheless, if the dearth of primary-school teachers knowledgeable about science coupled with the requirement that the multicultural dimensions of the subject be addressed in the curriculum, the task ahead for primary-school teachers is indeed challenging.

Setting Your Agenda

Tackling these issues as an individual teacher can be difficult but success is largely dependent on our attitudes. Our view of science needs to be open and flexible and our approach to cultural diversity should be based upon using this wealth of experience and material to enrich and deepen the science that we teach. We will find this easier if we work alongside colleagues.

The concept of 'challenges' is important. It is essential to challenge our preconceptions. This will help us to become clearer about what we understand by cultural diversity and science and, equally importantly, what these understandings imply for children in our schools and for the effective delivery of NC science.

Responses

Making NC Science Accessible and Effective

Planning for science is essential. Below, the topic of 'shops' is examined and illustrated in Table 7.2. This can provide opportunities for integrating both science and cultural diversity. The left-hand column asks a number of questions which ought to be answered at the planning stage and identifies demands from the National Curriculum for science. The next column highlights those issues which must be addressed for culturally diverse science to occur in the primary years.· Exemplification is given in the third column and, finally, reference to the strands within the Attainment Targets are identified.

Developing a Cultural Sensitivity

Two areas requiring specific attention when planning science for ethnic-minority groups of children are the language difficulties they may be experiencing and the religious and cultural backgrounds of the children. All children are entitled to have their beliefs treated with understanding and respect. They should not be pressured into departing from the principles of their faiths. If we are going to meet this challenge successfully, we need to know about the children we are teaching and their backgrounds. Areas of conflict or complication must be addressed, but it is important to work from a basis of celebrating diversity rather than focusing on differences. This is easily stated but less readily achieved. By their natures, science and the scientific method often confront and oppose, for example, religious beliefs.

Areas of particular cultural sensitivity include: food, life processes, clothing, relationships and cultural traditions. In National Curriculum science these topics include large areas of Attainment Targets 2 and 3 (AT2, level 3a — Know the basic life processes common to humans and other animals.). Considerable sensitivity will therefore be required.

Food is a popular topic in the primary phase of education. It might precede, follow or be part of the example of shops given in Table 7.2. Teachers here have the opportunity in science to deal with the aspects of Attainment Target 2 which includes the variety of life, the processes of life and human influences on the earth as well as the opportunity to introduce the concept of food as a source of energy. Cooking is an ideal way to look at changes of state resulting from heating and cooling. The range and variety of foods eaten by many ethnic groups in our schools provides us with an excellent opportunity to celebrate diversity. There are many customs relating to food which have their roots in religion and festivals and about which we should be aware if we are to ensure that all children feel comfortable with the topic (see Chapter 4). Most of us are aware that many religions put restrictions on the food that its followers are allowed to eat, but relatively few realize that some religious and cultural groups also put restrictions on utensils used in preparing food and on the vessels in which the food can be cooked. We need to remember, for example, not just that the Hindus do not eat beef and that Jews and Muslims do not eat pork but that the Hindus cannot cook in earthenware vessels or Jews cook meat in vessels that have been contaminated by milk. Sometimes children will be reluctant to eat anything in school because they are afraid that

Table 7.2: *Planning a Topic for Science and Cultural Diversity for a Year 3 Group*

FOCUS IN PLANNING	ISSUES FOR CULTURAL DIVERSITY	EXAMPLE — SHOPS	NC STRANDS
What science have the children done previously? • examine records • consult colleagues • consider children's existing achievement • look at your Key Stage plans	• Do records exist for all the group? • Have all pupils had these experiences? • Can the teacher be specific? • Are there clues in records of other areas? • Is there, evidence of cultural diversity featuring previously?	• previous topic on food where the class made Indian food • previous teacher stresses need for more observation • recent celebration of Diwali by the class	
What context will allow the science required?	• Will this be sufficiently motivating? • Is it relevant to all cultures? • Is it acceptable to all cultures?	• Yr 3 term 2 — theme — SHOPS visits to shops which represent and stock foods from a variety of cultures, shopkeepers invited back to school	
What time, resources and organization, are available, appropriate?	• Will you have time to talk to individuals? • Will there be variety and flexibility to suit *all* the children?	• four or five sessions per week • some whole-class work, some integrated group work	
What elements of the Programme of Study will be covered? Key Stage 2 — AT1 — PoS • use and develop scientific knowledge and understanding • raising, promoting and answering questions, seeking solutions	• any other Key Stage PoS relevant? • start from pupils' knowledge and understanding • use science and technology from a range of cultures • — observation and brainstorming — encourage confidence	• determining sources of goods, raw materials etc. • examining signs and labels, use of colour	S i L 2–5 S i and iii L 1–4

(Continued on next page)

FOCUS IN PLANNING	ISSUES FOR CULTURAL DIVERSITY	EXAMPLE – SHOPS	NC STRANDS
• first-hand observations	• careful use of language especially terms like fair testing and variables, use clear examples	• observing products, signs clothing, organization	S ii L 1–3
• explore with increasing precision • sorting and grouping	• have high expectations but remain sensitive	• accurate weighing, measuring • sorting and grouping vegetables	S ii L 3
• fair testing, identification of variables	• develop from ideas — strongest paper? — unfair tests! • do not assume competence with language	• examine and test fabrics for use in protective clothing	S ii L 4 and 5
AT3 — PoS • natural and man-made materials	• do not assume familiarity with materials and their uses	• opportunity to examine, test and classify materials	S iii L 3
• compare and classify materials	• provide opportunity to develop vocabulary i.e., strength, rigid, layers, stretch, compress, soak etc.	• exploring and making packaging	S i L 3 and 4
How will I structure the activities?	• visit a range of food or clothing shops • value the child's own language? • stress similarities • be sure that all participate	• visit shops presenting different cultures • interview shopkeepers • construct and test bags • examine materials used	
What language can be developed?	• use of own language • involvement of parents etc. • share language with monolingual peers • use a form of process writing, talking, writing a draft, talking, redrafting • use Information Technology, text handling, databases, simulations, Logo	• questioning, discussing, instructions, predicting, estimating, sequencing, recording, suggesting, comparing • new and special vocabulary abbreviations, symbols, questions and answers, secondary sources, choosing appropriate forms of language and the appropriate language, recounting events	

(Continued on next page)

Table 7.2: (Cont.)

FOCUS IN PLANNING	ISSUES FOR CULTURAL DIVERSITY	EXAMPLE – SHOPS	NC STRANDS
	• create the right atmosphere; this is our science and our language		
What resources will we use?	• is there racism in attitudes, stereotyping? • is cultural diversity valued? • is science in other cultures recognized? • is linguistic diversity celebrated?	• materials collected in shops • collection of foods, clothing, promotional material	
What cross-curricular links will be useful?	• don't assume that the links which appear obvious to you are obvious to others	• English cultural bias in advertising and promotional material • geography — sources • technology — materials, making	
What opportunities for assessment exist?	• is it meaningful? Is it skewed? • take care that the child is not disadvantaged by language • provide opportunity to communicate through art, movement etc.	• assessment of AT1, Strand ii through observation of the investigations above • assessment of AT3, Strand i L3a and L4a	

they will inadvertantly do something that is forbidden. It should be remembered also that Sikhs, Muslims and people of many other cultures and religions eat with only their right hands.

When observing changes of state through cooking, we should be sensitive to the experience the children are likely to bring to the situation. Are they, for example, familiar with jelly? Investigations into food should be relevant to their own lives. It would not be appropriate to test fabric for its suitability as a tea cosy if the child was unfamiliar with the article and its purpose. Tensions will always exist between extending and deepening pupils' experiences and respecting their cultures.

Typically, an examination of different foods is likely to form part of this work. A Hindu boy over 7 years of age would not be allowed to taste food once tasted by others. Smelling and tasting potato crisps is potentially a scientifically productive activity. Some children may not be familiar with the different flavours and others may not be able to take part in this activity because of religious reservations. In some cultural groups children are not likely, for religious reasons, to eat food from fast-food chains and so it might be inappropriate to ask them to do an investigation into the packaging of such food.

Dress is often dictated by religious demands. A Sikh boy will not be willing to remove his steel bangles (kara) even if the activity is messy (a child from year 1 mixing food) or if the wearing of it is thought by the teacher to be dangerous (when for example using tools).

Cultural differences can also affect the way a child reacts to the activities offered. Teachers cannot assume that all young children will have had a wide range of toys available (perhaps for economic reasons). Some children will therefore need a lot of play opportunities before they are familiar with the objects being handled (McCann, 1990). Energy and forces are often taught through the medium of toys and some children will need a longer period of unstructured play before being able to consider these concepts.

Tools which seem everyday to some may be quite unfamiliar to those from another culture. Activities regarded as 'normal' may be done quite differently by others. For example, a common British custom is to make tea by boiling a kettle and then pouring the boiling water over tea leaves in a tea pot. An Asian child may make tea by boiling the water and tea together in a pan on the hob. We need to be aware that our methods are neither universal nor right and that other methods are as valid as our own.

The Islamic religion disapproves of singing and dancing and so topics such as sound and music need to be treated sensitively. Islamic law forbids any representation of the human form. When the Standard Assessment Tasks were introduced in 1990 a real problem was presented to teachers when trying to assess whether the children recognized the names of different parts of the body. Pictures could not be used. A teacher who was not aware of this might have found that the child was uncooperative, perhaps appearing not to know. A more appropriate approach might be to point to the various parts of the body and ask for the names, or ask the pupils to point to the named parts of themselves or their peers.

Assumptions about experience are as dangerous as oversights. A child coming from the subtropics might be expected to know about the weather in those regions. This could be far from the case if, for example, the child emigrated in early life. Similarly, even where a child has experienced European winters, if that child's parents are unfamiliar with European traditions, as is quite likely even after many years residence, the child may not know about snowballing, sledging, building snowmen etc.

It is of course wrong to consider such cultural characteristics only in terms of restrictions. Each culture brings riches. The festivals of Diwali, Christmas, Hannuka and Eid each provide opportunities for primary-school science topics including light and colour, clothing, food.

When teaching all children we should ensure that what we teach is within their social context and that what we teach is at the appropriate level. We must also guard against lowering our expectations. The Swann report (Committee of Inquiry, 1985) claimed that teachers' low expectations of black pupils and stereotyped assumptions about their abilities often held back pupils' achievement.

All children need sensitive teachers who are informed about:

- the child;
- the culture; and
- the topic to be taught.

Language in Science Teaching

Language is a key factor in scientific learning. Scientific language can act as a barrier to a wide range of youngsters, including, bilingual learners, those for whom English is a second language and those whose culture does not share words and ideas. In science, everyday words are used specifically e.g., flow, switch, charge, power. There is also technical language e.g., terminal, positive, cell. Described by Hoyle (1987) as the *lingua franca* of the science world, this language forms a significant barrier. Pupils may, she says, eventually learn to cope with this language if regard is paid to their ideas and their language. An example from assessment is science Attainment Target 1 makes the point. At level 1 children are required to describe familiar and unfamiliar objects in terms of simple properties, for example, shape, colour and texture. A child whose first language is not English might describe a pebble as being soft when smooth is meant.

At one level, the particular language used to develop a concept is not a central issue. Many children to whom English is a second language or who are bilingual, learn scientific concepts in their own language and are later able to use English; however for some this may occur much later when English is a second language. This is very significant for teaching, learning and assessment. Hannon (1991) stresses how close the link between science and language is when developing the multicultural dimension. This is because of the cognitive links between words used to represent concepts are crucial irrespective of language. An excellent compendium on overcoming difficulties in learning and teaching bilingual pupils taking the National Curriculum has recently appeared (Cline and Frederickson, 1992).

Harlen (1992b) reminds us of 'the value of children discussing with each other, exchanging ideas and developing their own views through the act of trying to express them and explain them to others.' (p. 100). If children do not have a common language in which they are sufficiently skilled to do this, their conceptual development may be impeded. Language learning is now presented as being closely bound up with all other learning that is going on. Discussion enhances scientific understanding and it may be beneficial for children to exchange their ideas in their own language. Group work with children who speak a common language can support a non-English speaker and enable all children to share their ideas and participate more fully.

In reports from the Children's Learning In Science (CLIS) project at the University of Leeds time taken by teachers to establish children's understanding was seen as essential. This has been backed up by recent enquiry of the Science Processes and Concept Exploration (SPACE) project at the Liverpool University and King's College, London where a phase of elicitation was advocated. Thus teachers are encouraged to consider how learning of concepts takes place, to accommodate and challenge children's alternative understandings. Cultural diversity might account for some of these (AT2, Strand ii — Variation and the mechanisms of inheritance and evolution) but restricted English language may inhibit the elicitation. It is necessary to formulate questions in such a way that the children are able to respond (Harlen, 1992a; 1992b). Can another child be used to translate the question? Can the child reply in pictorial form? Is the child's oral competence superior to his/her writing capability?

Townend, Petrenas and Street (1991) recognize that:

the science curriculum can offer great opportunities for the linguistic development as well as the conceptual development of all pupils, provided that the demands are recognised and pupils are supported in meeting them.

Language whether verbal or non-verbal, has a crucial role to play as a communicator of either positive or negative attitudes about different people, situations and developments. It is therefore of paramount importance that we look to our attitudes and at the language we use as a foundation for our teaching . . . (Townend, Petrenas and Street, 1991, p. 52)

Cultural Diversity in the All-White School

In Thorp's work (1991) all white primary schools are first asked to consider if they are 'all white' and then are advised to approach the issue of cultural diversity in science through the context of the whole curriculum. Without an immediate multicultural community to draw on as a resource, a school may be at a disadvantage. Worse still, there may be colleagues, governors or parents who see this as a non-issue or even harbour racist views or ambivalence preventing a committed whole-school approach.

In this situation primary-school science is a considerable asset, a vehicle for children to examine the world, to draw comparisons between diversity in nature and diversity in culture. As noted earlier, tensions will always exist both within and between cultures between the aims of extending an understanding of science and respecting a culture's beliefs. The 'creationist' versus the 'evolutionist' argument is but one example of a very powerful and divisive religious/scientific controversy (Desmond and Moore, 1991).

Capitalizing on the Cultural Diversity in Your School or Classroom in Relation to National Curriculum Science

First of all, preparation involving research is required:

- read as widely as possible about cultural diversity;
- look carefully at your school situation; and
- gather as much relevant information as possible about the cultural groups represented.

What view of science do you present to the pupils?

- How is science education carried out?
- Are minority groups considered and actively catered for?
- Who does the science? — the teacher? all the children?

How are minority groups viewed?

- As a problem?
- As an enriching element of the community?
- Does the school have a relevant multicultural policy?

How much do you and fellow teachers know about the children's cultures?

- Are the children's cultures valued?
- How are teachers able to find out about the culture of minority ethnic groups?

Consider an action plan to take you/your colleagues forward:

- approach local 'experts';
- involve the community in some science projects;
- invite parents in; and, where appropriate,
- link science to culturally valued events.

More than any individual strategy, your overall approach to science and cultural diversity will be the deciding factor. The following responses characterize successful personal and professional development by teachers of science in primary schools.

Table 7.3: Summary of Responses: Science

Ensure the following:

- Staff development to give teachers the opportunity to learn and explore both scientific and multicultural terminology issues and acquire relevant information.
- Active engagement with the issue of cultural diversity just as we intend children will be active and engaged by the science.
- Agreement on a science policy which embraces the notion of antiracism and cultural diversity through:
  — choice of topics — make them relevant to all the children;
               — provide children with the opportunity to challenge stereotyped images and
               — be sensitive to the needs and aspirations of others.
  — the learning environment — use the children's everyday scientific and social experiences.
  — activities — make sure that cultural diversity is represented.
  — resources — check that these are suitable, familiar and available.
- Make the science policy part of a whole-curriculum approach to cultural diversity.
- Make use of knowledge and understanding required in National Curriculum Programmes of Study and Attainment Targets.
- Make use of science as a medium for challenging, enquiring about and celebrating diversity.
- Consult 'Access to Information on Multicultural Education Resources' (AIMER)
- Consult National Educational Resources Information Service (NERIS).
- Become informed through a desire to understand and actively promote cultural diversity in and through science.

References

ASSOCIATION FOR SCIENCE EDUCATION (1993) *The Whole Curriculum in Primary Schools: Maintaining quality in the teaching of primary science*, London, ASE.

CHILDREN'S LEARNING IN SCIENCE PROJECT (1988) *CLIS in the Classroom*, Leeds, CSSME.

CLINE, A. and FREDERICKSON, N. (1992) *Bilingual Pupils and the National Curriculum: Overcoming difficulties in teaching and learning*, London, UCL.

COMMITTEE OF INQUIRY INTO THE EDUCATION OF CHILDREN FROM ETHNIC MINORITY GROUPS (1985) *Education For All*, Cmnd. 9453, London, HMSO.

DEPARTMENT OF EDUCATION AND SCIENCE (1988) *Science for Ages 5–16: Proposals of the Secretary of State*, London, HMSO.

DEPARTMENT OF EDUCATION AND SCIENCE (1989) *Science in the National Curriculum*, London, HMSO.

DEPARTMENT OF EDUCATION AND SCIENCE (1991) *Science in the National Curriculum 1991*, London, HMSO.

DEPARTMENT OF EDUCATION AND SCIENCE (1992) *Science, Key Stages 1, 2 and 3*, London, HMSO.

DENNICK, R. (1992) 'Analysing multicultural and antiracist science education', *School Science Review*, 73, 264, pp. 79–88.

DESMOND, A. and MOORE, J. (1991) *Darwin*, London, Michael Joseph.

DRIVER, R. (1983) *The Pupil as Scientist?*, Milton Keynes, Open University Press.

HANNON, C. (1991) 'The Multicultural Dimension in the Science of Food', in PEACOCK, A. (Ed) *Science In Primary Schools — The Multicultural Dimension*, London, Macmillan, pp. 28–37.

HARLEN, W. (1992a) 'Research and development of science in the primary school', *International Journal of Science Education*, 14, 5, pp. 491–503.

HARLEN, W. (1992b) *The Teaching Of Science*, London, David Fulton.

HAWKING, S. (1988) *A Brief History of Time*, London, Bantam Press.

HOYLE, P. (1987) 'Science education in and for a multicultural society: some language issues', in DITCHFIELD, C. (Ed) *Better Science: Working for a Multicultural Society*, SSCR Curriculum Guide 7, London, Heineman Education Books / Association for Science Education.

JENKINS, A. (1991) 'The Green Revolution: A "Triumph" of Science?', in THORP, S. (Ed) *Race Equality and Science Teaching*, Hatfield, Association for Science Education, pp. 130–1.

KELLY, G. (1955) *The Psychology of Personal Constructs*, New York, Norton.

McCANN, A. (1990) 'Culture and Behaviour: A Study of Mirpari Pakistani Infant Pupils', in WEBB, R. (Ed) *Practitioner Research In The Primary School*, London, The Falmer Press, pp. 183–201.

PEACOCK, A. (1990) 'Building A Multicultural Dimension into Primary Science', *Primary Science Review*, 12, pp. 11–12.

PEACOCK, A. (Ed) (1991) *Science In Primary Schools — The Multicultural Dimension*, London, Macmillan.

PEACOCK, A. (1992) 'What can we learn from other countries about teaching science investigation to primary children?', in NEWTON, L. (Ed) *Primary Science: The Challenge of the 1990's*, Clevedon, Multilingual Matters Ltd., pp. 20–7.

PIAGET, J. (1930) *The Child's Conception of Physical Causality*, New York, Harcourt Brace and Co.

PUMFREY, P.D. (1960) 'The effects of an heuristic approach to science teaching in the top two forms of a junior school', Diploma in Child Psychology Dissertation. University of Birmingham School of Education.

PUMFREY, P.D. (1962) 'Junior School Science', *Educational Review*, 14, 2, pp. 142–51.

REID, D.J. and HODSON, D. (1987) *Science for All*, London, Cassell.

SIRAJ-BLATCHFORD, I. and SIRAJ-BLATCHFORD, J. (1991) 'Science and Cultural Relevance', *Primary Science Review*, 17, pp. 16–17.

THORP, S. (Ed) (1991) *Race Equality and Science Teaching*, Hatfield, Association for Science Education.

TOWNEND, C., PETRENAS, A. and STREET, L. (1991) 'Supporting language learning through doing science', in PEACOCK, A. (Ed) (1991) *Science In Primary Schools — The Multicultural Dimension*, London, Macmillan, pp. 51–79.

Chapter 8

Foundation Subject: Technology (including Design)

Stuart Powell

Context

Consequent upon recent revisions to the National Curriculum, Technology and English are now the only subjects to retain Profile Components, defined by the NCC (National Curriculum Council) in an (as yet) unpublished resource pack, as 'groups of ATs (Attainment Targets) brought together for the purposes of assessment and reporting'. Technology has two Profile Components, viz., 'design and technology capability', and 'Information Technology Capability'. The former has four ATs, the latter only one, and interestingly the name of the AT for Information Technology is identical to that of its Profile Component. The reference to 'capability' in both components emphasizes that technology is a subject concerned with practical action, drawing on knowledge from a wide range of subjects.

The four ATs for Design and Technology do not, as in mathematics for example, arbitrarily divide the subject into discrete parts, rather they provide a process based framework for the delivery of the subject. The ATs reflect stages in the design process, similar to the mode of operation adopted in science, referred to as the 'scientific method' or, as with Ma1 for mathematics, problem-solving strategies which might be deployed in almost any open investigation. The ATs or stages in Design and Technology, within the order for Technology 1990, are defined as: Identifying needs and opportunities (Te1), Generating a design (Te2), Planning and Making (Te3), and Evaluating (Te4). The numbering one to four does not imply a sequence. Indeed, good design practice often dictates that existing products are first evaluated in order to identify opportunities for innovation. The process, rather than being linear, is therefore cyclical and affords the opportunity to revisit stages to effect improvement and, more importantly, to reinforce learning in youngsters who will be engaged in a complex activity. At the time of writing, a review of the content and structure of the Design and Technology Profile Component has been ordered, and the likely outcome is a reduction in the number of ATs from four to two, these being Designing (Te1) and Making (Te2). This revision, however, does nothing to alter the nature of the way in which designers behave or the fundamental philosophy which underpins the activity, i.e., the design process will be retained.

Information Technology has five strands, viz., Developing Ideas and Communicating Information, Handling Information, Modelling, Measurement and Control, and Applications and Effects. Information Technology will be used within Design and Technology, but may also be used within all other subjects of the National Curriculum. It is a tool to be used *by all*. In determining the subject level for Technology for reporting purposes, Profile Component 1 (Design and Technology Capability) and Profile Component 2 (Information Technology Capability) are not afforded equal weighting, the weighting being three to one in favour of the former. The current review of the Technology Order specifically excludes the information technology Profile Component, this being judged successful in its *modus operandi*.

The Order specifies contexts in which the teaching of Design and Technology must occur, viz., Home, School, Recreation, Community, and Business and Industry. There exists within this list an incline of difficulty, and indeed the National Curriculum Council in its Non-Statutory Guidance suggests that 'pupils should begin with the familiar' (National Curriculum Council, 1990, p. A2, 2.3).

At Key Stage 1, pupils are likely to relate more readily to concepts which draw upon their knowledge of the home than to unfamiliar contexts such as Business and Industry. Later within this KS, design activity will make connections with the school environment and so on. Thus whilst few pupils in the primary phase will have more than a superficial knowledge of business and industry, all should have experienced design activity related to the community and this affords an opportunity to relate work not only to its historical roots but also to the different cultures which exist within our society. Pupils are, in relation to AT4, required in statute to evaluate the outcome of their own work and the processes used, and also the work of others, *including* products from other times and cultures. Within the primary phase, pupils will use materials, tools and processes to effect change in a purposeful and planned manner. Materials will include textiles, graphic media (such as paint, paper and photographs), construction materials (such as clay, wood, metal and plastics) and food. The Programmes of Study (PoS) divide Design and Technology products into three categories: Artefacts, Systems and Environments. The latter provides a rich source of study of our surroundings made, or developed by people.

Primary schools employ a range of delivery strategies in relation to technology. By far the most common is the integrated project or topic approach in which a study of, say, castles gives rise to work involving many subjects. For example, history, geography, mathematics and technology. Topic work may, of course, have any one of these subjects as the clear starting point, but few schools, because of a lack of confidence or experience amongst staff, choose to focus on technology. Many employ making skills to good effect for model making of a product associated with the topic, but few staff use modelling techniques with children as part of pedagogy in design. Sadly, even fewer recognize the distinction. Occasionally pupils are taught specific technological skills divorced from the process of design and, whilst there exists the opportunity to apply these skills at some later stage, this approach is perfectly valid. Technology projects which start with a clear design brief or instruction to children are most likely to result in a successful outcome and surprisingly, despite the specificity introduced at the start, imaginative and innovative approaches by children usually dominate the activity. However, very young children often respond better to carefully structured situations rather than tasks. For example, with the inclusion of stories, tapes, maps, lists, boxes, fabric material, games etc., children will constructively play games of their own making in an environment of their own design.

Challenges

Design work can benefit from the contributions of different cultures, and the SoA (Statements of Attainment) instance numerous examples where pupils are required to consider cultures other than their own. *The Design and Technology Working Group Final Report* (Department of Education and Science, 1989) states:

> Cultural diversity has always been a feature of British life . . . The different cultural and linguistic backgrounds of pupils are now becoming valued properly as a means of developing a richer learning environment for all.
> The teaching of Design & Technology . . . will require perception and sensitivity from teachers. Design & Technology has its technical language, aspects of which may have no counterparts in the mother tongues of some young children in schools. Children from different ethnic backgrounds may bring . . . different beliefs and practices, especially when food materials and environmental designs are involved. The variety of cultural backgrounds of pupils can broaden the insight they all have into the range of appropriate, alternative solutions to perceived problems. There are rich opportunities here to demonstrate that no one culture has a monopoly of achievements in Design & Technology. Appreciations of this kind could both contribute to better international understanding and yield direct economic benefits in later life. It is equally important that schools where there are few or no ethnic minority pupils ensure that their parents understand the cultural diversity of modern society and are aware of the diversity existing in areas in which they may later live or work. Design & Technology, like other subjects in the curriculum, has an important

part to play in preparing pupils for life in a multi-cultural society. (DES, 1989, p. 7, paras 1.44–1.46)

One of the challenges is to explore ways in which the subject technology can both benefit from, and contribute to, perceptions of our multicultural society. Multicultural education usually involves the study of a variety of different cultures and has this as its focus. This approach can often be racist in outcome by making cultures other than British appear unusual, different or strange. Teachers often feel handicapped by a lack of knowledge of the cultures of children from minority groups within our society. It should be remembered that cultures overlap and cannot be packaged into totally discrete components. Moreover, culture is subject to dynamic change as different cultures interact with one another. Simply imparting cultural knowledge therefore is not, on its own, a prerequisite for the active participation of all pupils for life in a multicultural society. Technological methodology has much to offer the primary curriculum in terms of a generic strategy for combating anti-racist teaching and a second challenge is, therefore, to identify the characteristics of the technology curriculum which may inform whole-school development planning in relation to multicultural education. A model which values the experiences of everyone in the class and also those experiences not represented within the cohort, is based on the concept that all people have common needs and that these needs may be satisfied in different ways through different experiences. In stressing the similarity, before acknowledging differences, all children are more likely to respond positively. Sealey, writing in 1983, comments that all too often the term multicultural is used as a euphemism for teaching about other cultures, thus marginalizing perfectly valid experiences simply because they differ from the norms of majority group perceptions. She identified three challenges:

Table 8.1: Summary of Challenges: Technology

- Harness technological contributions from different cultures.
- Improve teacher perception and sensitivity of the contributions of minority group culture.
- Provide experiences which permit pupils to conceptualize language and mores with which there is no parallel in their mother tongue and culture.
- Inculcate respect for different beliefs and practices in addressing technological problems.
- Influence parents to accept the need for the multicultural dimension to education.
- Prepare pupils for life within our multicultural society by demonstrating the complementary nature of different technologies.
- Educate teachers appropriately in multicultural educational pedagogy.
- Identify those characteristics of technology which may inform the whole-school multicultural policy.
- Appreciate technological diversity across cultures, whilst recognizing similarities in the problems addressed.

How do we ensure that we are basing learning on the child's real experiences rather than our (the teacher's) perception of them? . . . If children are exploring concepts through their own experiences, are all those experiences valued equally? . . . How can we ensure that we emphasise the similarity of human experience without overlooking the wealth of diversity? (Sealey, 1983)

Responses

The 1990 Order for Technology in the National Curriculum, DES, contains, within the Statements of Attainment, many references to consideration of the multicultural dimension. There are statements which specifically address this issue and it is useful to consider these statements in relation to current practice. Within Te1 at level 4 pupils are required to:

4f) know that in the past and in other cultures people have used design and technology to solve familiar problems in different ways, (p. 4).

The example given in the Order suggests that pupils should:

Know some ways people in different countries irrigate their crops and get water into their homes, (p. 4).

Within Te2 at level 3 pupils are required to:

3c) draw from information about materials, people, markets and processes and from other times and cultures to help in developing their ideas, (p. 7).

The example given in the Order suggests that pupils should:

Gather information on different types of ethnic food and people's preferences when planning a party, (p. 7).

Within Te4 at level 2 pupils are required to:

2b) make simple judgments about familiar artefacts, systems and environments, including those from other times and cultures, (p. 15).

The example given in the Order suggests that pupils should:

Comment on appearance and usefulness of a range of cutlery, ranging from a child's curved spoon to chopsticks, (p. 15).
3a) discuss their design and technological activities and their outcomes with teachers and others, taking into account how well they have met the needs of others, (p. 15).

The example given in the Order suggests that pupils should:

> Discuss whether the preferences of others have been taken into account when making food for a festival. Have people with different needs or interests been satisfied? Have people from different cultures been considered? (p. 15).

Other SoA from Te4 are:

> 4c) comment upon existing artefacts, systems or environments, and those from other times and cultures, including appearance and use of resources, (p. 16).
>
> 5c) understand that artefacts, systems or environments from other times and cultures have identifiable characteristics and styles, and draw upon this knowledge in design and technological activities (p. 16).

Clearly there is much scope for consideration of the lifestyles of a variety of cultures and such a profile is to be warmly welcomed, but the teaching of these issues must start with consideration of the similarity of children's experiences. For example, a study of fashion in clothing should first challenge basic assumptions such as: Why are clothes worn? Are certain items of clothing worn for particular events? Are the clothes that one would wear for sport different from those that would be worn for school, work, or protective purposes? Why would the clothes worn to celebrate a special occasion, for example, a wedding, differ from those worn for recreative purposes? Why is ceremonial dress worn at particular times? How many different types of uniform exist?

Having related design to function, one can then question style and its interaction with other design criteria. Design practice requires pupils to explore the influence of the environment. Consideration might be given to the relationship between climate, colour and materials. Fashion is a fascinating area of study for children of all ages and offers exciting cross-curricular links. Sadly, often before children reach school age, they possess a vocabulary which mimics the rhetoric of their, at times, ill informed elders. Observations however, suggest that they do appear to accept their peers irrespective of cultural differences. The acquisition of knowledge about design criteria should, therefore make a significant contribution to their informed understanding of cultural diversity.

Of the SoAs above four (forming almost half of the SoAs at KS1 and KS2) appear within Te4 (evaluation). The Non-Statutory Guidance for the subject explains that:

> 2.14) Evaluation occurs throughout technological activity, not only after a product has been made. Pupils should evaluate their work at every stage so that it improves progressively, (p. A4 2.14)

2.15) Two strands of development occur throughout Te4, and pupils are required to evaluate:

i   the outcomes of their own work, and the processes used;
ii the work of others, including products from other times and cultures, (p. A4 2.15).

2.16) Progression requires pupils to consider:

*   an increasing range of criteria;
*   more detailed criteria;
*   criteria further from their own experience, (p. A4 2.16) (National Curriculum Council, 1990).

Evaluation is crucial to design activity and it is important that in the early Key Stages teachers take the lead and discuss with children the selection of effective criteria for evaluation. Discussion of these factors is more likely to result in children offering reasoned argument rather than personal preference when engaged in the process of evaluating their own work or the work of their peers. This strategy is also more likely to encourage children to respect themselves and others and to break down ill-founded prejudices. The notion of progression, identified in 2.16 above, requires children to build up a concept by making sense of their own experiences, so that they are then able to transfer understanding by asking similar questions about situations outside their understanding. The concept of evaluating the process, in addition to the product, is fundamental to design methodology and results in a deeper understanding by children of the nature of personal prejudice.

Rather than imparting a fixed body of knowledge, and the existing Order has been criticized by some for not doing so, Technology has at present the potential to harness the enthusiasm of the individual pupil, and to allow the individual to follow interests which make sense to them, rather than adopting the interests of others. Tolerance of other people's interests grows from the quest for knowledge of matter which will inform the growth of our own interests and it is essential that children are afforded the opportunity to develop, test and evaluate hypotheses which make sense to them. The National Curriculum Science Non-Statutory Guidance states that:

In their early experiences of the world, pupils develop ideas which enable them to make sense of the things that surround them. They bring these informal ideas into the classroom and the aim of science education is to give pupils more explanatory power so that their ideas can become useful concepts. Viewed from this perspective, it is important that we should take a pupil's initial ideas seriously so as to ensure that any changes or development of these ideas, and the supporting evidence for them, makes sense and, in this way, become 'owned' by the pupil. The ideas of young children can be essentially scientific in so far as they fit the available evidence, even though they will tend to be limited to concrete, observable features and fall a long way short of, or even be inconsistent with, formal theories. Inevitably, pupils' ideas will develop as their experience, and their skill in interpreting that experience, widens. (National Curriculum Council, 1989, p. A7 6.2)

The concept demands that science and more particularly, technology, is seen as a response to human need and should demonstrate the validity of technology in relation to specific cultural contexts.

Reference has been made previously to the legitimacy of teaching specific skills in isolation from the design process and this assertion may appear to conflict with the philosophy of allowing a child-centred approach. There must of course be a balance between the two in order to structure effective learning. Consideration of a practical example related to a specific technique may, however, be useful in establishing procedural imperatives when engaged in this sort of activity. Above all, the activity must capture the imagination of pupils, be relevant to the Programmes of Study and inform future design activity. A typical KS2 activity for pupils engaged in Te3, cited in the exemplar material at level 4, within the SoA for design and technology is to 'choose tie and dye as a means of producing their design on fabric'. Pupils will not choose to select this medium unless they are first taught about the equipment, process and craft skills involved, and in these circumstances it is required that the teachers introduce such matter as syllabus content. Those who question the lack of specificity in the existing Order, arguing for a revision, misunderstand what design education is about.

Tie and dye is one of the simplest and quickest ways of patterning fabric and is practised throughout the world. The technique is at least 5000 years old. Teachers in the Stockport area, are privileged to have access to an invaluable resource, 'The Calabash', an arts and craft centre which focuses upon the work of a group of Nigerian textile designers. One facet of their work is known as Adire-Eleko, and has been produced for centuries by the Yoruba tribe of Nigeria. Yoruba people are known for travelling and trading in their crafts and today their influence can be seen the world over. They use traditional dying techniques which are simple and effective, producing results which fire the imagination of children, enthusing them to imitate the skill of the originator. The contribution of such groups is noted, not because they represent a minority cultural interest which should be fostered, but because they represent a unique resource, expert in their art, and eager to impart their skills and knowledge of specific processes. The inclusion of such experiences does not marginalize their work by making it appear different, unusual or strange. It is not offered to raise awareness of 'other cultures', it is included quite simply because it is the best available example of the traditional technique. Modern attempts to imitate the process fail to produce such spectacular results. Many such groups exist throughout the country, covering a wide range of specialisms. The arts council can provide details of such groups within your area. Similarly, a deal of expertise resides at the Commonwealth Institute

Resources Information Centre. Its catalogue of materials and services bearing on multicultural aspects of design and technology is invaluable.

The self-esteem of all pupils is of particular importance to their educational development. A child's perception of society is conditioned by the predominantly Eurocentric diet of education which they receive. Surely, as teachers, we must question the basic assumptions we make when planning to involve non-teaching assistants (usually parents) in our teaching programmes? Too frequently pressures of time dictate that any offer of help is readily accepted, rather than specific contributions based upon expertise in a particular area being actively sought. It is vitally important that, when planning the experiences of children, consideration is given to the range of activity, and that individuals able to make a specific contribution are identified. It is equally important that those presenting skills inputs reflect both a balance in gender and in the range of cultures within society. Self-esteem is developed in children by building confidence. Role models are important to children, but of greater importance is the confidence which comes from mastering a particular skill or technique and, unless we are able to access the specialist talents of people within our society, we disadvantage our children. Parental involvement within the classroom is important but the parental contribution is rarely planned in terms of specific skills and is certainly complementary to, rather than a replacement for, the properly structured activity for which I have argued.

Food is an important material cited within the technology Order and topics based upon food appear to offer a natural introduction to multicultural initiatives. A simple investigation of the different sorts of bread available locally, for example, is likely to reveal products as diverse as pitta, croissants and poori. Why does this range exist? How do they differ? These are questions of legitimate concern to the teacher helping pupils to meet the SoA in the Order. Similarly, an understanding of the reasons for Muslims not eating pork, or Jews not eating lamb are of equal importance. It is not adequate to suppose that introducing children to different tastes, different dishes, will effect an understanding of cultural diversity. Sadly, this may be the only outcome when differences are accentuated. Most children, and indeed many adults, have an in-built resistance to sampling new foods and negative images are easily formed. In this area of technology, probably more than in any other, it is possible for the teacher, quite unwittingly, to exclude many children from active participation. The problem is compounded by the fact that few primary schools are suitably resourced for working with food, and those that are usually staff such activity only with the help of well intentioned parents who may not be familiar with the dietary requirements associated with different cultures and religious faiths. Vegetarian and indeed vegan diets are increasingly common for a variety of reasons and respect for the beliefs of such children is vitally important.

The preservation of food is an area rich in common experience the world over, and may form a better entry into the topic. Preservation techniques vary and comparisons of the relative merits form useful links with the science curriculum. The equipment required is very basic and the testing provides a focus for work which may be revisited over a period of weeks. Hygiene is of vital importance in food preparation or preservation and offers yet another common point of entry into the subject.

Above all else design education places emphasis on the worth of the individual and the unique contribution which each has to offer. At primary level, the inventive ideas of pupils will probably not make a new contribution to the sum of human knowledge but we should never forget that, for the pupil, each step will be new and the child will need constant reassurance and praise as he or she treads an uncertain path. Similarities between human experiences should be explored before acknowledging differences, and there should be positive intervention wherever opportunities exist in order to raise the self-esteem of pupils.

Table 8.2: Summary of Responses: Technology

- Use design and technology to solve problems in a variety of ways, drawing upon the experiences of other cultures in analogous situations.
- Draw from information about materials, people, markets and processes typical of other cultures.
- Evaluate familiar artefacts, systems and environments including those from other cultures.
- Discuss design and technology activities and outcomes with pupils, taking into account how well they have met the needs of various cultural groups.
- Recognize contributions typical of different cultures and harness these whenever appropriate.
- Develop the concept of variety by initially considering similarities in technological problems addressed.
- Consider the impact of the environment upon design practice.
- Be sufficiently flexible as to allow individuals to follow interests which have relevance to the task as perceived by the pupil.
- Present pupils with relevant technological and design skills and experience before requiring them to apply these in a design situation.
- Select techniques on merit rather than on cultural bias, bearing in mind contextual constraints to technological and design solutions.
- Ensure that the contribution of non-teaching assistants is consistent with the desired objectives.
- In relation to design and technology as whole school issues, emphasize the worth of the individual and the uniqueness of his or her contribution, thus raising pupil self-esteem.

References

ASSOCIATION FOR SCIENCE EDUCATION (1981) *Science in Society (Book D)*, Food, ASE.

BATESON, P. and SHEPHERD, T. (1988) *The Water Game: A Topic Based Computer Simulation*, London, Centre for World Development Education.

DEPARTMENT OF EDUCATION AND SCIENCE (1978) *Primary Education in England: A Survey by HM Inspectors of Schools*, London, HMSO.

DEPARTMENT OF EDUCATION AND SCIENCE (1985a) *Education for all: A Report of the Committee of Inquiry into the Education of Children from Ethnic Minority Groups, (The Swann Report)*, Cmnd., 9453, London, HMSO.

DEPARTMENT OF EDUCATION AND SCIENCE (1985c) *Better Schools*, Cmnd., 9469, London, HMSO.

DEPARTMENT OF EDUCATION AND SCIENCE (1987) *National Curriculum Task Group on Assessment and Testing (TGAT), A Report*, London, HMSO.

DEPARTMENT OF EDUCATION AND SCIENCE (1988a) *Science for Ages 5–16*, London, HMSO.

DEPARTMENT OF EDUCATION AND SCIENCE (1988b) *Science for Ages 5–16: A Statement of Policy*, London, HMSO.

DEPARTMENT OF EDUCATION AND SCIENCE (1989) *Design and Technology Working Group Final Report*, London, HMSO.

DEPARTMENT OF EDUCATION AND SCIENCE (1989b) *Responses to Ethnic Diversity in Teacher Training*, London, HMSO.

DEPARTMENT OF EDUCATION AND SCIENCE (1990) *Technology in the National Curriculum*, London, HMSO.

DEPARTMENT OF EDUCATION AND SCIENCE (1992) *Technology: Key Stages 1, 2 & 3, A Report by HM Inspectorate on the First Year 1990–91*, London, HMSO.

DEPARTMENT OF EDUCATION AND SCIENCE/NATIONAL CURRICULUM COUNCIL (1988b) *Mathematics for Ages 5 to 16*, London, HMSO.

DEPARTMENT OF EDUCATION AND SCIENCE/NATIONAL CURRICULUM COUNCIL (1988c) *Science for Ages 5 to 16*, London, HMSO.

KLEIN, G. (1984) *Criteria for Selecting Classroom Materials, in Resources for Multicultural Education*, London, Schools Council Publications/SCDC.

NATIONAL CURRICULUM COUNCIL (1989) *Science Non-Statutory Guidance*, York, NCC.

NATIONAL CURRICULUM COUNCIL (1990) *Technology: Non-Statutory Guidance (Design and Technology Capability)*, York, NCC.

NATIONAL CURRICULUM COUNCIL (1990) *Technology: Non-Statutory Guidance (Information Technology Capability)*, York, NCC.

PEACOCK, A. (Ed) *Science in Primary Schools: A Multicultural Dimension*, London, Macmillan.

SCHOOLS CURRICULUM DEVELOPMENT COMMITTEE (1985) *Topic Work Resource Bank*, London, SCDC.

SCHOOLS COUNCIL (1983) *Primary Practice, Working Paper 75*, London, Methuen.

SEALEY, A. (1983) *Primary Projects: A Multicultural Approach in Issues and Resources. A Handbook for Teachers in a Multicultural Society*, AFFOR.

TANN, S.C. (Ed) (1988) *Developing Topic Work in the Primary School*, London, The Falmer Press.

Chapter 9

Foundation Subject: History

Julie Davies

Context

The National Curriculum now makes history teaching mandatory on a profession which has had little experience of teaching it and with meagre resources at its disposal. In fact, history has been, and probably still is, the least taught subject in the primary school. HMI surveys of 1978 and 1989 found little evidence of it and where it was being taught it was being done badly in 80 per cent of infant classes and 66 per cent of junior classes seen. Insufficient emphasis was given to history, in HMI's view, and the inadequately planned curriculum was ill-resourced and under-equipped. History was largely relegated to a bolted-on fragment of a topic whose central thrust was some other area (DES, 1989). The reasons for this situation vary. Some teachers maintained that the way history was taught to them using a 'chalk and talk' description of the past which they had to learn and reproduce for an exam, was not an experience they would want to repeat with primary-school children. Unless children could be engaged in active, first-hand learning experiences, some teachers felt, they would not retain much of what they were taught. Others argued that young children's historical thinking is severely limited by the stages of cognitive development they are going through and that history should be left until they are older. Each of these views rests on a premise of both the nature of children's learning and that of history. One over-simplified view of the latter is that history is about the past and, as such, is a transferable package of agreed knowledge from teacher to taught. However, history is arguably at least two things: the past, and the study of the past. The neglect of the latter definition may have contributed to history being largely disregarded or badly taught.

Into this vacuum came the history in the National Curriculum document (DES, 1991). It must be remembered that the history curriculum was designed by a group of people who had never taught in primary schools (one primary teacher was brought on to the committee at a late stage) and it was their priorities for history teaching which became the curriculum. It seems incongruous that the history to be taught in our primary schools should have received the national attention it did, given the marginalization of it in primary schools. It was one of the most discussed and most heatedly debated subject of the National Curriculum. The relative importance of various periods in history, their inclusion or omission caused a great deal of discussion. This is no doubt because history is recognized as having an important part to play in shaping people's views of themselves, of their own cultural roots and of society at large. However, the content and form of the Programme of Study (PoS) and Attainment Targets (ATs) are the products of what the working party perceived as the purposes of history teaching and so it is useful to analyse them from this viewpoint.

There are two main aims of school history:

- to help pupils develop a sense of identity through learning about the development of Britain, Europe and the World;
- to introduce pupils to what is involved in understanding and interpreting the past. (NCC, 1991, para. 1.2)

Taking the first aim and applying it to the PoS reveals the content to consist of around 50 per cent British history. Given that Britain is a multicultural society encompassing many minority ethnic groups, is this a reasonable balance? The argument for such a curriculum rests on the belief that helping all British children of all ethnic origins to make sense of a past that is their collective heritage should be the prime purpose of teaching history in schools. The history working group made this point clear:

> Britain has always been in one way or another a multicultural society. In drawing up our recommendations we have acknowledged this fact. In our view an ethnically diverse population strengthens rather than weakens the argument for including a substantial element of British history within the school curriculum, although it places a high degree of responsibility on the manner in which material is presented. (DES, 1990, p. 184)

This argument appears to be assimilationist and at odds with the 'personal identity' focus. The prescription and nature of the content of history teaching has also been critically received as detrimental to the first main purpose of school history. There is no doubt that ensuring history teaching reflects the multicultural nature of modern British society is one of the most intractable problems in schools today. Yet its solution is important because of the unique contribution history can make in bringing about a better understanding of our multicultural society. The importance of the choice of content to support this aim was recognized in the Swann report:

> Historical skills alone will not eradicate prejudice or create universal toleration; related to appropriate content, they can at least make some

considerable contribution towards giving tolerance an intellectual cutting edge to challenge prejudice. History, if not a sufficient, is certainly a necessary condition for helping young people to live with a degree of understanding in a multicultural society. (Committee of Inquiry into the Education of Children from Minority Ethnic groups, 1985, p. 319)

The assessment procedures inherent in the ATs are based on the other key purpose of school history, namely that of the study of history. The ATs make it imperative that children are introduced to the skills by which historians come to their interpretations of the past. The document emphasizes that the PoSs and ATs are complementary and that it is only through demonstrating the latter with evidence drawn from the former that children can be awarded the Statements of Attainment. This emphasis on methodological practices and historiography encourages the view of history as interpretive rather than a fixed body of knowledge. Having described the context of the history document, it is pertinent to look at the challenges that primary schools face in implementing it in multicultural Britain.

Table 9.1: Challenges to Teaching National Curriculum History for Cultural Diversity

- The commitment, confidence, knowledge and expertise of the teacher.
- The size and scope of the Programme of Study at Key Stage 2.
- To help children develop a sense of identity through learning about the development of Britain, Europe and the World.
- Resourcing the history curriculum to accommodate the development of children's critical understanding of the nature of historical evidence and of different interpretations of the past.

Challenges

History in the National Curriculum has to be taught within the context of cultural diversity. This poses significant challenges to the average primary teacher who is already overstretched with nine areas of the curriculum to cover and who, in addition, has to come to terms with teaching a subject he or she has largely ignored until now. A major challenge to the effective teaching and learning of history in the primary school rests on the commitment, confidence, knowledge and expertise of the teachers. Teachers who have not previously taught history in any focused sense (the vast majority in primary schools), will feel vulnerable when confronted with the National Curriculum history document because it calls into question their previous teaching emphases. They often tended to bolt on, in an *ad hoc* fashion, bits of history as they seemed to suit the title of the topic being studied. A classic, though not apocryphal, example of this was the teacher who was doing a topic on 'flight'. Under the history heading for this was one item 'The Flight into Egypt'.

Faced with the demands of the PoSs, teachers who had this approach to history may well feel their past practice cavalier, if not irresponsible.

The track record of primary history teaching generally is fairly poor and when the multicultural dimension is included, the picture becomes bleaker

> the majority of British schools made little attempt in teaching history to reflect Britain's multiracial society, or to teach pupils something about the origins and backgrounds of the various — especially minority, communities that form British society. (Committee of Inquiry into the Education of Children from Ethnic Minority Groups, 1985, p. 234)

Inevitably, the teachers' own past as well as the history that has been taught to them, and in what way, can be stumbling blocks to the delivery of a broad and balanced history curriculum which includes different types of history: local, British, European and non-European. For example, teachers will not be able to offer their children a wide range of stories about people from the past at Key Stage 1 unless they can access non-European stories as readily as those from Britain and Europe.

The PoSs themselves are challenging in both their stipulated size and scope, especially at Key Stage 2. There is just one PoS for Key Stage 1 to be taught throughout Years 1 and 2. It involves looking at personal, family and local history, stories about the past and the way of life of people in a period in the past beyond living memory. Children must also be introduced to a range of historical sources. This unit, though challenging, is viewed covetously by KS2 staff who have to teach collectively nine units in four years, consisting of *core* study units which must include:

CSU 1   Invaders and Settlers: Roman, Anglo-Saxons, and Vikings in Britain
CSU 2   Tutor and Stuart Times
CSU 3   Victorian Britain}
either or both
CSU 4   Britain Since 1930}
CSU 5   Ancient Greece
CSU 6   Explorations and Encounters 1450 to 1550.

and *supplementary* **study units**, which consist of either three or four units which should complement or extend the core study units. The templates the teachers are given to work to in each unit are daunting in their implications for time, expertise and resourcing in an already overcrowded curriculum.

The challenge of meeting one of the two main aims of school history — to help pupils develop a sense of identity through learning about the development of Britain, Europe and the world — is related to the level of teacher knowledge and understanding of history which is wider than a narrowly

British perspective. It is incumbent on the teacher to try to ensure all the children of all ethnic origins can make sense of a past that is their collective heritage. The challenge is, therefore, to analyse the body of knowledge in the PoSs in terms of its relevance to all children, remembering the diversity inherent in our society. In addition, there is a need for teachers to be able to show the links between local, national and world history and how they affect each other in various ways. Ultimately, the teacher's own knowledge of these issues will affect the curriculum the children are given.

Each history study unit has certain key elements which have to be taught at all ages and stages. Two of these are particularly pertinent to the multicultural dimension. Firstly, children must be introduced to the study of history from a variety of perspectives in a balanced way: political, economic, technological and scientific, social, religious, cultural and aesthetic (PESC). Secondly, pupils should be taught about the social, cultural, religious and ethnic diversity of the societies studied and the experiences of men and women in those societies. The same challenge to the teacher's personal level of knowledge exists here but also brings in the challenge of how the subject is taught.

At Key Stage 2 there is a problem of curriculum overload in terms of volume of content within each study unit. The presence of this may encourage the transmission approach to the teaching of history by which the teacher identifies what she considers to be the important knowledge, skills and understanding about a period and finds ways of transmitting it to the children. The alternative — the transformation approach — is for the teacher to provide the learning experiences, evidence and materials which will help to introduce pupils to what is involved in understanding and interpreting the past. The ATs presume the latter approach for the purposes of assessment, with their emphasis on interpretations of history and the handling of sources as well as children's knowledge and understanding of history. The challenge, then, will be to accommodate the apparent tension between the PoSs and the ATs through whole-school planning. Allied to this is the problem of which teaching strategies to use in primary-school history. The debate about subject-specific lessons or a topic work approach needs to be resolved to the satisfaction of the staff if effective teaching and learning of history is to take place.

How to handle the content of history is a crucial factor, bearing in mind the purposes of history teaching which also include the following:

- to contribute to pupils' knowledge and understanding of other countries and cultures;
- to understand the present in the light of the past; and
- to train the mind in disciplined study.

First and foremost, teachers face the challenge of encouraging primary school children to look at the nature of historical evidence in a critical, analytical way. More specifically, they need to alert children to the factors which have contributed to the evidence being preserved and to the possibility that it is incomplete. For example, if the Benin study is used, source material examples are given as early accounts by Portuguese, Dutch and English people, including a description of the Benin Court by the Dutchman Olfert Dapper. That these accounts present an incomplete picture should become clear to the children when they are encouraged to think about AT2: 'Interpretations of history'. The reason for this source material's preservation would be discussed through assessment of AT3.

Teachers need to be aware that history teaching can *increase* prejudice and the challenge is to use content which will help minimise this. For example, the myths and misconceptions about people of immigrant origin in Britain today are based partly on the belief that immigration is a very recent phenomenon. Finding source material within the 'Invaders and Settlers' unit and others which refutes this is a necessary but difficult duty, given the pressures on primary teachers today. The challenge is to combat racist stereotypes and ethnocentric attitudes through the rigorous examination of whatever content is available.

A further challenge involves the search for appropriate resources. Inadequate history teaching was found to coincide with an over-reliance on textbooks and secondary source material. The content of some textbooks has been scrutinized and found to be based on a selection of evidence which is lacking in balance and gives false strength to a case (Gill, 1987). Shortage of money has led some schools to continue to keep on their shelves books which are so out of date as to give misinformation, as well as portraying racist images of people. Besides good quality secondary-source materials, it is essential that children have access to primary and secondary-source materials to develop their skills as budding historians. Finding this in the local, national and European context is a challenge for primary-school teachers, given the lack of any previous resourcing of history. Making sure that the study of the non-European and world dimensions are covered through primary source material is an even greater challenge. The danger of bias, through omission of different view points, will be ever present where source material is scant and one-sided. The challenges just described are resolvable given the responses listed in Table 9.2 and discussed in the following section.

Table 9.2: Challenges and Responses: History

Challenges	Responses
1	1,3,7
2	1
3	2,3,4,5
4	2,3,5,6

Responses

In order that all aspects of the history curriculum may be taught in a coherent, balanced way to ensure continuity and progression from Year 1 to Year 6,

Table 9.3: *Responses to the Challenges of Teaching National Curriculum History for Cultural Diversity*

- Whole-school planning to incorporate all aspects of the history curriculum in a coherent, balanced way to ensure continuity and progression from Year 1 to Year 6.
- The methodology of the historian, epitomized in AT2, can be employed to ensure history addresses cultural diversity in the past as well as the present.
- Issues of bias, Eurocentrism and omission can be addressed through appropriate handling of content (ATs) and INSET.
- Anachronism can be tempered through restrained use of empathy.
- The critical analysis of evidence (AT3) will heighten awareness of the importance of primary and secondary sources, socio-cultural context.
- Resourcing the history curriculum effectively and comprehensively can be done but will require time to find and collate materials and develop expertise in their use.
- Teacher knowledge and understanding of history and how it is to be taught can be extended through appropriate INSET.

whole-school planning is essential. Important policy decisions in the two key areas of how history is to be taught and which content is to be used must be made after informed and open debate. While the sheer quantity of National Curriculum requirements makes single-subject teaching impossible as a method to fulfil all of them, the deficiencies of a loose topic framework are well-known (Alexander, Rose and Woodhead, 1991). Focused and carefully planned subject-biased topic work might be a way of getting the best of both worlds with a history curriculum post-holder to add weight to the demands for INSET and resourcing of the subject for cultural diversity. The second, more intractable, issue is that of the sheer amount of history children are expected to cover. It is totally unrealistic, given the demands of the rest of the National Curriculum plus the cross-curricular themes, skills and dimensions (see Volume 4 in this series). This means the staff will have to select within the study units and decide which aspects of the content should be given more emphasis at the expense of other aspects. A major consideration here should be the inclusion of the multicultural dimension in whatever content is chosen. While most of the history curriculum is set out in the core study units there are still some choices to be made from the supplementary units and these need careful consideration. Section C necessitates a choice from Ancient Egypt, Mesopotamia, Assyria, The Indus Valley, The Maya or Benin.

There is one central criterion for choice: whichever unit is chosen there must be opportunities for children to behave like historians: to handle evidence; draw tentative conclusions about it; and understand how there may be different interpretations of what they are studying. If the evidence to which they have access is only textbook-based, then that may be one reason for not choosing that particular period of study. The unit based on local history (B) should be handled much more rigorously than the local environmental study that was so common in primary practice in the past. It can be used very effectively to investigate how the locality has evolved and to make use of the children's own cultural capital, including their languages, religions and histories. There is an opportunity here to trace local, national and world links to and from the school's locality. This can be used to demonstrate to children that the British experience has always been diverse and culturally changing and that our pluralist society has a pluralist history.

> If it can be truly said that we need to look to the past to understand the present, then we need to look to local-national-world links in the past to understand both the present complex international scene and the diverse communities within the national and local boundaries. (Collicot, 1986, p. 112)

This approach will bring cultural diversity and balance to a unit that could remain purely parochial or Anglocentric. Whole-school planning will also help achieve balance between the various types of history: social, political, cultural and aesthetic, religious, economic, technological and scientific. This will encourage the investigation of other cultures in a way which will minimize the emphasis on the strange or exotic within them by drawing out the similarities that exist between societies in the past and the present.

The methodology of the historian, epitomized in AT2: 'Interpretations of history', encourages the development of the ability to understand that history is not an agreed, unchangeable body of knowledge transmitted from one generation to another. Rather it demands an active, problem-solving approach to historical content which takes on board the contingent nature of any facts or opinions assembled and commented on by historians. This view of history as process involves the study of history as a detective story where clues and evidence are scrutinized and interpreted and tentative hypotheses are proffered as a result. Fundamental questions such as 'Why have we got the history we have in the forms we have it?', are raised. This increases our critical awareness of how some knowledge of the past has been disregarded, distorted and/or marginalized.

History methodology is thus characterized by scrupulous respect for evidence and disciplined use of the imagination. For example, 5-year-olds at level 1 will be discussing the history stories they are told in terms of whether the characters are fictional or real people. The idea of myth and legend is introduced as they ponder whether Dick Whittington, Boadicea or Toussaint L'Ouverture existed or how accurate is the information known about them. At level 3 children are expected to be able to distinguish between fact and a point of view which is a very direct way of exposing the degree of bias implicit in historical interpretation of the past. For example, the Roman historian Tacitus's description of the Celts as 'savages' needs to be viewed in part, at least, as part of the rationale for imperialism and conquest, while his comment on Boadicea's resistance reveals his preoccupations 'What makes matters worse is that all this ruin is brought about by a woman'. This approach leads us into a discussion of the sufficiency, partiality and reliability of the evidence on which judgments are based. For example, the core unit 'Explorations and Encounters 1450–1550' could be used to reinforce the

151

perception of Europe as the centre from which all human curiosity, initiative and enterprise radiates. This is especially true if only European voyages are mentioned for there is an implication then that somehow the rest of the world is lagging behind. Handling the unit from a more global point of view would mean seeing exploration as part of the natural curiosity of the whole human race and making mention of the voyages to Zanzibar of Cheng He, a fifteenth-century Chinese Moslem, in ships three times as large as European vessels. The Mercator map used could also be analysed for its misrepresentation of Europe as the centre of the world. Finally, the views of all the peoples affected by Columbus's voyages should be discussed. What did the Caribs and Arawaks think about Columbus's seizure of the Caribbean? If their voice is lost from the historical sources then the fact that their population fell from 360,000 to less than 40,000 within twenty years could be used as a discussion point.

Anachronism, which involves looking into the past with present-day values very much in mind, can be addressed through AT2 when the view that people in the past were inferior to those living today is discussed. Encouraging children to recognize that every society has or had its own set of values and traditions and through disciplined use of empathy giving them the cognitive and emotional capacity to identify with somebody else and to understand their position (but not necessarily supporting or adopting it) is important. Through this approach, investigating other cultures (removed in time and place) can help children avoid the false generalizations which breed hostility, bigotry and racial conflict in present-day society.

There are three issues which need to be addressed through sensitive use of the content of the PoS in conjunction with AT1 'Knowledge and understanding of history'. The first of these is the problem of Eurocentrism and how it can affect the delivery of a balanced curriculum which is permeated by a multicultural dimension. Besides widening children's perspectives through setting study units in their world setting, as has already been described, there is further opportunity at Key Stage 1 through the use of narrative in history teaching. The teacher is free to use stories from any time and any culture to inform children about the past. For example, the story of Jamaican Mary Seacole's determination to nurse the sick in the Crimea could be used effectively here. Her repeated efforts to get permission to work with the wounded could be sequenced on the key events of her life. The exploration of the reasons for the army's refusal to let her work for the sick could be compared with the treatment of her contemporary Florence Nightingale. Level 2b would be addressed through this while level 2c would need to incorporate the present-day experiences of people of different races in their quest for jobs. Choosing one of the supplementary units such as food and farming would encourage a wider cultural perspective than the Eurocentric or national with an emphasis on the cultural importance of food. The origins of various food stuffs would naturally include a world dimension: tea from China, coffee from Turkey; potatoes from America; and cloves from Zanzibar, for example.

In order to combat the second problem of bias in handling evidence, it is necessary to have knowledge of the issues and an understanding of the spectrum of different view points. For example, the belief that black presence in Britain is a post-World War II phenomenon needs to be examined in the light of the evidence of which the following are two examples. The Romans brought black regiments with them and North African troops guarded Hadrian's Wall which was inspected by the black Emperor Septimus Severus. Statistics from the War Office reveal that one third of soldiers who fought for Britain in the two world wars were from the Commonwealth and one-eighth of these were black.

This leads into the third problematic area of omission in the balance of history teaching in a culturally diverse society. The identification of omission such as the blackness of Ancient Egyptians described by Herodotus is a useful exercise in itself for it highlights the ethnocentric basis of our culture. Similarly, the fact that Greeks, such as Plato, travelled to the great universities of Africa can be used as a balance to the idea that Greek culture and learning had no African connections. The knowledge that the Vikings were great traders who visited Byzantium which was at that time considered the centre of the world, redresses the idea that Britain was, in fact, the centre of the world. Similarly, the finding of a Buddha figure in a Viking grave can give pause for thought as to the religious diversity of those people. All these attempts at obtaining a multicultural balance within the history curriculum subscribes to the view that careful historical thinking is the implacable enemy of unexamined and stridently asserted stereotypes (HMI, 1985, p. 32).

Through the development of children's ability to acquire evidence from historical sources and to form judgments about their reliability and value (AT3) the issues of bias, Eurocentrism and omission will be naturally raised in discussion. The National Curriculum demands that children be allowed to learn about the past from a range of historical sources, including: artifacts, pictures and photographs, music, adults talking about their past, documents and printed sources, buildings and sites and computer-based material.

Two problems immediately spring to mind in ensuring the multicultural dimension is given appropriate consideration.

1) Where are these sources obtained?

As one of the main purposes in teaching history to young children is to give them a sense of personal identity then it will be necessary to look for sources within the community that the school serves. This is particularly relevant to the PoS for Key Stage 1 which deals with family history and history within living memory and for the study units based on Victorian times and life in the 1930s. Artifacts are plentiful in every home and garden. Children will bring in pieces of clothing, books and toys which can be handled in a historical way to discuss change and continuity, causation and time. Similarly, pictures and photographs are readily available to be used. The older members of the community are treasure troves of memories and opinions potentially available to be interviewed about their experiences. The local built environment is near at hand, familiar yet interesting to budding historians. Written sources do not have to be marriage or birth certificates. They can be local newspaper accounts of famous local events or sporting stories; they can be postcards and letters from different periods, or the school log, old advertisements, recipe books or catalogues. Needless to say, the ethnic make-up and backgrounds of the school population will be naturally and effectively appraised through these activities. If all the children happen to be monoethnic, then the fact that the community should form part of the study can be used by the teacher to bring in source materials from other cultures within that community. History from the Victorians onwards is relatively easy to deal with in this manner.

2) How can resources be used?

The collection of resources should facilitate the teacher in teaching and assessing the children's historical understanding through first-hand experiences using primary or secondary sources wherever possible. Having said that, there is still a good deal of INSET to be done to ensure that teachers use the resources in a historically accurate way to develop children's historical understanding. Too often, the activity can end up as a useful oral language session or an inspiring art-and-design experience rather than a session which extends children's historical concepts. To keep a check on how resources are used and the effectiveness of this, it helps to have clarified, through staff meetings, the purpose of any materials introduced into the classroom for the teaching and learning of history. The requirement that children be taught about the cultural and ethnic diversity of past societies means that when resources of a study unit are planned this aspect must be considered.

The central importance of the quality of the teacher's expertise will be a recurring theme as a response to the challenges of teaching history in the context of cultural diversity. The Department for Education has perceived this and is planning twenty day courses to upgrade teachers' knowledge of history and to develop their expertise in National Curriculum assessment (DFE, 1992). The appointment of a coordinator for history in each school will also raise the profile of history as well as encourage whole-school planning for a cohesive balanced delivery of a subject whose importance has been largely ignored. Through INSET teachers will be empowered by the provision of help with resourcing for local, national and world history as well as educating in the methodology appropriate for the teaching and learning of history for cultural diversity.

References and Resources

Below is a very brief and indicative section on resources with key publications where appropriate. Each heading could be profitably worked on to build up a resource file of how to use the various types of evidence listed in the 'Responses' section to facilitate the teaching of history in a culturally diverse society. Helpful advice and information can also be obtained from:

Black Cultural Archives, 378 Coldharbour Lane, London, SW9.

1. **Artifacts, Portraits and Pictures**

    Morris, S. (1990) *A Teachers' Guide to Using Portraits*, London, English Heritage.

    Durbin, G., Morris, S. and Wilkinson, S. (1990) *A Teacher's Guide to Learning from Objects*, London, English Heritage.

    In addition, and useful for INSET purposes, English Heritage produce a Slide Pack 'Using portraits' which takes viewers through twelve slides with careful notes so that their observation skills are enhanced.

2. **Stories and Narrative**

    Department of Education and Science (1985) *History in the Primary and Secondary Years*, London, HMSO.

    Department of Education and Science (1989) *Aspects of Primary Education. The Teaching and Learning of History and Geography*, London, HMSO.

    Cox, K. and Hughes, P. (1990) *Early Years History: An Approach Through Story*, Liverpool Institute of Higher Education, Stand Park Road, Liverpool, L16 9JD.

    Farmer, A. (1990) 'Story-Telling in History', *Teaching History*, January, 1990.

    Little, V. and John, T. (1988) Historical Fiction in the Classroom, *Teaching of History*, Series No. 59. The Historical Association, 1988.

    Sets of books are also available from:

    Madeline Lindley, Early Years History: An Approach through Story, 79 Acorn Centre, Barry Street, Oldham, OL1 3NE.

    Stories for Time Book Box from:

    Badger Publishing Limited,

    Unit One, Parsons Green Estate, Boulton Road, Stevenage, Herts, SG1 4QG.

3. **Oral History**

    Purkis, S. (1987) *Thanks for the Memory*, London, Collins Educational.

4. **Buildings**

    For further information on this primary source see the English Heritage series of videos and accompanying booklets for various historic sites. In addition they produce a series of videos which show how a historian needs to be like a detective in looking for clues and evidence in order to reach conclusions about buildings and objects. These can be fruitfully discussed in staff development time. Information for these and all English Heritage material can be obtained from:

English Heritage Education Service,
Key Sign House,
429, Oxford Street,
London, W1R 2HD
Telephone: 071 973 3442/3.

5 Written Sources

There is a rich variety of documentary material available such as school
log books, census returns, parish records, letters, inventories and government reports, marriage and birth certificates and wills. In addition, news-
papers, directories, advertisements, posters and other printed matter
provide useful material on which to work.

One pack of documents which is a good model of how to make the
past accessible to children has been produced by Charlotte Mason College
and Cumbria Archive Service and is called *Could do Better. Children at School
1870–1925*.

6. Living History

This involves children in a dramatic reconstruction of an event in the
past. It is useful means by which children can enter into the lives of
people from the past.

7. Information Technology

Its first and most significant contribution to the history curriculum lies in
the data bases that can be created to deal with the material generated from
studies involving the local community such as census returns or school
rolls.

The second area where IT can enhance the history curriculum is
through the series of computer-aided learning programmes becoming
readily available from publishers. They need careful appraisal to ensure
they will fully support the aims of the history curriculum.

8. TV and Published History Schemes

One important piece of information needs to the borne in mind here.
HMI found that where there was poor primary history practice there was
also over-reliance on TV programmes and published schemes. There is
good material on the market, of course, but there is also a lot that is not
suitable for teaching history as effectively as a resource bank built specifically to meet the needs of a particular set of children tackling a particular
study unit.

References

ALEXANDER, R., ROSE, J. and WOODHEAD, C. (1991) *Curriculum Organization
and Classroom Practice in Primary Schools: A discussion paper*, London,
HMSO.

COLLICOTT, S. (1986) *Connections: Haringly Local — National — World Links*, Haringey, Community Information Service in association with the Multicultural Curriculum Support Group.

COMMITTEE OF INQUIRY INTO THE EDUCATION OF CHILDREN FROM MINORITY ETHNIC GROUPS (1985) *Education for All*, Cmnd. 9453, London, HMSO.

DEPARTMENT OF EDUCATION AND SCIENCE (1985) *Education for All: The Report of the Committee of Inquiry of Children from Ethnic Minority Groups*, London, HMSO.

DEPARTMENT OF EDUCATION AND SCIENCE (1989) *Aspects of Primary Education: The Teaching and Learning of History and Geography*, London, HMSO.

DEPARTMENT OF EDUCATION AND SCIENCE (1991) *History for ages 5 to 16: Proposals of the Secretary of State for Education and Science*, London, HMSO.

DEPARTMENT FOR EDUCATION (1992) *GEST 1993–94: Designated Courses for Enhancing Primary Teachers' Subject Knowledge*, London, DFE.

GILL, D. (1987) 'Education or Propaganda?' *Multicultural Teaching*, 5, 3, pp. 51–6.

HER MAJESTY'S INSPECTORATE (1985) History in the Primary and Secondary Years, London, DES.

JENKINS, K. and BRICKLEY, P. (1991) 'Always historicise: Unintended opportunities in National Curriculum History', *Teaching History*, 62, pp. 8–14.

POURCE, E. (1985) 'Together — The Forgotten Contribution of the Black Commonwealth on the Two World Wars', *Multicultural Teaching*, 3, 3, pp. 21–6.

SHAH, S. (1987) 'History and Inter-Cultural Education', *Teaching History*, 4, 8, pp. 16–21.

Chapter 10

Foundation Subject: Geography

Diana Rainey

Context

Everyone who is involved with young children will appreciate how crucially important both the pre-school and primary stage of education can be. To give a child a sense of individuality, to value that individuality within the community and to instill within a child a purpose for his or her actions are essential parts of the educational process. The attitudes and habits that the child learns in these early years will shape the development of a lifetime. The inclusion of geography as a foundation subject in the National Curriculum provides a vehicle whereby pupils can utilize the cultural diversity that characterizes most urban schools.

The Education Act 1944 lists as the central purposes of education 'spiritual, moral, mental and physical development' (section 7). The Education Reform Act 1988 adds 'cultural development' to this list and DES Circular 5/89 states that 'It is intended that the curriculum should reflect the culturally diverse society to which pupils belong and of which they will become adult members.' Further guidance given by the National Curriculum Council documented in the *Whole Curriculum* (1990) suggests that 'a commitment to providing equal opportunities for all pupils, and a recognition that preparation for life in a multicultural society is relevant to all pupils, should permeate every aspect of the curriculum.' It then goes on to state that 'in order to make access to the whole curriculum a reality for all pupils, schools need to foster a climate in which equality of opportunity is supported by a policy to which the whole school subscribes and in which positive attitudes to . . . cultural diversity are actively promoted'. It continues: 'Introducing multicultural perspectives gives pupils the opportunity to view the world from different standpoints, helping them to question prejudice and develop open mindedness. Teachers have a major role to play in preparing young people for adult life; this means life in a multicultural, multilingual Europe which in its turn is interdependent with the rest of the world'.

Teaching about other people and other places is part of the very essence of geography. The whole of Attainment Target 2, 'Knowledge and understanding of place', and Attainment Target 4, 'Human geography' deals with the the study of place and the study of the lives of the people within different societies all over the world. The study of distant places applies to the Programmes of Study for both Key Stages 1 and 2. The Statutory Orders for Geography require that pupils at Key Stages 1 and 2 study people and places locally, nationally and globally. Children are required to study their own locality and another locality in the UK. Britain is itself a culturally diverse society and any locality study will include the children finding out about the lives of people living in that locality, their religion and their cultural backgrounds. The children themselves will form part of the phenomena that they are studying so the study is bound to be relevant and meaningful to them.

During the last fifteen years we have seen a great change in the way geography is being taught in primary schools. In 1978 the National Primary Survey reported that in most schools geography was taught as part of topic or thematic work. The standards of work in geography were found to be generally unsatisfactory. After HMIs National Monitoring Survey which took place between 1982 and 1986 standards appeared to have risen marginally, but not significantly. HMI found improvement in some areas, notably the increased proportion of schools with a teacher designated special responsibility for geography, and the increased number of schools with written guidelines for geography. In the examples of good classroom practice observed by HMI and identified in case studies, strong leadership in geography and the existence of a well thought-out policy document for the teaching and learning of geography, featured predominantly. These case studies can be found in *Aspects of Primary Education: The Teaching and Learning of History and Geography* (DES, 1989). They are examples of good practice which schools can emulate. The final case study incorporates multicultural education, but more could probably be made of the issues surrounding cultural diversity.

Documented evidence concerning the teaching of geography in primary schools since the introduction of the National Curriculum has yet to be published. From the experience of visiting a number of schools to observe students on teaching practice, involvement with teachers through geography INSET and generally talking to students and teachers, it can be concluded that the teaching and learning of geography is changing in response to the National Curriculum. With the introduction of the Statutory Orders many schools reviewed their history and geography curricula during 1991–2 and evaluated the needs of the schools in these areas. Looking at data that has been collected through involvement in research, as yet unpublished, involving the implementation of Key Stage 2, it is apparent that geography has not received the amount of INSET time and attention as has science or indeed history with its emphasis upon content. The planning cycles of some schools, which had previously been generated through the science curriculum, were modified in order to accommodate history and geography and some then received more of an emphasis upon the humanities. It is indeed interesting that the so-called

Table 10.1: Geography: Challenges

- To develop a school geography policy which takes into account the cultural diversity of our society.
- To ensure that the teaching and learning of geography takes place with consideration of the school's policy on multicultural education and the school's antiracist policy.
- To make adequate provision for teachers to examine their own views, attitudes and classroom practices to ensure there is representation of different cultural viewpoints.
- To ensure that there are adequate resources for the teaching of geography and that these resources are examined for cultural bias.
- To make sure that the places chosen for study will adequately reflect cultural diversity.

'great debate', in which teachers were accused of devoting too much time to the studying of the humanities and too little on science and technology, should occur at a time when HMI found the teaching of history and geography in primary schools to be unsatisfactory.

It is within this context that the challenges presented in improving the quality of the geographical education to which a child is entitled can be identified. This should be regardless of whatever ethnic majority or minority group to which he or she belongs and should capitalize upon the value of diversity.

Challenges

Within a context of cultural diversity, the primary-school teacher is faced with several challenges in order to develop good quality geographical education within his or her classroom and within the school as a whole. In attempting to provide geographical education we must not only look at the content of lessons, textbooks and resources but also at the attitudes of teachers in teaching different groups of pupils. This can not be effectively dealt with by one teacher alone. The whole staff of the school need to be aware of the variety of teaching strategies required to help young pupils develop an awareness and better understanding of the cultural and ethnic diversity within our society. Teachers will need to closely examine their own prejudices and attitudes in order to then get children to appreciate the significance of people's attitudes and values in the context of particular environmental or social issues which they have investigated. Examples of ways in which this can be attempted can be found in Deam, R. (1984)

Table 10.1 summarizes the challenges involved in developing a geography curriculum that fully takes account of the nature of our culturally diverse society and the entitlement of children growing up within it. The greatest challenge of all will be that of finding an adequate amount of time so that teachers are able to fully discuss the issues involved, develop and evaluate classroom practice.

Responses

Responding to the above challenges is not as easy as it might first seem. All evidence from HMI reports in all subject areas demonstrates the importance of effective leadership in curriculum coordination whether it be the leadership of the headteacher or an individual subject coordinator. One of the most important tasks that the geography coordinator will have to carry out is the drawing up of a policy document for the subject. Writing this document without consultation with the rest of the staff is likely to lead to a document on paper only and its ideas will not take root in classroom practice. As discussed earlier in this chapter, geographical education which prepares children for life in a culturally diverse society must include the exploration of similarities and contrasts between pupils' values and attitudes through geography. This will involve teachers examining their own practice to see which values and attitudes they are consciously or unconsciously encouraging in children.

Each school should agree, explicitly, what values and attitudes it wishes to promote. To do this effectively, it will also need to consult with parents and the wider community. All this consultation and discussion will take a great deal of time. By talking to teachers it can be established that in responding to the ERA teachers in primary schools have found the process of implementing curriculum change and modification very demanding. It is essential that the existing curriculum of the school receives a thorough audit in all curriculum areas and this is a time-consuming process. The very nature of the task involves the likelihood of some policy documents being 'rushed in' without sufficient consultation amongst the staff, very much in the same way as the National Curriculum itself was brought into being. For this reason it is important that policy documents be the subject of review procedures and that each area of the curriculum is reviewed in turn as part of the school's development plan.

The requirements of the school in terms of providing every child in the school with the geographical education to which he or she is entitled under the terms of the National Curriculum will have to be evaluated. These needs will vary from school to school but it is highly likely that all primary schools will require that a considerable amount of time be set aside for in-service education in order to enable the responses necessary to take place. A summary of responses to the challenges posed in implementing the geography National Curriculum is set out in Table 10.2.

During the remainder of this chapter it is intended to expand upon the above responses in as realistic a way as is possible during this period of great curriculum development and change. If the members of the staff of the school have all been given the opportunity to contribute their ideas then it is more likely that the policy document produced will contain a true picture of both current and future work in geography. The document will vary a great deal from school to school but it might contain:

Table 10.2: Geography: Responses

- To ensure that the school geography policy document is arrived at through discussion with the whole of the staff of the school and is subject to review.
- To ascertain whether all the staff are familiar with the agreed policy on multicultural education and that the school has both an equal opportunities and an antiracist policy that have been developed through adequate discussion.
- To develop a checklist for planning so that teachers can examine their syllabus, theme, or unit plan for geography and ensure that there is plenty of opportunity for issues to be examined by children with open-mindedness and taking into consideration different points of view.
- To examine and evaluate the resources that are used in teaching geography collectively so that any stereotyping or cultural bias is less likely to go unnoticed.
- To decide with colleagues which places should be studied and ensure that there is no cultural imbalance.

- a written statement showing the aims and objectives for geography;
- a topic or unit plan which shows the place of geography within the whole curriculum;
- a list of available resources;
- a list of places where members of staff can get help: local planning offices, County Records Offices, etc;
- a list of suitable places for class visits;
- details of any school recording system for geography;
- details of the local secondary-schools syllabus for geography in Y7;
- suitable TV broadcasts; and
- suitable books, both fiction and non-fiction, with a geographical content.

Any statement of aims and objectives in geography will need to include a reference to cultural diversity and any other field in which unfair discrimination exists, and the promotion of those values underpinning equality of opportunity. For example those:

- which encourage a positive attitude to disability;
- which reject racist and sexist views;
- which give regard to personal worth and self-esteem;
- which encourage responsibility to both the community and the environment; and
- which encourage tolerance of other religions, races and ways of life.

It might be that such a statement include cross-references to the school's policies on both multicultural and antiracist issues. It is insufficient for children to be taught merely geographical knowledge and facts about other cultures. They should be taught in a way that incorporates mutual respect and understanding of different ways of life.

In their document *The Practical Curriculum* the Schools Council (1981) made the following observations:

Schools have a great capacity for a social, personal and moral education. But they should neither seek, nor be charged with, total responsibility. In these areas above all the influence of home, neighbourhood and contemporary society is strong. In these areas, too, the pluralism of contemporary society may be reflected in differing views among the teachers in school . . . each school ought to decide what values and attitudes it wishes to emphasise. These are matters which teachers should discuss with their pupils, parents and the local community. (Schools Council, 1981)

The ERA 1988 curriculum requires a more explicit accountability of teachers and schools in delivering to all pupils the geographical knowledge, skills and understanding specified.

In teaching their pupils then, teachers must give the children the opportunity to explore their own values and attitudes and become aware of the values and attitudes of others. In everyday-language, teachers need to be aware of the messages that they convey to the children. For example instead of saying 'we believe . . .' it may be more appropriate to say 'Christians believe . . .' It is necessary to examine our own racial awareness in order that we are able to foster positive attitudes in children. If the school has an antiracist policy then it is important that the policy is carried out, so that, for example, any racist remark or incident is dealt with appropriately. Advice on such issues can be obtained from the various agencies concerned with racial equality (see Table 10.4). Most LEAs have policy documents that schools are expected to follow. There still exists amongst some parents and teachers the view that it is not necessary to use multicultural teaching in schools containing no ethnic-minority pupils. This view needs to be challenged and school policies should reflect the view that adequate planning to include learning about other cultures, apart from being a requirement of the ERA, is even more important where the children have no direct contact with children whose culture is different from their own. The geography curriculum provides an excellent vehicle for this to take place.

In choosing topics or units of work to study we have an opportunity to foster cultural pluralism. It will be possible to use the backgrounds of all the children in a class (or school) but at the same time it is important that the individual children's feelings and thoughts on the matter under consideration are treated sensitively. Most children enjoy having examples of their work displayed on the classroom wall, but for some children a personal piece of writing might be produced for a certain private audience only, perhaps only the teacher, and the last thing they wish is for it to be displayed for all to see. In the same way some ethnic-minority children may not enjoy teachers drawing attention to their different cultures and teachers will have to treat such children with sensitivity. Education for cultural diversity demands that every pupil's culture should be accepted and valued in its own right. It is important that we value the individual pupil who brings his or her cultural experiences

Table 10.3: Teaching about Minorities: A Checklist

- *Motives*
What are your motives for choosing to teach about a particular minority group? Is it merely because they appear colourful or quaint?
- *The present*
Will the study look at the present situation of the particular minority as well as the past and at the issues which confront its members today?
- *Status*
Will the study show the social and economic status of the minority group and its disadvantaged position in society as regards the majority?
- *Prejudice*
Will the study acknowledge the presence of prejudice and discrimination in majority/minority situations?
- *Origins*
Will the study consider the origins of the minority situation, e.g., colonization, migration, separatism?
- *Empathy*
Will the study attempt to foster sensitivity and empathy for the minority experience? Will it attempt to combat prejudice in any way?
- *Culture*
Will the study look at the minority group's culture and history in a positive way, including views of minority members themselves?
- *Victims*
Will the study make it clear that the minority group itself is not the problem, or will it blame the victims for their own oppression?
- *Response*
Will the study show the breadth of minority response to discrimination, ranging from despair to direct action?
- *Self-esteem*
What will be the likely effect of this study on the self-image and self-esteem of children from that, or other, minority groups?

Source: Fisher, S. and Hicks, D. (1985) *World Studies 8–13: A Teacher's Handbook.*
Note: This list has a value in relation to all subjects in the curriculum.

into the school and, by implication, the cultural group from whom he or she comes. If this does not take place, then we can turn cultural differences into cultural disadvantages. In planning a geographical topic or theme Fisher and Hicks (1985) provide a useful checklist for teaching about minorities. This is shown in Table 10.3.

The National Curriculum sets out the categories of places to be studied. By the end of Key Stage 1 pupils should have studied a minimum of three locations:

- the local area;
- a locality in the UK which offers a contrast to the local area; and
- a locality beyond the UK.

By the end of Key Stage 2 pupils should have studied a minimum of four locations:

- the local area and the home region;
- a contrasting locality in the UK;

- a locality in an economically developing country; and
- a locality in a European community country outside the UK.

Within these categories, the choice of a locality to study remains for the teachers to decide and it is in making these choices that teachers need to consider the issues already discussed surrounding cultural pluralism. If the school is an all-white school then it seems sensible to choose a contrasting area in the UK locality which has a school where ethnic-minority groups are represented. Perhaps the school could find a contrasting school to 'twin' with, so that the children could exchange letters, data, photographs etc. Teachers could contact Cheshire Twinning in order to find such a school (the address can be found in Table 10.4). By using 'real people' and exchanging 'real' views and ideas the dangers of stereotyping can be avoided. It also seems sensible to choose as an overseas locality a place that can offer some link with an ethnic-minority group within the school and here links with National Curriculum history might be appropriate. As in all things, the question of giving a balanced view of a culture is important. It is interesting that, although most Australian children know the names of Indian native Americans, until recently they were not familiar with the names of the indigenous Aborigines who also resisted colonization (Manuel, 1992). In a UK school, where the majority of the population is black, it is important that the culture of the white indigenous population is also examined. Geography is important in helping pupils to build an informed and balanced view of the world and their place in it.

In the geography Non-Statutory Guidance, the writers acknowledge the rich resource of cultural diversity and suggest that teachers use the knowledge and experience of pupils from ethnic-minority backgrounds to help select places for study (NCC, 1990). In this way links with the local community can be made, relatives can visit the school and talk about their country of origin, children can be encouraged to bring in from home objects for discussion, displays can be set up in the classroom which reflect the multicultural nature of our society.

The geography curriculum enables pupils to consider the similarities and differences between individuals, groups and communities. Geography helps pupils to understand these similarities and differences by explaining the reasons for them. By asking geographical questions such as 'Why do people move?' and 'Where do people come from?' it is possible to show children both the diverse and common elements of their family histories.

The varied and changing patterns of relative wealth and poverty both in the UK and overseas, and the economic reasons for these, are significant facts in which the geography of an area plays an important role. The identification and exploitation of natural resources is an issue of great importance to an understanding of the present and the future. The patterns of occupations that develop as a consequence, are equally so. Appreciating such patterns, and their effects on migration to and from this country and others, is important if pupils are to be helped to understand the dynamic relationships between various aspects of physical, economic and social geography. Why is the UK an increasingly multicultural society? Why do people wish to immigrate here? Why do others emigrate?

Within an area of this country, a city, a locality, a primary school or a classroom, geographically-related patterns of movement can also be identified and explored. Which pupils are arriving or leaving? From whence are new pupils coming or to where are they going? Why are such movements taking place? Are there geographical patterns that can be identified? What has caused such patterns? What could change them?

The effects of geographical variables on internal patterns of migration are well documented by the UK Office of Population Censuses and Surveys in their many publications. Similar information exists concerning the development and distribution of occupations and the products associated with them. The interplay between history, geography and economics cannot be ignored at the level of the locality, the nation, or the world. Such interactions raise many complex equal-opportunity issues. In Volume 1, Chapter 11, these controversial issues are helpfully explored and promising educational strategies outlined (Gill, 1993). The interpretation of geographical patterns in all their variety is significantly affected by the ideological framework within which such considerations take place. Geography is not a politically neutral subject. In education it must be handled with due care.

The National Union of Teachers produced a booklet in which antiracist guidelines were considered in relation to the various subjects comprising the National Curriculum (NUT, 1992). When it was published, the document received a considerable bruising by certain sections of the press. Despite this, indeed, *because* of the press reaction, the ideas presented in the NUT document merit consideration.

'The geography syllabus appears at first sight to be overloaded with requirements about the UK and European countries' (p. 7). It is suggested that topics such as:

- patterns of settlement;
- immigrants' geographical origins;
- employment patterns; and
- mapping perspectives

can be used to make explicit and explore issues related to ethnic and cultural diversity.

Within the PoS for 'Knowledge and understanding of places' there are many opportunities for studying the similarities and differences between the school's local area, home region and a variety of other localities including the economically developing countries from which members of many minority ethnic groups or their families migrated. Interdependence of groups through the import and export of a vast range of goods and services can be explored.

The reasons why some countries are economically advantaged and other disadvantaged can develop in parallel.

The human geography Attainment Targets bearing on population movements, settlements' journeys and communications provide opportunities for drawing on the experiences of immigrant groups, provided that the tensions faced by British-born children of parents from overseas are appreciated. In many senses, such children are 'caught between cultures' and their self-concepts develop in an educational context that can easily underestimate the difficulties that different cultural value systems present.

A consideration of the implications for resource management includes topics such as 'sustainable development, stewardship and conservation'.

It is clear that NC geography is not a curricular 'island': its links with other aspects of the foundation subjects and the cross-curricular themes are clear: History and Environmental Education make the point.

'Teachers can draw on the experiences of pupils and their families to enrich understanding of aspects of geography and make it more relevant to students' (ibid., p. 7).

Handling similarities and differences has to be managed sensitively, particularly if the area where the child lives is not viewed in a positive way by the teacher. By asking the children what they believe to be the positive attributes of where they live, teachers can avoid conveying their own, perhaps negative, perceptions to the children. Children might see advantages of which the teacher may not be aware. The Non-Statutory Guidance suggests a common-needs approach where similarities are looked at first. We all need food, shelter, clothes, love and beliefs; depending upon circumstances and different influences e.g., different climates, traditions, histories or environments; what we do and how we behave is largely fashioned.

> Topics, such as houses and transport, can help pupils to understand that people have common needs which are met in different ways according to local circumstances. Shelter and transport systems will be created according to local climate, environment and economic activities, for example. Considering similarities first and differences second can help to promote positive images and challenge myths, stereotypes and misconceptions. (NCC, 1990, para. 5.27)

Teachers need to find out what perceptions children have about a place they are to study. It may be that they have misconceptions, based upon cultural stereotyping, of which the teacher is required to be aware. One easy way to get some idea about how much children know is to get them to 'brainstorm' and tell you all they can about a particular locality. It is often surprising to discover where children's ideas come from and, at the same time, it heightens teachers' awareness of the importance and difficulty of ensuring that the investigations that they carry out with the children are free from bias through gender, culture, race or any other form of stereotyping. Some children, for example, have ideas about India that are based upon cowboy and Native Indian films. One 8-year-old child at a Warrington primary school thought that Macclesfield was in Scotland because it began with 'Mac'.

In deciding which places to study, teachers will need to consider the resources available to do so effectively. In studying the local area there will be less difficulty as the children are able to go 'out into the field' and large-scale local maps etc. are relatively inexpensive. The teacher can tailor-make the materials used and in so doing provide for cultural diversity. This becomes more difficult as the children are required to study places further away when first-hand experience is no longer possible. The places chosen will depend upon the availability of resources and, in order that the children receive accurate images, it is important that the materials used are examined for racist stereotypes and negative images of the developing world. Children see images of poverty through the media and sometimes can be led to believe that we in the western world have to 'help those who are unable to help themselves'. Children became very aware of the famine in Ethiopia through news coverage and the publicity surrounding 'Live Aid' and 'Band Aid' during the 1980s but were they aware of all the work being done by the Ethiopians themselves? Many schools are involved in fund-raising activities for the Third World and much of the information that we receive from the media stresses poverty and disasters. It is important to counteract this impression.

Many of the world's greatest civilizations began in parts of what we now would term 'the developing world'. Teachers need to examine the teaching materials that they use. In teaching the topic 'Homes', for example, they need to ensure that they show photographs of a wide variety of homes in the locality so that not all the homes in an economically developing country are seen as poor. Teachers should try to focus upon the everyday lives of people in localities overseas using real people and real events. The ideal solution is to visit the locality or 'twin' with a school in a locality overseas so that information can be exchanged and the children can come to know the children in the 'twin' locality in a very real way. Unfortunately this is not always possible and so teachers have to rely on other resources such as locality packs published by various aid agencies, those connected with the Development Education Project, professional groups such as the Geographical Association and those listed in Table 10.4. Most of these organizations have attempted to address the issues with which we are concerned in this chapter but teachers have to continually ask themselves about the images and ideas that these packs portray. The Chembakolli pack, for example (produced by Action Aid) provides some excellent photographs and ideas for teaching about a locality in India. Some PGCE students, however, whilst using the pack commented upon the fact that the drawings of people in the pack portrayed very sad people. Was that the message that ought to be conveyed to the children? Photographs will of course convey more accurate information but it is important that an accurate picture and not an incomplete picture is exhibited. Teachers should ask

Table 10.4: Sources of Information and Advice

Access to Information on Multicultural Education Resources (AIMER)
Faculty of Education and Community Studies,
The University of Reading, Bulmershe Court,
Earley,
Reading, RG6, 1HV.

Catholic Fund for Overseas Development,
2, Romero Close,
Stockwell Road,
London, SW9 9TY.

Centre for Global Education,
Longwith College,
University of York,
York, YO1 5DD.

Centre for World Development Education,
Regent's College,
Inner Circle,
Regent's Park,
London, NW1 4NS.

'Cheshire Twinning',
Langley Education Centre,
Main Road,
Langley,
Macclesfield SK11 OBU.

Christian Aid,
P.O. Box 100,
London, SE1 7RT.

Commission for Racial Equality,
Elliot House,
10–12 Allington Street,
London, SW1E 5EH.

**Commonwealth Institute: Centre for Commonwealth Education and Culture in
    Britain,**
Kensington High Street,
London, W8 6QN.

Geographical Association,
343 Fulwood Road,
Sheffield, S10 3BP.

Institute of Race Relations,
2–6 Leeke Street,
King's Cross Road,
London, WC1X 9HS.

National Association of Development Education Centres,
6, Endsleigh Street,
London, WC1H ODX.

Table 10.4: (Cont.)

Office of Population Censuses and Surveys,
St. Catherine's House,
10 Kingsway,
London, WC2B 6JP.

Oxfam,
274, Banbury Road,
Oxford, OX2 7GZ.

Save the Children,
Mary Datchelor House,
17 Grove Lane,
Camberwell,
London, SE 5 8RD.

themselves and also get the children to ask 'Why did the photographer take this photograph?'

In providing maps and other geographical materials, conveying a balanced view should be a priority for teachers. For example, several world-map projections should be shown to the children so that they become aware of the distortions possible. The National Curriculum document contains two world maps that have been prepared using a modification of Gall's projection which is an equal-area projection, but still contains some distortions.

An attempt has been made to give examples of the kinds of responses that teachers can give when faced with the challenges of the National Curriculum and cultural diversity. There is only one way forward and that is through a whole-school planning approach so that collectively teachers can decide firstly which places can be studied and, secondly, what issues can be focused upon to provide opportunities for developing community understanding, economic and industrial understanding and for environmental education.

References

BALE, J. (1987) *Geography in the Primary School*, London, Routledge and Kegan Paul.

CHESHIRE COUNTY COUNCIL (1992) *Cheshire Twinning*, Chester, Education Services, CCC.

DEEM, R. (Ed) 1984 'Schooling, work and unemployment', in *Conflict and Change in Education*, (E 205), Milton Keynes, Open University Press.

DEPARTMENT OF EDUCATION AND SCIENCE (1978) *Primary Education in England: A Survey by H.M. Inspectors of Schools*, London, HMSO.

DEPARTMENT OF EDUCATION AND SCIENCE (1986) *Geography 5–16, Curriculum Matters 7*, London, HMSO.

DEPARTMENT OF EDUCATION AND SCIENCE (1989) *Aspects of Primary Education: The Teaching and Learning of History and Geography*, London, HMSO.

DEPARTMENT OF EDUCATION AND SCIENCE (1991) *Geography in the National Curriculum*, London, HMSO.

FISHER, S. and HICKS, D. (Eds), (1985) *World Studies 8–13: A Teacher's Handbook*, Edinburgh, Oliver and Boyd.

GILL, D. (1993) 'Geography', in PUMFREY, P.D. and VERMA, G.K. (Eds) *Cultural Diversity and the Curriculum Volume 1. The Foundation Subjects and Religious Education in Secondary Schools*, London, The Falmer Press.

MANUEL, G. (1992) 'Aboriginal sin.', *Times Educational Supplement*, 14 August, p. 15.

MILLS, D. (Ed) (1987) *Geographical Work in Primary and Middle Schools*, Sheffield, The Geographical Association.

NATIONAL CURRICULUM COUNCIL (1990) *The Whole Curriculum, Curriculum Guidance No. 3*, York, NCC.

NATIONAL UNION OF TEACHERS (1992) *Anti-racist Curriculum Guidelines*, London, NUT.

THE SCHOOLS COUNCIL (1981) *The Practical Curriculum: Working Paper 70*, London, Methuen.

WALFORD, R. (Ed) (1985) *Geographical Education for a Multicultural Society*, Sheffield, The Geographical Association.

Chapter 11

Foundation Subject: Music

Jill Scarfe

Context

Background

The changes that had taken place in music education since 1945, from a curriculum based upon singing and musical-appreciation lessons to one which enabled the pupil in primary schools to enjoy a much more participatory role were outlined by Dorothy Taylor in her book *Music Now* as long ago as 1979. When in 1985, the General Certificate of Secondary Education national criteria for music was published the intention was to:

> foster a greater understanding of music through more direct experience of the creative processes involved. (DES, 1985, p. 1)

and one of the aims was to:

> develop a perceptive, sensitive and critical response to music of different styles in a cultural and historical context. (DES, 1985, p. 3)

This reflected the changes which had already taken place in the thinking of many primary teachers. However, when these changes were enshrined in the interim report of the National Curriculum music working group, they were met with considerable opposition (DES, 1991a).

The following fifteen months saw a heated debate, vocally expressed by some of our country's leading musicians and educationalists. This chapter is too short to air all the arguments but the following are central to the multicultural music debate.

> On this curriculum, pupils will be able to study music for 10 years without gaining a sound knowledge of either the history or the technique of Western classical music, which is surely one of the greatest achievements of our civilisation. (O'Hear, 1991)

Table 11.1: *Music: Changing Attainment Targets*

Consultation report (2 January 1992): AT2: Knowledge and understanding	The development of knowledge and understanding of musical history and theory, including the ability to listen to and appraise music. (NCC, 1992a, p. 23)
Draft Order (27 January 1992): AT2: Listening and appraising	The development of the ability to listen to and appraise music, including knowledge of musical history, (DES, 1992a).
Final Order (April 1992): AT2: Listening and appraising	The development of the ability to listen to and appraise music including knowledge of musical history, *our diverse musical heritage, and a variety of other musical traditions.* (DES, 1992b, p. 5)

After the publication of the draft proposals a year later produced a pendulum swing of concern, Marland wrote in the *Education Guardian*:

> the non-statutory examples of the aspects of study for music are unexpectedly Eurocentric, with only a single mention of 'calypso' to balance 27 Western composers. (Marland, 1992)

This debate has been reflected in the changes apparent in the documents published by the DES to Attainment Target 2, as outlined in Table 11.1. These general requirements, enshrined in law, are particularly welcome.

Opposition to the earlier interim report of the National Curriculum music working group appeared to be for three reasons. Firstly there is a lack of understanding as to what music education is really about, secondly, the function of world music within that curriculum is misunderstood and thirdly, the music of other cultures is unfamiliar to many writers on education. For example:

> In a classroom with many West Indian or Asian children, there is some justification for broadening the curriculum to embrace Caribbean and Indian traditions, though it is a rare teacher who can enthuse equally knowledgeably about ragas, reggae and Rigoletto. (Morrison, 1991)

The insistence upon a Euro-classical music curriculum, except for those pupils whose families may have their origins in other parts of the world, not only denies the value of the musics of other cultures, it also ignores the value to each pupil of his or her own popular cultures. Such a curriculum could deny many pupils equal access to the music curriculum and thus access to a successful music education.

Early attempts by music teachers to consider the cultural diversity of our society were often criticized as token gestures which failed to acknowledge the depth and richness of our many cultures.

As Houlton pointed out, it is necessary for any curriculum acknowledgment of a child's culture to take account of the complexity of his or her cultural experiences.

> It needs to go further than promoting diversity at the level of 'clothing, calypsos, cooking and customs' or . . .' sarees, samosas and steelbands'. (Houlton, 1986, p. 27)

However, the main feature of the last twenty years in music education has been the climate of innovative change. The music curriculum is much the better for it. The study of 'world musics' offers a range of opportunities to excite and stimulate the pupil's musical education which is too valuable to lose. It is now up to teachers to build upon the possibilities and opportunities enshrined in the National Curriculum.

The intention of this chapter is to show ways in which the curriculum can be planned to give full and effective value to our culturally diverse society whilst promoting learning for all, including the musically very able, of any culture.

The Current Scene

In March 1992, the National Curriculum Council submitted its recommendations to the Secretary of State, and in April 1992, the following Attainment Targets and Programmes of Study became part of the final Order appropriate for assessing a pupil's performance at each Key Stage and for preparing for the pupil's development.

There are two Attainment Targets AT1 'Performing and composing' and AT2 'Listening and appraising'. The Secretary of State wishes that the proposed Attainment Targets should be weighted 2:1 in favour of the first target.

> Attainment Target 1: 'Performing and composing', requires the development of the ability to perform and compose music with understanding.

> Attainment Target 2: 'Listening and appraising', requires the development of the ability to listen to and appraise music, including the knowledge of musical history, our diverse musical heritage, and a variety of other musical traditions.

Further the non-statutory guidelines state that:

> The National Curriculum in music is designed to be flexible, manageable and straightforward . . . should be sufficiently flexible for teachers to choose an approach which suits the needs of their pupils. (NCC, 1992b, E1)

If the National Curriculum Council continues to support the Orders for music by including statements such as 'choose an approach which suits the needs of their pupils' quoted above, there is every reason for teachers to feel that they can provide rewarding and imaginative musical experiences for their children, allowing both teachers and pupils to encounter, better appreciate and understand the musics of many traditions.

Despite current moves to increase subject-specialist teaching in NC Years 5 and 6, teachers in primary schools require a wide range of skills and knowledge plus the ability to teach all the core and foundation subjects in the National Curriculum. Music is one of the subjects which appears to cause great concern and, at present, music provision at primary level is very patchy. Sometimes, but not always, there will be a music specialist who has responsibility for coordinating music throughout the school. Even when there is such a specialist, the classroom teacher is expected to cover some aspects of the music curriculum (Mills, 1989; 1993).

As stated by the Inspectorate in their document *Aspects of Primary Education: The Teaching and Learning of Music*:

> Overall, policies for teaching music and planning work received less attention than most other subjects in the primary schools visited. (DES, 1991b, p. 11)

One of the main causes for this is a lack of confidence in this curricular area amongst primary teachers.

> If they [teachers] feel ill at ease in the arts and unable to organise these essential experiences for children, it may be because they were denied them as children . . . It is not surprising that they tend to maintain the practices which nurtured their success and to limit their involvement in the areas which they themselves were educated to neglect. (Gulbenkian Report, 1982, p. 57)

In addition to bringing from their own childhood to their teaching career a lack of confidence in the area of music, there is as yet very varied provision for initial teacher training in music for the generalist teacher.

> The HMI survey *Quality in Schools: the Initial Training of Teachers*, carried out between 1983 and 1985 . . . found 'inadequate provision for the expressive arts in virtually all the institutions. (Gulbenkian Report, 1989, p. 6)

There is even less support for the teaching of world music, of which many teachers may have little knowledge. So strongly did the working party of the Arts Education for a Multicultural Society project feel on this matter that, as one of their recommendations, they stated:

inclusion of world music be one of the criteria by which BEd and PGCE courses are judged in validation and accreditation. (AEMS, 1989, p. 12)

Primary pupils themselves have very varied experiences and bring to schools their very different musical skills. Some are developing considerable skills playing an instrument; others have no such experiences. Many are very knowledgeable about popular music. Some may have experience of Euro-classical music. They will have brought to school varying attitudes received at home and from the media with regard to music, its status in their education and the place of world musics within that. They may have come to expect that only pupils with instrumental skills will be able to benefit from any form of musical education and those pupils with instrumental skills may find that they have greater musical knowledge than their class teachers. These factors may all have a negative effect upon the teachers' willingness to teach music.

The emphasis in the curriculum may vary according to the ethos of the school. The concerns of governors and teachers in church schools, inner-city schools, rural schools or schools where children may have, between them, more than fifty mother tongues, have been shown to be different. (Gaine 1987, p. 126). Post-ERA 1988, has this situation developed greater homo-geneity in relation to music as a NC, foundation subject?

Within the fertile ground of primary education, where the enquiring mind of the child, regardless of its cultural background is still excited by new experiences, pupils can best be introduced to a wide range of musics. It is true to say that no child comes to the study of music value-free, but the primary-school teacher has a unique opportunity to help the child, in an exploratory, developmental way, towards an understanding of those values and how they may be developed.

The argument of this chapter is that it is perfectly possible for all these pupils to have equality of opportunity in music education by implementing the principles outlined in the National Curriculum for music.

Challenges

Implementing the National Curriculum for music in a manner which will create a fully integrated curriculum rather than a monocultural scheme with 'added bits', and will also ensure equal access for all pupils regardless of their cultural background, poses several challenges. This next section will examine two areas: the natures of music education and of world musics.

The following six challenges are linked to in the next section of this chapter.

1. Music teaching can be effective only when the nature of music itself is understood and the development of students respected. (Swanwick, 1988, p. 141)

One of the many advantages possessed by the generalist primary teacher who has a love of music but lacks knowledge, is a response to the sounds and colours of music which has been uncluttered by theoretical knowledge. Dry sterile analysis which ignores the very nature of the music can be the death of musical aesthetic education. However

> when analysis is conceived as an active, involved exploration of the living qualities of music, and when analysis is in constant and immediate touch with musical experience itself, it is the essential means for making musical enjoyment more obtainable. (Swanwick, 1981, p. 65)

Just as teachers refer to music as something which 'they like', so do their pupils. They talk of the music which they choose to listen to, as something which they enjoy, which makes them 'feel something'. Music communicates 'feelings' to which the listener responds, uncluttered by conventional language or symbols. It is the organization of these sounds that we refer to as music, sounds to which the pupil responds. But to be worth responding to it must 'say something' to the listener. This is where the 'non-specialist' can communicate at the most important level with the pupil. There is ample documentary evidence to show that much school music has failed to fulfil this need in the past (Paynter, 1982).

> 2. As salt adds flavour to a stew, losing its character as grains of salt but adding a particular flavour to the stew, the symbol must be dissolved in the musical sounds, losing its character as a symbol but adding its symbol-flavour to the whole piece. (Reimer, 1970, p. 32)

If music is 'organized sound', then it is possible to separate out and thus recognize the various elements, of which it consists. It is the relationship between these elements that create music's particular expressive qualities. When hearing Chopin's 'Funeral March' the listener may respond by saying the music feels heavy, drab, morbid, unrelenting. If however one of the elements were to be changed (e.g., changing the pace to fast instead of slow) the whole character of the music changes, because the relationship between the elements has been changed. We may teach the pupils to recognize the elements, but it is the mixture of these elements, the flavour, that creates the expressive qualities to which they respond, not the individual elements themselves. To illustrate this, two diagrams are included. Figure 11.1 shows an adaptation of Bruner's spiral of learning (London Borough of Harrow, 1988, pp. 16 and 17). It demonstrates how pupils' awareness of music increases as the elements are visited and revisited and their response is heightened by this developing awareness. Figure 11.2 shows how these elements interrelate, creating the sounds we recognize as music.

Figure 11.1: The Spiral Curriculum: An Elevation, Showing the Progression of Musical Development

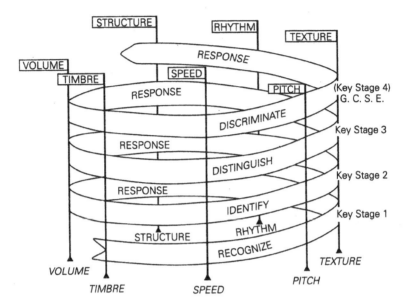

3. Artists have always been 'magpies', appropriating aspects of styles and traditions other than their own. Thus, the history of European artistic adoption of foreign influences is not at odds with an educational policy that advocates the study of a wide range of musical styles and traditions. (AEMS, 1989, p. 5)

First, it is necessary to question the belief that Euro-classical music is part of a separate culture, untouched by outside influences. During the early debate on music in the National Curriculum, Professor Scruton recommended, as the basis of a suitable music curriculum, the classical music tradition,

> not only the highest achievement of European culture, but also a universal language of the human spirit. (Scruton, 1991)

What is not always understood is that the 'European classical music tradition' has been continuously influenced by other cultures. Gregorian chant, the basis of so much 'western music' absorbed early African church music and adapted early Jewish synagogal patterns. The medieval troubadours, worked alongside gypsies from India; Haydn delighted in the music of Hungary and Croatia and the music of Mozart exhibits Turkish Janisary influences (Sadie, 1980). Debussy and countless other respected composers of the late nineteenth and twentieth century have openly acknowledged the debt they owe to other musical cultures (Griffith, 1978). Even if we were to exclude from the class-room, music by latter composers such as Boulez, Messiaen, Stockhausen and Steve Reich, by playing Debussy's *Prélude à L'après-midi d'un faune*, Rimsky-Korsakov's *Scheherazade* and music by the English composer Holst such as the 'Hymn of Jesus' and 'Neptune' from the 'Planet' Suite, we would still be play-ing music influenced by the peoples of Asia.

The inclusion of world music will not discourage a study of Euro-classical music. Indeed it will help pupils better to reflect upon and understand their own culture, whatever that might be, and ensure that we have a better educated society

4. when western musicians speak of 'primitive music' they are gen-erally discussing music which is interested in other matters than those with which our music is concerned. (Small, 1980, p. 49)

The various world musics are concerned with different aspects of organ-ized sound than is the Euro-classical tradition. Whilst this means that they may be 'different', they are certainly not inferior. Unfortunately, because they are 'different', they are often misunderstood. There has been little education about world musics in music colleges and even less in teacher-training estab-lishments. The inclination to dismiss other musical cultures as 'primitive' may come from lack of familiarity and understanding. The intrinsic qualities of various world musics therefore need to be valued. As the eminent American musicologist Bennett Reimer so clearly put it:

Trying to respond musically to sounds in an unknown style is like watching a game being played in which none of the rules or regula-tions or purposes are known to the person watching . . . (Reimer, 1970, p. 101)

Each musical culture uses musical features in its own particular way. The affective qualities experienced by the participator have come from the same selection of musical elements as other musical cultures, but blended in its own way.

This demonstrates that music is not an international language, enabling the speaker in one language to communicate easily in another. If it is under-stood that the ingredients are the same, and that it is merely the way they are put together that creates the differences, the rules can soon be understood and the music appreciated.

5. No child should be expected to cast off the language and culture of the home as he crosses the school threshold . . . (DES, 1975, para. 20.5)

This is as true for music education as it is for any other subject in the National Curriculum. If pupils are to learn satisfactorily, the differing musical experiences which they bring to the classroom should be acknowledged. If a music curriculum is devised which ignores their own understanding of how the ingredients of music are organized, however that might be, they will be denied equal access to educational opportunities as outlined in the document.

6. We become more sensitive to the central concepts of pitch and rhythm variation, of timbre and texture change, by seeing them work over a range of styles and periods. (Swanwick, 1981, p. 118)

The premise of this chapter is to maintain that the inclusion of world musics in the curriculum is necessary to enable all children equal access to that curriculum. Of equal importance is to demonstrate that such a curriculum would be not only academically sound, but that by broadening the content to include music from as wide a range of cultures as is practicable, educational progression and development will be positively enhanced. The richness of the cultural diversity of our society has given opportunities for developing the range, width and depth of our teaching. Cultural diversity presents new opportunities and challenges; it should not be seen as bringing to the teaching profession yet another problem.

The questions must arise: which styles, which periods? Paul Zec uses a music education example when discussing the necessity to select curricular material according to criteria which are educational and rational (Zec, 1981, p. 40). Having compared a cross rhythm in a symphony by Beethoven to a similar cross rhythm in African music, he suggests that multicultural music educators:

find examples for appreciation and performance from as broad a range of cultural experience as possible — which reflect as well as possible the interplay between what is common to all music and how each music idiom handles the commonly fundamental structures. (Zec, 1981, p. 40)

This can be done by starting with just those elements in music which the pupil finds most appealing in the culture he or she is most used to. This culture could be music of the local community or it might often be the latest genre of popular music. The teacher may then proceed to examine these elements in a diversity of cultures.

This approach not only dismisses the idea that cultural diversity is a problem, it also demonstrates that the multicultural approach to curriculum development can actually strengthen pupils' understanding of these commonly held fundamental musical structures and elements.

Responses

In the previous section, beliefs and attitudes which make change in curriculum practice difficult to achieve have been described. This section will look at

Figure 11.2: *Concepts Essential to the Understanding of Music*

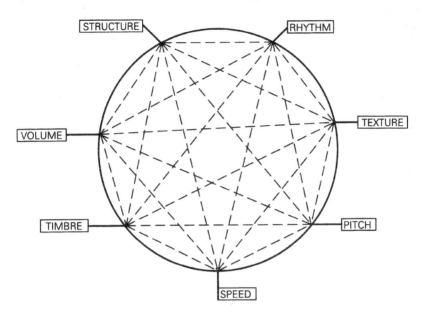

Note: The nature and significance of the relationships between these concepts vary between cultures. Sensitivity to such differences is necessary if the listener is to understand and appreciate the resultant musical languages.

ways in which those beliefs and attitudes may be changed and teachers in primary schools may develop strategies to include world music as an integral part of the curriculum, to the benefit of all children. (The numbers relate to the same numbers in the previous section.) This is followed by a list of resources which will enable teachers to implement these strategies. Finally, there is an adaptation of a planning model from the National Curriculum Non-Statutory Guidelines which explores Chinese music and develops understanding of commonly fundamental structures.

1. Throughout the world, music serves a utilitarian purpose. There are songs of praise, work songs, songs to celebrate special festivals, music to help children to sleep, music to wake them up. The list is virtually infinite. Music which has a purpose also creates a specific response, (lullabies have different expressive qualities than does military music). Discussion of the use of this music in different cultures and ways in which the necessary expressive qualities have been achieved, will deepen pupils' understanding.

2. Although all musics are concerned with the elements of melody, duration, texture, timbre etc. the ways each culture treats these elements are different. To understand and value the resultant musical languages, the pupils

need to develop sensitivity to these differences. Singing various songs and composing accompaniments to go with them will not only familiarize pupils with the way that an individual culture highlights a certain element, but will help the pupil to understand its function more readily when meeting it in another music. If, for example, the pupil invents a drone to accompany an Indian song, they will have a deeper appreciation of a Scottish bagpipe drone or a 'pedal point' playing in a Bach Fugue.

3. No culture stands still and no musical tradition can be unchanging. A few, like some European folk music have been passed on aurally, that is from singer to singer, not being written down. Others, like Indian and Chinese vocal music have notation systems and are sometimes written down and sometimes not. As has been shown, the music of Europe has been greatly influenced by other cultures. A valuable exercise would be a comparable study tracing the history of other world musics and what has influenced the changes and why. Suitable subjects might include:

- the music of the Maori people;
- the music of the people of China;
- music of the different peoples of South Africa;
- musical traditions of Brazil;
- Afro-caribbean musics; and
- Indian musical traditions.

4. To change negative attitudes to the inclusion of world musics in the curriculum, two problems need to be faced: firstly lack of familiarity with the sounds and, secondly, the development of knowledge and understanding about the cultures.

The best way that teachers can familiarize themselves with the music of other cultures is, quite simply, to listen to it. We become accustomed to various musics when we are young, by hearing and absorbing a selection of sounds we hear around us. However, what that music was, depended upon the choices of others and it is to that organization of sound which we heard when very small, that we respond. Now the teacher can make his or her own choice of music to listen to, and even if this listening is only in the background, the teacher will soon find that they have become conversant with what was previously incomprehensible.

When planning to introduce children to musics to which they are unfamiliar similar strategies may be adopted. Many primary schools play music during assembly time. Response to music introduced in this manner could first be discussed, (is it bright, dull, happy, sad, angry, gentle) by teachers with little or no technical knowledge of the music. As confidence is gained, reference to the elements of the music (Is the music high or low, fast or slow, quiet or loud?) will concentrate the pupils' thinking. Notes on the back of record sleeves often tell which instruments are playing and provide other interesting relevant details.

5. It is unwise to make assumptions as to what is the musical culture and experiences of pupils in school. Like teachers, pupils' musical exposure may range from devotional music to TV soap operas, reggae to ragamuffin, hassapiko to bangra. To respond constructively, the pupil must have had some experience upon which that response can be founded. It is therefore necessary to start from 'where the child is' wherever that might be.

It is often underestimated what a wonderful resource the pupils themselves can be. They, and the communities from which they stem, have many skills. It is essential that the teacher structures the pupils' Programmes of Study in such a way as to acknowledge these experiences and skills. The curriculum need not be seen as something imposed from on high. Teachers can gain much by combining their pedagogic skills with the pupils' knowledge and that of their families.

6. Once the pupils have grasped an understanding of musical elements as suggested above, their appreciation of how they work will be strengthened if they observe them working in context, over several cultures. Teachers could devise a module which looked at a specific element e.g., structure. All music consists of repetition and contrast, tension and resolution, and the ability to recognize these characteristics in differing musical cultures helps the music seem less strange and makes it more accessible. This also strengthens the pupils' understanding of the music of their own culture. The musics chosen should start with the music most accessible to the pupils concerned, should include music from the different cultures which make up Britain today (AT2: our diverse musical heritage) and music of the peoples of Africa, Asia, the Americas, Australasia, and Europe (AT2: a variety of other musical traditions). It was the conclusion of the AEMS working party that such a model would

> help to avoid two main dangers — exoticism and tokenism— by virtue of the fact that attention is focussed on the similarities, as well as the distinctive differences, in the 'handling' of musical concepts cross-culturally. (AEMS, 1989, p. 6)

A curriculum model which starts by encouraging response to the sounds of the music itself, develops first an understanding of how those sounds are organized and then a knowledge of the function of, and place in, the society of that music, can challenge existing stereotypes and cultivate a proper regard for the musics of those societies.

The National Curriculum Council has published non-statutory guidelines which include advice on planning. The following plan is based upon 'Model A' to be found on D5 of the Non-Statutory Guidance. It takes as its unit title 'Music of the People of China' and follows the model on D7 as closely as possible. The notes in the plan are deliberately brief but, using the recommended books and the ideas described above, the generalist teachers

Table 11.2: NCC Model A: The Music of the Peoples of China — An Example

Model A

Unit no. 7	Title of unit:	Main focus of the unit:	PoS
	The music	AT1 Composing melodies - to the pentatonic scale - to words	(x1) (x11)
Class/year: 6			
Duration: 4 wks	of the	AT2 Identifying some features of Chinese music	(1) (v)
	peoples of		
Term: Summer	China	General requirements: group work	

Playing and singing (by ear, from signs and notations)	• learn songs and sing them from memory Fukien Boat Song, Lantern Song .. • Perform 'Song of Happiness' from Chinese notation	AT1 (1) (11)
Controlling sounds made by the voice and a range of musical instruments	• sing words clearly and sing longer phrases in one breath • Play tuned percussion notes together and in the correct place in the song	(111) (1v)
Performing with others	• play suggested percussion parts to accompany songs • rehearse group pieces and perform to class	(v) (v11)
Composing, arranging and improvising	• compose a melody on the pentatonic scale CDEGA using step wise mvt. & intervals, as discovered in songs • Using these notes, compose a melody to fit the words of an unknown song.	(x11) (x1)
Refining, recording and communicating musical ideas	• record melodies using note names e.g CDEGA with c̄ or c̣ for pitch, or use Chinese notation. • improve melodies through group discussion	(x111)
Listening and identifying elements and structures	• knowledge of pentatonic scale & sound of intervals • knowledge of how to construct a melody - repetition • Listen to other folk songs, identifying large & small intervals	AT2 (1)
The history of music: its composers and traditions	• listen to the music of the peoples of Japan, Korea, Vietnam. • listen to songs from Hong Kong film music	(111)
Appraising music: appreciation of live and recorded music	• Respond to the instrumental qualities & textures of 'The River Flowing'. • Listen to the tune of the folk song which provided the words for the pupils compositions, discuss.	(v)

Outcomes—tasks:	End of key stage statements:	Criteria for success:	Resources:
Learning folk songs. Writing melodies. Discussing music from Asia.	1 d 2 b	Pupils should be able to write a simple melody using intervals Pupils should be able to describe some features of folk music	'Dragon Boat' by Gaik See Chew 'Music Around the World' book and tape.

should be able to adapt this unit to suit their class and then make further adaptations to include other music of their choice.

Resources

Until recently there was a great shortage of useful material for the teaching of world music in schools. Now, most good music-education suppliers have a relevant section in their catalogues. Local record shops can often supply recordings valued by pupils, and popular in many different communities.

The music working party of the Arts Education for a Multicultural Society (AEMS) project, chaired by Professor Blacking and David Peacock, produced a report on music education *Breaking the Sound Barrier.* This document reviews aspects of music and multicultural education including rationale, strategies for curriculum development, teacher training, sources and resources, assessment and recommendations. It also has a valuable list of classroom resources and books and is available from:

AEMS, 105 Piccadilly, London W1V OAU.

In addition to the material listed in the AEMS publication *Breaking the Sound Barrier* teachers may consider developing strategies for the teaching of world music using different sets of resources:

- Song collections.
  A review of the major catalogues will reveal books of folk songs from many parts of the world.
- Books which include information about world music:
  Music Around the World (Peter Dunbar-Hall and Glenda Hodge, Science Press) contains many facts about the origins of the musics and how they are constructed. It is accompanied by a cassette featuring examples of the music discussed.
  The New Grove Dictionary of Music and Musicians contains comprehensive details of different world music traditions.
- Resource material which not only contains information about different musics but also provides suggestions as to how they may be used in the classroom:
  Dragon Boat (Gaik See Chew, Chester Music) not only includes Chinese folk songs suitable for schools and information about Chinese music, it also provides information about the people who would sing these songs.
  Silver Burdett and Ginn Music (Simon and Schuster International), a music course in four parts covering the ages 4–14 years, is based upon sound multicultural and cross-curricular principles, providing a comprehensive range of materials for use in performing, composing and listening.

Books such as Jean Gilbert's *Festivals*, June Tillman's *Oxford Assembly Book* (both OUP) and *Light the Candles* (June Tillman, CUP) have material which can be a valuable resource for teachers, providing material suitable for performing, composing, listening and appraising, supported by useful background information.

Music File (Mary Glasgow Publications Ltd) publishes resource material which is added to each term. This caters mainly for older children but it has had several sections which have concentrated on the use of various world musics which primary teachers would find of interest to themselves and which they could then adapt to use with younger children.

- Story books which are accompanied by a tape.

The Singing Sack (A and C Black) has song stories from around the world. Each contains a simple song (recorded on tape for teachers who lack confidence to teach the song and sung by musicians from the relevant culture).

Look Lively, Rest Easy (A and C Black) offers a similar selection to the above, but might be suitable for younger children.

- Books for the instrumental performer.

Trentham Books are developing a series of books which embrace various world musics. Their first publication in this series was *Play Pan: Learn Music the Steel Band Way* (Terry Noel and Jill Scarfe) which outlines the development of music in Trinidad in addition to developing skills in listening, composing and performing. They have recently published *Play Tabla* ('Frances Shepherd and Sharda Sahai), an approach to playing tabla based on tried and tested methods used in schools.

Further resources may be borrowed from:

The Commonwealth Institute Resource centre, Kensington High Street, London W8 6NQ.

One resource which should not be overlooked, is that which may be provided by the pupils themselves and their families. In addition to their personal skills as performers, many have contacts with other musicians in the community and possess or have access to a wide range of recorded material.

There has not been the opportunity, in this chapter, to explore cross-curricular principles, the instrumental services, extended curricular activities and links with the music profession, business and industry. These important areas should be sensitively covered by schools when ensuring that curriculum practices are in line with the requirements of the National Curriculum for Music (Glower and Ward, 1992).

References

ARTS EDUCATION FOR A MULTICULTURAL SOCIETY (1989) *Breaking the Sound Barrier*, London, AEMS.

DEPARTMENT OF EDUCATION AND SCIENCE (1975) *A Language for Life* (The Bullock Report), London, HMSO.

DEPARTMENT OF EDUCATION AND SCIENCE (1985) *General Certificate of Secondary Education. The National Criteria, Music*, London, HMSO.

DEPARTMENT OF EDUCATION AND SCIENCE (1991a) *National Curriculum Music Working Group Interim Report*, London, HMSO.

DEPARTMENT OF EDUCATION AND SCIENCE (1991b) *Aspects of Primary Education, The Teaching and Learning of Music*, London, HMSO.

DEPARTMENT OF EDUCATION AND SCIENCE (1992a) *Music in the National Curriculum: Draft Statutory Order*, London, HMSO.

DEPARTMENT OF EDUCATION AND SCIENCE (1992b) *Music in the National Curriculum*, London, HMSO.

GAINE, C. (1987) *No Problem Here: A Practical Approach to Education and 'Race' in White Schools*, London, Hutchinson.

GLOVER, J. and WARD, S. (1992) *Children, Teachers and Learning: Teaching Music in the Primary School*, London, Cassell.

GRIFFITH, P. (1978) *A Concise History of Modern Music*, London, Thames and Hudson.

GULBENKIAN REPORT (1982) *The Arts in Schools: Principles, Practice and Provision*, London, Calouste Gulbenkian Foundation.

GULBENKIAN REPORT (1989) *The Arts in the Primary School: Reforming Teacher Education*, London, Calouste Gulbenkian Foundation.

HOULTON, D. (1986) *Cultural Diversity in the Primary School*, London, Batsford.

HARROW, LEA. (1988) *'Music in Harrow Schools and Colleges'*, Harrow, Harrow Education Department.

MARLAND, M. (1992) 'New world for the arts?' *Education Guardian*, 21 January.

MILLS, J. (1989) 'The generalist Primary Teacher: a Problem of Confidence' *British Journal of Music Education*, 6, 2, July.

MILLS, J. (1993) *Music in the Primary School*, Cambridge, Cambridge University Press.

MORRISON, R. (1991) 'A generation drummed out', *The Times*, London, 13 February.

NATIONAL CURRICULUM COUNCIL (1992a) *National Curriculum Council Consultation Report: Music*, York, NCC.

NATIONAL CURRICULUM COUNCIL (1992b) *Music: Non-statutory Guidance*, York, NCC.

O'HEAR, A. (1991) 'Out of sync with Bach, the emphasis on pop, rock and heavy metal in the National Curriculum threatens our musical tradition', in *Times Educational Supplement*, London, 22 February.

PAYNTER, J. (1982) *Music in the Secondary School Curriculum*, Cambridge, Cambridge University Press.

REIMER, B. (1970) *A Philosophy of Music Education*, New Jersey, Prentice-Hall.

SADIE, S. (Ed) (1980) *The New Grove Dictionary of Music and Musicians*, London, Macmillan.

SCRUTON, R. (1991) 'Rock around the classroom, contempt for traditional values now extends to the teaching of music', in *Sunday Telegraph*, London, 10 February.

SMALL, C. (1980) *Music — Society — Education*, London, John Calder.

SWANWICK, K. (1988) *Music, Mind and Education*, London, Routledge.

SWANWICK, K. (1981) *A Basis for Music Education*, Windsor, NFER-Nelson.

TAYLOR, D. (1979) *Music Now*, London, Open University Press.

ZEC, P. (1981) 'Multicultural Education: What Kind of Relativism is Possible?', in JAMES, A. and JEFFCOATE, R. (Ed) *The School in the Multicultural Society*, London, Harper and Row.

Chapter 12

Foundation Subject: Art

Rita Ray and Judith Piotrowski

Context

Multicultural education is not defined by a uniform set of concepts but is a kind of kaleidoscope. It changes its aspect depending upon which point of view is being considered. Similarly, there are many notions and definitions of multicultural art. It may be seen, for example, as the process of drawing on the arts of many cultures or as the provision of an art curriculum which takes into account the ethnic diversity of a school population. The latter view suggests that schools which do not have ethnic diversity need not pay much attention to multicultural art. There is also confusion between the more general concept of multiculturalism seen as a component of the school's equal-opportunities policy and the provision of an arts curriculum which includes content from other cultures. The primary arts curriculum may derive part of its rationale and aims from the school's policy statement concerning equal opportunities and multicultural education.

The concern of this paper is to describe the current position of primary art education and to suggest ways of translating abstract policy aims into practical courses of action consonant with the requirements of the ERA 1988. Multicultural art education will be considered in two broad categories: the multicultural dimension which underpins art policy making in primary schools; and the recognition and appreciation of cultural diversity and its expression in primary school arts practice.

The Multicultural Dimension

Multicultural art should be part of a school's environment and ethos rather than being 'done' as an isolated project, though there may be times when there is a special focus on aspects of art from other cultures. As Eisner and Ecker point out:

Table 12.1: Art Attainment Targets

AT1: Investigating and making:
- Recording what has been seen, imagined or remembered: visual perception.
- Gathering and using resources and materials.
- Using different materials and techniques in practical work.
- Reviewing and modifying work.

AT2: Knowledge and understanding:
- Knowledge of different kinds of art and the development of visual literacy.
- Knowledge of different periods, cultures and traditions in art and the work of influential artists.
- Applying knowledge of the work of other artists to their own work.

There is no art in which there is only a single tradition. (Eisner and Ecker, 1966)

The arts curriculum should look beyond the valuing of art from other cultures only insofar as it has influenced the western tradition e.g., Cubism and African masks. It is important that art be seen in its sociocultural setting and not allowed to become disembedded from its multicultural contexts.

At primary level, especially at Key Stage 1, we are concerned with teaching 'through the arts', that is, using the arts as part of a thematic approach, rather than teaching art solely as a subject 'to the arts'.

The Gulbenkian report, *The Arts in Schools*, 1982, states: 'The arts of other cultures should inform arts teaching at each level of the curriculum'. (p. 109) It elaborates this to say that multicultural arts education should be pursued because it

a   helps pupils understand cultural diversity by bringing them into contact with the attitudes, values and institutions of other cultures as well as exploring their own;
b   emphasises cultural relativity by helping them to recognise and compare their own cultural assumptions and values with the others;
c   alerts them to the evolutionary nature of culture and the potential for change; and
d   encourages a cultural perspective by relating contemporary values to the historical facts which moulded them. (Gulbenkian Foundation, 1982, p. 40)

There is very little reference to these views in the National Curriculum documents. Both the statutory and non-statutory components have to be scanned carefully to find mention of multiculturalism. The art working group states:

In the short time available to us . . . we were not able to consider fully all the issues . . . we therefore focused our attention on recommendations for Attainment Targets and Programmes of Study and deferred consideration of such issues as . . . equal opportunity, gender and ethnic diversity (DES, 1991, para. 1.7)

Although one of the underlying assumptions of National Curriculum is that it is a curriculum for all, it would inspire confidence to know that the deliberations of the working party had a positive underpinning of multicultural awareness. It is unfortunate that equal opportunities and multicultural education seem to be an afterthought in the devising of art National Curriculum; indeed there is no explicit reference to these issues in the Non-Statutory Guidance. The group feels that the issue of multicultural education has been dealt with in two 'tag-on' paragraphs 10.10 and 10.11, in the final report. The statements contained in these paragraphs can only reflect a superficial token coverage of the subject.

We wish to emphasise the educational benefits and opportunities presented by a multicultural world. We believe that art education offers particular scope to enrich learning and celebrate the differences between Western and non-Western art forms and cultures. All pupils should be given some access to good art, craft and design from a number of cultures. Teaching should be aimed at bringing non-Western art into the mainstream. Pupils should be encouraged to appreciate and value in its own right art, craft and design from other cultures, as well as being introduced to the work of a range of artists, craftworkers and designers currently working in the United Kingdom.

Some aspects of art are widely practised and valued in one culture but not in another. For example, drawing from direct observation in order to achieve an accurate representation is commonly found in Western art, but has not been considered so important in some other cultures. Art may be produced to fulfil a variety of needs, influenced by social, economic, religious and personal factors which differ in emphasis according to the particular culture. Diverse views and influences exist within ethnic groups. A greater understanding of these views and of issues such as racial stereotyping can be achieved through the study of the work of artists, craftworkers and designers from other cultural traditions. (DES, 1991, p. 56)

Art in primary schools takes many forms and its priority usually depends on having an informed, interested and influential member of staff. HMI reports reveal a wide range of practices. Art is often given a supporting role as a means of illustrating topics and providing displays rather than reflecting challenging curriculum activities and embodying plans for progression and continuity.

Cultural Diversity and Primary-School Practice

Support for multicultural education is given by ERA (section 1 (20 (a)) which is further reinforced by the DES:

> More [that is, than the 'Foundation Subjects'] will, however, be needed to secure the kind of curriculum required by section 1 of the ERA. The whole curriculum for all pupils will certainly need to include at appropriate (and in some cases all) stages . . . coverage across the curriculum of . . . multicultural issues. (DES, 1989, para. 3.8)

The final report of the arts working party sets out what is common in cases of good practice (2.7). There is no mention of multicultural art but there is emphasis on the development of pupils' confidence and skill and the valuing of individuals' responses. To this end it is vital to create an environment which promotes attainment in art for all pupils. At the same time there is a need to get away from themes rooted in restricted emotive ideas which emphasize art as therapy and stress emotional development and personal growth at the expense of cognitive and imaginative engagement with art.

A school-based action research project undertaken by Amrik Varkalis (1992) showed how attainment in art improved dramatically once the pupils' home language was used in the art lesson. It was as if 'permission' had been given to draw upon their home background. Pupils progressed from making poor drawings from the object, in western tradition, to detailed drawings of the same subject embellished and enlivened by a more 'surface pattern' approach. (This is, of course, a short, simplistic account of the project.) As Wittgenstein (in Barrett, 1966) remarked, 'What belongs to language is a whole culture.'

A culturally diverse curriculum is appropriate regardless of the ethnic make-up of the school. Where teachers wish to focus on cultures embraced within the school, skill and sensitivity will be reinforced by a considered and agreed school policy. Care must be taken to avoid emphasizing cultural differences in a way that polarizes groups.

In order to effect change in practice there must be shifts in arts and aesthetic theory. Muddled messages have filtered through to primary practice from the realms of specialism. Recent developments in action research in the classroom go a long way to empower primary practitioners and to facilitate the development of a rationale which reflects current primary practice. In this way theory and practice are reciprocally related. Art has been dogged by outmoded theories which persist in the field of education. Essentialist views, derived from the ideas of Plato, gave the impression that art attainment is the result of inborn ability rather than the acquisition of skills which can be taught and learned. This view masks our awareness of the diverse approaches to art which are implicit in various cultural traditions. For example, western art traditionally values originality whilst other cultures may value the continuation

Table 12.2: *Challenges: Art*

- Developing policies and curriculum planning which will enrich pupils' art experience by reflecting the historical and contemporary cultural diversity of British society.
- Enabling children to understand something of the relative significance of the use of imagery across cultures.
- Avoiding cultural stereotyping by increasing background knowledge about the artefacts of different cultures.
- Resisting presenting children with a series of separate study units of the art of various cultures.

and refinement of existing skills. On reflection, the complementarity of these two polarized positions is not difficult to appreciate.

Art has its own set of skills, knowledge and terms which can be taught and learned in a systematic way. In the past (and in some cases, in the present) art has not been seen as an area of potential development but as a fully formed inborn capacity. Teachers have seen children's art productions as sacrosanct, not to be viewed in the same way as, say, writing. Early attempts at writing are praised and valued as communication. Later, children are encouraged to make drafts and to develop a range of writing skills appropriate to the specialist area of English and to reflect and enhance other areas of the curriculum. Art, too, has several roles to play in the primary curriculum. Like English, it is a specialism *and* a cross-curricular theme.

Art may be seen in the same way as writing, i.e., as a subject which has recognizable stages and which can be made into a coherent structural teaching and learning programme. Such an approach would break down the non-interventionist view of children's art. Organizing the subject in this way would make it easier to build multicultural experiences into the planning of the arts curriculum. Added to this, the pursuit of excellence is frequently confused with elitism so that pupils have been denied access to a range of art in the interests of an ill-considered and often spurious concept of 'relevance'.

According to Heard (1990), teachers' beliefs and expectations are key factors for positive learning outcomes in multicultural learning situations. It is not envisaged that in-service training would bring about an immediate change in teachers' beliefs, rather they should learn to be aware of the effects of their beliefs. Does cultural diversity mean equal acceptance of the different belief systems and the associated artistic traditions that are part of our cultural heritage? It might help to refer to Wittgenstein's view of concept categories: that different belief systems and cultural traditions are like the fibres which make up one rope, the rope of all human culture.

Challenges

1. Developing policies and curriculum planning which will enrich pupils' art experience by reflecting the historical and contemporary cultural diversity of British society:

We are challenged to do justice to the cultural diversity of British society, to explore the art-forms and images presented by the many cultures represented in British society and to do so in a way that explores the values of both western (or European) art and non-western art. Children need to be able to appreciate the messages of the so-called 'mainstream' art which surrounds them in their daily lives but they should also 'recognise that no one culture has a monopoly of artistic achievement' (DES, 1991). It is important that the values and principles of western art, are explored. The danger exists that western values, images and contexts remain unexplored and unquestioned.

2. Enabling children to understand something of the relative significance of the use of imagery across cultures:

Children need to be able to discuss use of the language of art (line, tone, colour, form, pattern, texture, shape) and to identify the messages and images within art from a variety of cultures. This appreciation of images within their cultural context is stressed by different sources. 'The Arts 5–16' (NCC, 1990) refers us to the Gulbenkian Foundation report when it insists that children need to understand that there are different ways of seeing

> events that may be steeped in significance within one culture may have no significance within another (Gulbenkian Foundation, 1985, p. 37).

In a similar vein, the DES *Art for Ages 5–14* (1991) highlights the fact that different cultures make differentiated use of the variety of art forms and techniques.

> Some aspects of art are widely practised and valued in one culture but not in another. For example, drawing from direct observation . . . is commonly found in Western art, but has not been considered so important in some other cultures. (DES, 1991, p. 56)

Images in art-work, the techniques and skills of the different art forms are influenced greatly by their social, technological, religious and historical context, e.g., images of mother and child, of power, of harmony in nature.

3. Avoiding cultural stereotyping by increasing background knowledge about the artefacts of different cultures:

Whilst there are usually identifiable traditions and approaches in the art work of a variety of cultures, individual cultural groups are not homogeneous. This aspect needs to be explored to avoid cultural or racial stereotyping. Such diversity of views and influences within ethnic groups is acknowledged by DES in *Art for Ages 5–14* (1991, para. 10.11). It is suggested that a greater understanding of this issue can be achieved through the study of the work of artists, craft workers and designers from a variety of cultural traditions, e.g., the diversity of American, European, African or Asian art. The artistic traditions, related to the characteristic religions of cultural groups provides a promising avenue (see Chapter 4).

4. Resisting presenting children with a series of separate study units of the art of various cultures:

There are real dangers in adopting an approach to multicultural education in art which assumes the fundamental primacy and significance of western art and presents the art of non-western cultures as separate study units. It is unfortunate that throughout the National Curriculum art and the DES *Art for Ages 5–14* the term 'other cultures' is used. To value the contribution of all cultures to the experience of art, we need to avoid any implicit reference or suggestion by default that western art is more important or 'correct' and hence that the art of non-western cultures is not as valid. It is of course virtually impossible because of the curricular time restrictions to address the full range of art from other cultures. However, by including art forms from a variety of cultures, children can be helped more fully to appreciate the cultural diversity of their world and their place within it.

Responses

Any attempt to recommend courses of action must take into account constraints of time and finance and the degree of priority given to the resourcing of particular subjects. Some measures require a change of perspective or an increase in understanding. Teachers need access to a knowledge base, technical expertise and art resources and materials if they are to fulfil the requirements of National Curriculum art and, consequently, multicultural art. The primary teacher is already weighed down by the role of polymath and will be assisted by well-prepared and time-saving support. Differentiated provision will be needed to provide for the teacher's varying needs in the areas of both art *and* multicultural education.

The following courses of action would go some way towards answering the identified challenges.

1. In-service training

Published packages containing reproductions of artworks from many cultures, background information, instructions about practical skills and guidance on linking projects to art Attainment Targets will be of considerable help to the general primary teacher and the art coordinator. The art coordinator should be able to relate in-service materials to school policy to create a plan

Table 12.3: Responses to Challenges 1, 2, 3, 4: Art

- In-service training.
- Focused thematic planning.
- Organization of resources.
- Identification of multicultural opportunities in the Programmes of Study.
- Mastery of language and key terms.
- 'Artists in schools' schemes.
- Valuing of children's home culture and language.

for multicultural art and art in a context of cultural diversity, reflecting the particular school and community as well as embracing the notion of Britain as a culturally diverse society.

2. Focused thematic planning

Teachers and coordinators will have the task of examining the representation of cultures in planning cross-curricular topics and themes. Awareness raising of non-European art is equally important for schools with little or no representation of ethnic minorities. The distinction must be made too between culture as a process and as a product of human existence. The development of societies is a dynamic process. Children need to learn about several aspects of a culture and art is one way of seeing views of culture reflected over a period of time.

3. Organization of resources

Resources for multicultural art form a part of National Curriculum resources. The emphasis on a range of skills encompasses the need for materials which will enable children to engage with modes of expression from and about other cultures, both as a focus of art and as a component of cross-curricular topics. LEA sources of books and reproductions — school-library service, artefact loan schemes — are subject to the changing situation brought about by LMS and other sources are not yet established. Suppliers of artefacts to educational establishments might find it useful to institute a loan scheme to replace the funded schemes. What follows are some such useful sources:

- Access to Information on Multicultural Educational Resources (AIMER) is a further valuable source of information (see Chapter 1, Table 1.1)
- Commonwealth Institute, Kensington High Street, London W8 6NQ.
- Design Council (Education Section), Design Centre, 28, Haymarket, London, SW1Y 4SU. (Tel: 071–839–8000).
- Jackson Contra-banned, Unit 2, Gatehouse Enterprise Centre, Albert Street, Lockwood, Huddersfield, HD1 3QD. (Tel: 0484–530855)
- National Association of Arts Centres, Room 110, The Arts Centre, Vane Terrace, Darlington, DL3 7AX.

- Ginn, Publishers, Bucks (1992) Approaches to Art: *Teachers' Resource Book. : Group Discussion Book.*
- Additional sources: Thames and Hudson, Publishers, London (1987) series including the following titles: *African Art* (Frank Willet) *The Art of Mesoamerica* (Mary Ellen Miller) *Chinese Art* (Mary Tregear) *Indian Art* (Ray Craven) *Islamic Art* (David Rice) *Japanese Art* (Joan Stanley Baker)

4. Identification of multicultural opportunities in the Programmes of Study

AT1 KS1 Example Opportunities:

- make drawings of people wearing traditional costumes at special events or festivals;
- make a painting or a model based on a memory of a family occasion;
- collect and compare cards given on special occasions and design and make one of their own; and
- make a collection of teacups and saucers and compare their shapes and decoration, describe the colour and feel of different fabrics they have collected (or similar functional utensils, pots, containers).

AT1 KS2 Example Opportunities:

- talk about familiar objects in use at school and in the home;
- talk about artefacts and buildings used for a variety of occasions and purposes;
- consider how themes such as 'Mother and child' are expressed in different kinds of art e.g., icons, sculptures of Henry Moore . . . and in African tribal art;
- compare the different ways that animals and plants are represented in different times and cultures;
- draw children playing; and
- compare the way they (the children) use colour in drawings and paintings of flowers with the work of other artists.

AT2 KS2 Example Opportunities:

- look at how faces are depicted for a variety of purposes e.g., portraits, stamps, gargoyles etc;
- compare the way in which the design of clothes has changed over the centuries or in different cultures e.g., sportswear, uniforms, working and ceremonial clothes;
- discuss the ways in which artists have depicted the English landscape;
- talk about how subjects are illustrated in Egyptian wall painting, on Greek vases, Assyrian relief panels and in the Bayeux tapestry;

- discuss how Breughel the Elder depicted the everyday life of Flemish people in the sixteenth century;
- compare how nature is represented in Impressionist paintings by Monet, Pissarro . . . with the work of Turner, Constable and Hiroshize;
- compare the way that different artists have carved or constructed figures; and
- note the different ways in which the flower motif is used in textiles from a variety of cultures and times.

5. Mastery of language and key terms

A further area of study concerns the mastery of language and terms associated with a range of cultural expressions and the fostering of awareness that a society's most cherished ideas can be manifested in objects. As well as study- ing artworks, children can be introduced to media — especially television and film — architecture and street furniture, fashion and cooking. These topics could be linked to the study of literature, drama, maths and science from other cultures. The importance of developing a vocabulary with which to discuss cultural expressions cannot be stressed too highly.

6. Artists in schools schemes

The experience of having practitioners demonstrating expertise and working alongside pupils can be rewarding and enriching. There are artists from many cultural backgrounds working in Britain. Such practising artists can enhance attainment in art by initiating children into the use of different materials and techniques and by providing a role model. Teachers observing the results of such projects frequently have their expectations of children's attainment raised. They also gain ideas and recognize the possibilities inherent in a wider range of materials and techniques.

7. Valuing the child's home culture and language

The work of researchers and teachers such as Amrik Varkalis (op. cit.) indic- ates that encompassing a child's home culture in a natural way can promote better art attainment by validating the contribution each child brings to school. This will be further reinforced by having artists from different cultures work- ing in school.

References

ASSISTANT MASTERS AND MISTRESSES ASSOCIATION (1989) *Multicultural and Anti- Racist Education Today*, London, AMMA.
BOOTH, T., SWANN, W., MASTERTON M. and POTTS, P. (1992) *Learning for all: Curricula for Diversity in Education*, London, OUP/Routledge.

COHEN, L. and COHEN, A. (1986) *Multicultural Education*, London, Harper and Row.

DEPARTMENT OF EDUCATION AND SCIENCE (1989) *National Curriculum: From Policy to Practice*, London, DES and WO.

DEPARTMENT OF EDUCATION AND SCIENCE (1991) *Art for Ages 5–14*, London, HMSO.

DEPARTMENT OF EDUCATION AND SCIENCE (1991) *Art in the National Curriculum*, London, HMSO.

EISNER, E.W. and ECKER, D.W. (1966) *Readings in Art*, New York, Blaisell Publishing Company.

GULBENKIAN FOUNDATION (1985) *The Gulbenkian Report: The Arts in Schools*, London, Calouste Gulbenkian Foundation.

HEARD, D. (1990) 'How do teachers identify multicultural and cross-cultural pedagogical phenomena in and out of art classrooms?', *Education Review*, 42, 3, 1990, pp. 303–18.

HEWINS, H. and ETIENNE, C. (1989) 'Art, history, critical studies and anti-racism: so what's new?', *Multicultural Teaching*, 7, 3, 1989, pp. 41–3.

MACAULAY, P. (1992) 'Inspired by Rickshaws', *Child Education*, February, pp. 42–3.

MARLAND, M. (1989) 'Arts, cultures and the curriculum', *Multicultural Teaching*, 8, 1, pp. 21–7.

NATIONAL CURRICULUM COUNCIL (1990) *The Arts 5–16 Series: Practice and Innovation*, London, Oliver and Boyd.

NATIONAL CURRICULUM COUNCIL (1990) *The Arts 5.16 Series: A Curriculum Framework*, Essex, Oliver and Boyd.

NATIONAL CURRICULUM COUNCIL *The Arts 5–16: A Workpack for Teachers*, Essex, Oliver and Boyd.

NATIONAL CURRICULUM COUNCIL (1991) *National Curriculum Non-Statutory Guidance*, York, NCC.

VARKALIS, A. (1992) 'Bilingual and bicultural approaches to Art and Design', *Journal of Art and Design Education*, 11, 2, pp. 167–73.

Chapter 13

Foundation Subject:
Physical Education

Anne Williams

Context

In attempting to address issues of cultural diversity and physical education in the context of one brief chapter there is a danger of oversimplifying complex issues. Simply defining the terms could be a chapter if not a book in itself. The interpretation of education for cultural diversity adopted here is an education appropriate to a democratic, culturally pluralist society. A distinction has not been made between multicultural and antiracist education here, for while recognizing that for many, the two are far from synonymous, it should also be recognized that there are many interpretations of each. While at the extremes, there are significant differences in perspective between those espousing a multicultural approach and those supporting antiracist strategies, there is also a great deal of common or overlapping middle ground, and that it is within that middle ground that the emphasis of this chapter is located.

The focus will be upon Asian and Afro-Caribbean groups, while noting that these are two of many ethnic-minority groups living in Britain and that neither group is of itself, homogeneous. It should also be remembered that there can be a fine line between respecting culture and making stereotypical assumptions. Just as the Asian population is made of many different Asian cultures it is also made up of people with widely differing views about the extent to which they wish to retain elements of their own culture and the extent to which they wish to embrace western culture. If imposing white middle-class western culture upon all pupils is unacceptable, so is imposing any other specific culture, to the exclusion of others, upon pupils, since this runs the risk of simply trapping the child into a different form of racist knowledge. Thus a fundamental tenet of educating for cultural diversity in physical education as in other subject areas is that it involves understanding of, and respect for, a range of cultures.

Issues about race are of course inextricably bound up with those which concern gender and class and discussion of one in isolation from the others creates an artificial separation, and one which cannot always be maintained when discussing physical education. As will be illustrated later, there are a number of physical education contexts when the dominant issue is one of gender rather than one of race, and, of course, there are other situations when race and gender constitute mutually reinforcing phenomena.

Physical Education in the National Curriculum

This section will look at physical education in the National Curriculum from the perspective of cultural diversity and at some of the constraints which operate in the context of physical education in all primary schools and which have a bearing upon multicultural issues as well as on other aspects of teaching and learning.

Physical education in the National Curriculum has the following aims according to the Non-Statutory Guidance provided by the National Curriculum Council (NCC, 1992). Physical education contributes to the overall education of young people by helping them to lead full and valuable lives through engaging in purposeful physical activity. It can:

- develop physical competence and help to promote physical development;
- teach pupils through experience, to know about and value the benefits of participation in physical activity while at school and throughout life; and
- develop an appreciation of skilful and creative performance across the areas of activity.

Physical education can also contribute to:

- the development of problem-solving skills (e.g., by giving pupils the opportunities to make up and refine their own games);
- the establishment of self-esteem through the development of physical confidence (e.g., swimming at least twenty-five metres unaided);
- the development of inter-personal skills (e.g., helping pupils to be aware of their roles as members of teams and groups and taking account of others' ideas).

'Physical activity is combined with the thinking involved in making decisions and selecting, refining, judging and adapting movements. Through these activities, pupils should be encouraged to develop the personal qualities of commitment, fairness and enthusiasm.' (NCC, 1992).

These aims are to be achieved through the medium of six activity areas: games, gymnastic activities, dance, swimming, athletic activities and outdoor and adventurous activities. For the primary-school teacher, in addition to the requirement to teach every child to swim, the recommended emphasis is on games, gymnastic activities and dance, with relatively little time allocation to the remaining two activity areas, although all six are requirements at Key Stages 1 and 2. The Non-Statutory Guidance makes reference to the need for breadth and balance at all Key Stages, and to the need for differentiation to ensure relevance, success and challenge for all pupils.

The proposals for National Curriculum physical education based upon the recommendations of the physical education working group include some reference to cultural diversity (DES, 1991). It is noted that tensions may arise both between diverse cultural groups and between different generations and that children frequently have to cope with these tensions. It is recommended that schools should embrace the opportunities offered by diversity. 'These enable children to learn both to accommodate variety and difference from themselves, and to value the extension of their own experience which can be developed.' Preconceptions based upon stereotypes are highlighted. Reference is made to the inappropriateness of notions of 'national games or dance' given that we live in a multicultural society. The opportunities presented by learning a range of dance and games for the recognition of the richness and diversity of cultures are noted. The need for sensitivity to the ways in which culture and religion affect attitudes to aspects of physical education is also highlighted by paragraphs about issues such as physical contact, teaching groups, particularly those which are mixed-sex, and appropriate clothing. (Shaikh and Kelly, 1989; Carroll and Hollinshed, 1993).

The non-statutory guidance offered by the National Curriculum Council also makes reference to multicultural issues under a section which considers equal opportunities. The use of pupils' backgrounds and experiences to enrich the physical education curriculum and to extend the range of activities undertaken is recommended. Consideration of whether chosen activities might inhibit full participation because of, for example, physical contact is also recommended. Issues of respect for cultural and religious conventions and the need for awareness of religious observances such as fasting, which may limit participation in energetic physical activity, are also stressed.

On the face of it, the physical education curriculum appears to have the potential to cater for cultural diversity and to have formalized support for such an approach via the DES and the NCC. A closer examination of the relevant documentation however raises a number of questions. The first point to make is that the Non-Statutory Guidance which relates to equal-opportunity considerations has not been sent automatically to primary schools. This is apparently to assist in reducing the amount of documentation being sent to teachers in Key Stages 1 and 2. It is difficult to see how the omission of six pieces of paper will make a significant contribution to reducing the amount of paperwork with which teachers are currently being confronted. More seriously, and much more significantly, is the message given about priorities. Non-statutory guidance with respect to cross-curricular matters has simply not been made available to the primary-school teacher unless the headteacher specifically requests it. This does not simply omit issues which relate directly to cultural diversity. Health-related exercise guidance is also missing because, as a cross-curricular theme, it appears in the same section. In the context of cultural diversity where for some cultural groups there is little tradition of physically active play, the absence of recommendations about a health-related exercise which could be an important vehicle for negotiation with members of the community about the value of physical education, is particularly unfortunate.

To find further evidence of the importance, or lack of it, accorded to issues of cultural diversity, it is instructive to read the National Curriculum Council consultation report (NCC, 1991). The Secretary of State's proposals (DES, 1991) had recommended that for Key Stage 3, games plus either gymnastics or dance should be compulsory in each year of the Key Stage. This would have ensured at least a measure of balance within the curriculum. The National Curriculum Council recommends the removal of this recommendation and its replacement by a requirement that games should be the only compulsory activity. This is significant for a number of reasons, albeit that it refers to an age group which is outside the scope of this chapter. First, it ignores the potential of dance to utilize cultural diversity as a resource. It also goes against the majority view expressed in the consultation phase. Most telling is the justification for the games recommendation which has been retained in the Statutory Order.

> Council's recommendation that games should be a compulsory area of activity in each year of Key Stage 3 has the advantage of perpetuating the best of English traditions and cultural heritage. (NCC, 1991)

It should be added that it is the best of English male tradition which is being perpetuated. Klein's comment that the National Curriculum is 'monocultural, . . . narrow, elitist and nationalistic' (Klein, 1988) seems to apply as much to physical education as to other core and foundation subjects.

This is not to say that the committed teacher is not able to pursue anti or non-racist policies while teaching to the requirements of the National Curriculum, especially in the case of physical education at Key Stages 1 and 2. Nevertheless, the disappointment expressed by the CRE that National Curriculum consultation documents make no mention of the need for a curriculum which reflects the multicultural nature of British society has proved to be well-founded.

The Pupils

There is no shortage of evidence about the difficulties encountered within education by both Afro-Caribbean and Asian pupils. In order to understand how issues of race may impact upon the experience of individual children, it is important to recognize that school physical education is allied with, and relates to, sport and recreational activity in ways which are rarely found in other subject areas. Images of adult involvement in sport and physical activity are therefore potentially influential and will affect pupils' attitudes to physical education. There are many role models for Afro-Caribbean youngsters in the form of high-level participants, although fewer as coaches or administrators as acknowledged by the West Midlands Sports Council (West Midlands Council for Sport and Recreation, 1991). There are fewer Asian role models in fewer sports, and very few female role models, although this is beginning to change. Certainly at the level of recreational participation, the targetting of Asian women by those seeking to raise levels of participation has had some effect. In the long term, it may well be that the pupil's actual experience of physical activity at school will be a major factor determining whether or not an individual is predisposed to continue with physical activity either in a sporting or a recreational capacity once he or she leaves school. The pupils' experience of physical education in the primary school is a first and important step in this process. Indeed it may be argued that, particularly for girls, the establishment of positive attitudes to physical activity at this age is essential if interest and achievement are to continue through the secondary school.

The physical-education experiences of pupils from ethnic-minority backgrounds do not necessarily parallel their experiences elsewhere in the education system. Much has been written about the underachievement of Afro-Caribbean youngsters in British schools. However, far from being a part of this, physical education and sport have been an avenue for success for many such youngsters to the extent that physical education of sport has been seen as partly to blame for lack of academic success. There have been a number of examples of black sportsmen and women who feel that they have been pushed into sport on the assumption that they are incapable of achieving academically. If involvement in sport leads to long hours of training and frequent competition, it actually limits academic achievement by limiting the time available for other work. Cashmore (1982) offers a number of illustrations of this. Duncan cites evidence gathered for both the Rampton and Swann enquiries which showed that, 'the tendency is to stereotype black youngsters as being good at sports and music and nothing else and so shift them from other classes to do more music or sports. No wonder they are good at these . . . No wonder they tend to do badly in other areas' (Duncan, 1988).

For pupils from Asia, the situation is rather different. Physical education has been identified as a source of conflict between south-east Asian families and schools, mainly where families are Muslims but also at times from Sikh families. Here issues of gender can become inextricably intertwined with issues of race. Carrington and Williams (1988) reporting on a project which investigated secondary-school pupils, conclude that gender differences are heightened by ethnicity. Whereas Asian males appeared to be as involved in physical activity outside school as their white peers, and appeared to be as positive in their attitudes towards such activity, female participation among young Asians was minimal. This is of course not different from the situation in other cultures, but it is an illustration of the existence of a larger participation gap than that found elsewhere.

For some Asian parents, play has little educational significance and children therefore have few toys and spend little time on 'play' activities. Parents may also not have the money to purchase toys. Lack of play activity may result in limitations in motor coordination and physical skill in comparison with children whose opportunities for play have been rich. The child may thus be disadvantaged in physical education through limited previous physical-activity experiences. This disadvantage is likely to continue if the child is denied the opportunities of extra-curricular activity or informal play enjoyed by other children. This is not simply a multicultural issue. Girls are frequently disadvantaged compared with boys in the same way. What is important is that the teacher recognizes that a child's limitations may not be physical but may be due simply to lack of opportunity.

Challenges

A major challenge to many primary-school teachers is simply to offer an effective and relevant physical-education curriculum. There remain many teachers who lack confidence in their ability to teach the subject and who will, given the opportunity, avoid it. The education service as a whole therefore faces the challenge of supporting developments in physical education within the context of schools where confidence and expertise among the teachers may be low. In the context of cultural diversity, the main challenges are to provide a relevant curriculum for all pupils in a setting which provides opportunities for all pupils to succeed, and which promotes values such as respect for all and equality of opportunity. This demands an examination of curriculum content, of teaching approaches and of school procedures. For the purposes of this chapter, four strands will be identified.

The first is make multicultural education an issue for every school, rather than solely for those whose intake is racially mixed. It is still all too easy to find examples of schools in all-white communities which see multiculturalism as irrelevant. It is equally easy to offer over-simplistic suggestions. The educational principle of starting with the child and his or her community and of selecting experiences on the basis of their relevance to that child does not coexist easily with a philosophy of designing curricula which move away from the community value consensus. Attempted with insufficient forethought and planning, such strategies run the risk of reinforcing existing stereotypes rather than challenging them.

Second, it is important to recognize that many challenges facing the primary-school teacher are not simply matters of multiculturalism but are also matters of gender. The fact that team games are essentially masculine activities, certainly if viewed from the perspective of adolescent or adult levels of interest or participation, means that girls can be doubly disadvantaged. Grudgeon and Woods (1990) recount the way in which football served to integrate the boys in the school: 'In the playground, football predominates for the boys and there is no apparent racial discrimination. As Pradeep said 'it is all against all (boys that is) and that is exactly what it looked like!' Football then, on the one hand, appears to serve an integrating function. On the other however, it effectively ensures that playground activity is organized along gender specific lines and that the playground is dominated by the boys. Thus, girls who may already be disadvantaged through lack of experience of physical play, become further disadvantaged through lack of opportunity to gain that experience at playtimes.

In more general terms, girls are already likely to be socialized out of an interest in sports by the time they reach puberty, even where there is evidence of interest within the family. Where the family reinforces the view that playing games is unfeminine and undesirable, daughters are even less likely to retain an interest and see the curriculum as relevant to them. The challenge for the teacher is thus to provide a curriculum which motivates all. One of the ways in which the above may be achieved is by using the pupils themselves as a resource. Strategies for this will be considered in the next section.

A third challenge is to develop strategies which counter racism and prejudice and which challenge the use of stereotypes which can damage ethnic-minority pupils. There is no lack of evidence of racist behaviour from pupils, parents and teachers. Its elimination demands sensitivity, since the clumsy application of antiracist policies can increase hostility and prejudice rather than diminish them. Countering the institutionalized racism which manifests itself in school organization as much as elsewhere in life is even more difficult to achieve. The record of schools in setting levels of expectation which match the aspirations of black students and their parents is not a good one.

This is no mean challenge. It assumes that teachers themselves share a common concern for the inequalities and discrimination which result from racist attitudes and is, in effect, asking teachers to adopt attitudes and values which are 'ahead' of society as a whole. A frequent response to changes about provision made for multicultural education is to argue that the school provides a good education and that all children are treated the same. This generally means treating them all like white children and probably like white middle-class children. This will inevitably mean that all children's needs are not being equally met. The reality, of course, is that children from different cultures are all too frequently accorded different treatment. The fact that expectations of children vary according to a range of factors including social background, has been extensively researched. The stereotyping of Asians as hard-working and of West Indians as lazy and liable to cause trouble is well documented.

In the context of physical education there remain 'facts' derived from research which purport to demonstrate the Afro-Caribbean pupils have limited ability in swimming, or that Asian pupils have physical characteristics

Table 13.1: Summary of Challenges: Physical Education

- Access for pupils at Key Stages 1 and 2 to the requirements of National Curriculum PE.
- Provision of a PE curriculum which is relevant to everyone, including all ethnic groups, all social backgrounds and both sexes.
- Multiculturalism as an issue for every school.
- Appreciation of the links between gender issues and multicultural issues in the context of PE.
- Development of strategies to counter racism and to challenge the use of inappropriate ethnic stereotypes, whether from teacher, pupil, parent or governor.
- Development of appropriate teacher expectations including challenging research 'facts' purporting to demonstrate that particular groups have particular physical characteristics.

which give them a particular aptitude for racket sports. Although such research has been largely discredited, it continues to provide a pseudo-scientific rationale for perceived performance differences between different racial groups. The damage which is done is largely in relation to teacher expectations which result from such misinformation which then translate into unequal opportunities to achieve among different groups of pupils. Teacher expectations should be high of all pupils regardless of race or gender.

A fourth challenge involves consideration of the interests of all the ethnic groups present in the school. While accepting the undesirability of presenting any pupils with all-white images through books, pictures and role models, the effects are much less immediate in an all-white school than in a school whereby black pupils thereby have no role models. In the context of physical education, a narrowly focused curriculum which offers activities with which only white middle-class pupils, and probably only male pupils, can identify, cannot meet the needs of all.

A final challenge is to use the potential of physical education in promoting personal qualities such as respect for others and in other whole curriculum or cross-curricular areas such as language development.

Responses

This section will make various suggestions for practical strategies aimed at providing pupils with relevant physical-education experiences and with appropriate role models in a physical-education context, and will also consider how physical education might provide the context for addressing more general antiracist or multicultural issues.

There are a number of ways in which broadening of horizons may offer opportunities for a multicultural perspective, either subject specifically or more generally. Physical education can provide a context for visits between schools. Grudgeon and Woods (1990) describe visits made by 7-year-olds from an all-white rural village school (Garfield) to a multicultural urban school (Albert Road).

> Undoubtedly the greatest attraction at Albert Road for Garfield children was the apparatus. They have none at their school, and they had been told about the frames, ropes, boxes, horses, benches, bars and mats that filled the hall at Albert Road. So deprived were some of the Garfield children in this respect that one child asked her teacher, 'What is apparatus?' They had a few balls, a few hoops and a few skipping ropes which they could only use if it was fine. Consequently their coordination was dreadful. (Grudgeon and Woods, 1990)

Apart from providing an interesting alternative perspective on deprivation, such a visit clearly has potential for enhancing Albert Road pupils' self-esteem by placing them in a position where they can behave with confidence in a familiar environment. As far as the Garfield Road pupils are concerned, at a subject-specific level they are able to extend their experience, and at a more general level, they have the opportunity of learning from mixing with a group of pupils about whom they could have harboured many misconceptions and of broadening their own experience through learning about other cultures first-hand.

The content of the curriculum can also be considered in terms of its relevance to all pupils. At Key Stages 1 and 2 there is considerable opportunity for enabling pupils to use their own experience as a resource. For example, Key Stage 1 games includes: 'Pupils should be given opportunities to make up and play games with simple rules and objectives that involve one person and a limited amount of equipment, extended to working with a partner when ready.' For Key Stage 2 this is extended to: 'Pupils should individually, with a partner and in small groups make up, play and refine their own games within prescribed limits, considering and developing rules and scoring systems.' There is clearly potential here for the creation of games which relate to other than the conventional team games which constitute the curriculum of most secondary schools. For example, the Asian game *kabbadi* could serve as the basis of a made-up game just as well as soccer or netball. A variation of the games-making theme could be to ask the class to bring examples of games played by their families. Houlton (1986) describes the experience of Subash Sachdeva, a Leicester teacher in doing just this.

> My class then played these games for the rest of the school and the children and teachers were given the chance to ask questions. My children wrote about the games in different languages and also added some art work. We followed this up by inviting another class to join us in our PE/Games period. (Houlton, 1986)

Towards the end of Key Stage 2, when the programme moves towards small side versions of adult-game forms, the balance of games offered should be considered in times of its relevance to all pupils, including different cultural groups. For some cultures contact sports are not a tradition, therefore offering soccer and rugby will not in itself constitute the most relevant curriculum.

A balance between invasion, net/racket and striking/fielding games will also involve a range of games within which the interests of different pupils can be accommodated.

It should however be noted that a games-dominated curriculum, while possibly catering for male cultural diversity, is unlikely to be seen as relevant by female pupils, although role models from different cultures are now more readily available, for example the South Korean women's hockey team or the Jamaican netball team. The publicity which surrounded the gold medal performance by a Muslim woman at the Barcelona Olympics illustrates the potential conflict which can still exist between Muslim family and cultural values and sporting achievement (Carroll and Hollinshead, 1993). At a less emotive level, many girls still fail to make the kinds of connection between school games and adult recreational activity which are made by most boys. The balance between games and other activity areas should therefore receive careful consideration. Gymnastics and dance both offer opportunities for body-management work which may not simply be more enjoyable than games for some pupils but which may also be a more appropriate medium for acquiring basic-movement experience where this is lacking.

Dance is often seen as an area offering great potential for a multicultural focus (Gordon, 1986). Unfortunately it is also the area of physical education most often neglected, especially at Key Stage 2, because of lack of expertise among teachers. As already described, use of visiting teachers is one effective way of offering a multicultural focus. Groups such as Kukuma, a Birmingham-based Afro-Caribbean company, run many workshops in schools, providing role models, challenging gender stereotypes, and introducing young people to the excitement and physical challenge of dance.

Physical education also provides a context where racist behaviour such as name calling can and, of course, should be challenged. The fact that pupils are working in a less formal setting than that of many classrooms and interacting with each other means that there is plenty of opportunity for such comment. If ignored by the teacher, the message given is that such remarks are acceptable. It is therefore most important that name calling or any other racist comments are challenged publicly. Physical education is often promoted for its potential in the area of personal and social development and it is in this context that inappropriate or racist behaviour may best be challenged. It should however be emphasized that the personal and social qualities which it purports to develop will not simply appear as a by-product but need to be planned for and made explicit (Williams and Underwood, 1991). If this is done, through discussion with the pupils about the qualities needed for successful group work or partner work, such as patience, respect for others or tolerance, followed by praise when those qualities are shown as well as when physical performance or effort warrants it, then a context relevant to good-community relationships whether at school or outside will be fostered and a framework for behaviour will be created in which issues of racism may be raised and constructively addressed.

The availability of role models in the setting of primary-school physical education is often a difficulty in the context of both race and gender. Those available in the context of physical education tend to be white and male, despite the numerical supremacy of women among primary-school teachers, with the result that opportunities are more often available to boys than to girls outside school hours. All pupils are thus deprived of positive images of women and ethnic-minority role models. Local-community links may usefully be employed in this context. For example, in some areas there are sports-development officers, either supported by the local authority under its leisure and recreation services, or supported by the relevant governing body, such as a football-development officer employed by the football association, with a brief to develop youth sport. It may well be that through their auspices, black role models can come into school and be involved with the pupils. This may be through the development officer himself or herself if he or she is black, or through his or her contacts with local sportspeople who are prepared to come into school to promote their sport.

In a different physical-education context, a number of areas now have dance animateurs, or arts-centre based dancers with an education brief. Many major dance companies, such as Birmingham Royal Ballet, or London Contemporary Dance offer educational workshops in schools in the cities or towns where they are working. Any of these can offer the opportunity for pupils to work alongside and with black performers or teachers. All-white schools have invited Indian dancers to lead dance workshops. This has enabled pupils to relate to, and work with, people from a different background and to meet Asian people coming into school as professionals with particular skills. The use of Indian classical dance can enrich a range of curriculum areas and themes. The same strategy in a multicultural school has the added advantage of offering a positive role model to a particular group of pupils.

Where the above suggestions are not feasible, it should still be possible to provide pupils with appropriate role models in the form of display material. For both white and multicultural schools visual images of male and female performers from a range of physical activities which demonstrate that physical activity and sport can be the province of all, regardless of race or gender, can be a powerful tool in developing positive attitudes towards the involvement of all.

Finally, the relevance of physical education to all pupils will depend not only upon pupil perceptions of the programme offered, but upon that of their parents. In a small number of cases pupils have been withdrawn from physical-education lessons because they are seen to conflict with cultural demands and values. In many others relatively simple strategies, and ones which many would argue are good educational practice irrespective of cultural issues, can do much to allay family concerns, particularly where these strategies are combined with positive efforts to involve members of the community in decision-making and discussion. Requests for single-sex provision for pupils at Key Stage 2 should be met if at all possible, together with teachers of the same sex. This may well be relatively easily achievable by combining Years 5 and 6 and dividing them into two single-sex groups.

While clothing for physical education should be hygienic and safe, there is no reason why all pupils should not have the option of wearing tracksuits or churidar pyjamas (narrow lightweight trousers). While this is a cultural issue for female pupils, the option should be extended to all, whether in mixed or single-sex lessons. If at all possible, single-sex changing facilities should be provided.

Most importantly, parents should be informed of the physical-education procedures which prevail in the school, and where it is not possible to accommodate demands of some parents, pupils may have to be excused from the lesson. This should be a last resort. For example, where public swimming pools are used, it is not always possible to guarantee a single-sex environment because schools do not always have exclusive use of the pool.

Mention has already been made of the potential of physical education to contribute to personal and social education. The second cross-curricular area to which a significant contribution can be made in the context of education for cultural diversity is that of language development. It has been said that physical education is less language dependent than other subject areas and that, therefore, physical education for the bilingual child should not be a problem area. However, all too often the bilingual child who lacks sufficient understanding to follow the teacher's instructions is limited to copying other children. While this may be an acceptable start, it is far from satisfactory in the long term. Not only will the child underachieve in physical education but the opportunity to use physical education to enhance language development will be lost. Daley (1988) gives many practical suggestions of ways in which physical education can support language development. The primary-school teacher who is responsible for delivering the whole curriculum to a particular class is well placed for this sort of work. Words used in physical education can be reinforced in the classroom and vice versa. For example, work could focus on prepositions such as 'along', 'across', 'over', 'under'. Concepts such as 'large' and 'small' can be developed in physical education and in the classroom. Since children generally share equipment, space, or apparatus, many opportunities arise for communication in a context and for a purpose. As physical skills are repeated, so language can be practised or repeated alongside. The use of resource cards with pictures and words is another invaluable aid, and if used with the pupils' mother tongue as well as English, can assist the process of valuing that child's language as well as helping him or her to learn a second one.

Conclusion

Physical education in the primary school is a challenge for many teachers. It may be argued that much of what is suggested here is good educational

Table 13.2: Summary of Responses: Physical Education

- Appropriate balance between time allocation to different activity areas.
- Selection of curriculum content, e.g., choice of games, to be of interest to many different pupil groups.
- Interschool visits to promote understanding and mutual respect.
- Consistent challenging of racist behaviour.
- Exploitation of the potential of PE for personal and social development.
- Exploitation of the potential of PE for language development.
- Use of outside agencies in partnership work in order to provide a wide range of role models.
- Effective links and communication with parents.
- Sensitivity in matters of uniform and activity location to expectations of certain cultural groups.

practice and not specific to a multicultural context. We are still far from a situation where cultural diversity is an issue addressed by all schools. Education for a pluralist society must be the concern of every school and every subject including physical education. It must involve both educating all children about, and sensitizing them to, life in a multicultural society, and offering children from ethnic minorities an education which is both relevant and challenging. The curriculum leader for physical education can play an important role in ensuring that the subject is not omitted from debate and policy-making in this area. He or she will only be able to do this from a position of knowledge and commitment. This chapter and this series of books are a contribution to the knowledge needed.

References

ASKEW, S. and ROSS, C. (1988) 'Boys Don't Cry', *Boys and sexism in education*, Milton Keynes, Open University Press.

CARRINGTON, B. and SHORT, G. (1989) *Race and the Primary School*, London, NFER-Nelson.

CARRINGTON, B. and WILLIAMS, T. (1988) 'Patriarchy and ethnicity — the link between school physical education and community and leisure activities', in Evans, J. (Ed) *Teachers, Teaching and Control in Physical Education*, Brighton, The Falmer Press.

CARROLL, R. and HOLLINSHEAD, G. (1993) 'Ethnicity and Conflict in Physical Education', *British Educational Research Journal*, 19, 1.

CASHMORE, E. (1982) *Black Sportsmen*, London, Routledge and Kegan Paul.

DALEY, D. (1988) 'Language development through physical education', *in British Journal of Physical Education*, 19, 3.

DEPARTMENT OF EDUCATION AND SCIENCE (1991) *Physical Education for Ages 5 to 16*, London, HMSO.

DEPARTMENT OF EDUCATION AND SCIENCE (1992) *Physical Education in the National Curriculum*, London, HMSO.

DUNCAN, C. (1988) *Pastoral care: and anti-racist/multicultural perspective*, London, Blackwell.

GORDON, D. (1986) 'Multicultural education and the dance educator', in *Dance, The Study of Dance and the Place of Dance in Society*, Proceedings of the VIII Commonwealth and International Conference on Sport Physical Education Dance Recreation and Health, London, Spon.

GRUDGEON, E. and WOODS, P. (1990) *Educating All: Multicultural perspectives in the primary school*, London, Routledge.

HOULTON, D. (1986) *Cultural Diversity in the Primary School*, London, Batsford.

KLEIN, G. (1988) 'Editorial: the nature of the beast', in *Multicultural Teaching*, 6, 2, 3.

MODGIL, S., VERMA, G.K., MALLICK, K. and MODGIL, C. (Eds) (1986) *Multicultural Education: The Interminable Debate*, Lewes, The Falmer Press.

MATTHEWS, A. (1985) 'The Dilemma of Opposing Values', in *Multicultural Educational Review*, 4, pp. 18–20.

NATIONAL CURRICULUM COUNCIL *(1991) Additional Advice to the Secretary of State for Education and Science. Physical Education*, York, NCC.

NATIONAL CURRICULUM COUNCIL *(1992) Physical Education: Non-statutory guidance*, York, NCC.

POLLARD, A. (1988) 'Physical Education, Competition and Control in Primary Education', in EVANS, J. (Ed) *Teachers, Teaching and Control in Physical Education*, Brighton, The Falmer Press.

SHAIKH, S. and KELLY, A. (1989) 'To mix or not to mix: Pakistani girls in British Schools', *Educational Research*, 31, 1.

TUTCHELL, E. (Ed) (1990) *Dolls and Dungarees. Gender Issues in the primary school curriculum*, Milton Keynes, Open University Press.

WEST MIDLANDS COUNCIL FOR SPORT AND RECREATION (1991) *Equal Opportunity? Sport, Race and Racism*, A summary leaflet of a report by a working party of the West Midlands Council for Sport and Recreation, Birmingham, WMCSR.

WILLIAMS, E.A. and UNDERWOOD, M. (1991) 'Personal and social education through gymnastics', *British Journal of Physical Education*, 22, 3.

WILLIAMS, E.A. (1989) *Issues in Physical Education for the Primary Years*, Brighton, The Falmer Press.

The Race Relations Act and Education

Prabodh Merchant and Gajendra K. Verma

Earlier chapters have provided the ethnic, religious and cultural contexts which should be taken into account if the educational needs and aspirations of all students are to be properly fulfilled. In an increasingly competitive environment with the ever-present scarcity of resources it is particularly important that those with the formal responsibility of educating society are also aware of the legal context in relation to race and culture within which they need to carry out their work. It will be helpful therefore to look briefly at the development of race-relations law in this country over the past twenty to thirty years resulting from the changing racial, cultural and religious composition of the population.

Background to the Laws

While it is true to say that the UK has always had migrants who have been assimilated into the social and economic life of the country, these have been, up to the mid 1950s, generally of white-European origins. For these migrants difficulties in the main were those resulting from differences in language, religion and those flowing from newness: i.e., lack of contacts, availability of, and access to, goods and services. It was assumed that most, if not all, of the problems likely to be encountered by these migrants would resolve themselves without any special intervention by the State in a matter of a generation or two at most. The differences such as those relating to religion, custom and practice could be accommodated within the existing legal framework. Problems of race discrimination were thought to be virtually non-existent and could similarly be left to be dealt with by the common-sense application of existing public-order legislation supported by the innate sense of fair play on the part of the majority of the British people.

Post-war reconstruction of shattered cities and economies and the scarcity of labour in all the European countries necessitated a wider search for suitable labour. Thus, throughout of the 1950s various European countries actively encouraged recruitment of labour from their colonies or from countries newly given their independence. For the United Kingdom the most fruitful sources of labour were the islands of the Caribbean, and the newly independent countries of the Indian subcontinent. People from these countries were already familiar to the British and, as members of the Commonwealth, were free to enter the mother country without any restrictions. Throughout the 1950s people came to work and mostly returned to the countries of origin to visit the families whom they supported. As their prime concern was to obtain work, they were attracted to towns and cities offering opportunities for unskilled and semi-skilled work. Again, with the responsibility of supporting their families in their country of origin, it was important that living expenses in this country were kept to a minimum. This typically meant living in Victorian terraced housing shared with friends and relatives in the cheapest areas of town, close to mills, factories and transport depots where they worked. Inevitably, differences in priorities, culture, language, religion, and so forth caused friction between these newcomers and the white working-class residents.

Towards the end of the 1950s, in response to public clamour, the government made known its intention to introduce restrictions on the entry of Commonwealth citizens. This intention was translated in 1962 into the Commonwealth Immigrants Act. Commonwealth citizens entering the UK for work after the passing of the Act in mid-1962 needed vouchers. Dependents of those already in the UK were, however, allowed to come without vouchers. This had a significant impact on the nature of immigration and the pattern of their settlement in the UK. Initially there was a rush to beat the deadline of unrestricted entry. This was followed by a need for entrants of both the pre and post-period of the 1962 Act to take up permanent settlement and make arrangements for their families to join them here in the United Kingdom. Thus, by introducing an element of sponsorship, the voucher system reinforced bonds of friendship and kinship and provided a further incentive for the new entrants to settle among existing communities and into similar work areas. This change in the composition and pattern of migration had, in its turn, implications for the various services including the education service. The arrival of families with school-age young people into areas which were already the poorest in terms of housing, education, and social and environmental amenities created further tensions and friction.

The 1962 Act was followed in 1965 by the first of the three Race Relations Acts. The 1965 Race Relations Act created a race-relations board with powers to take up individual cases of overt discrimination in a very limited sphere of public life. The emphasis of the Act was on conciliation, with the reserve power to take those few who behaved in an illegal way to court. As yet there was no official acceptance of racial discrimination as a significant factor in the continuing disadvantage and harassment suffered by those who were now being euphemistically referred to as 'new-Commonwealth immigrants'.

The task of helping the newcomers to adjust to British society was largely left to the newcomers and voluntary groups such as the Joint Council for the Welfare of Immigrants, the National Committee for Commonwealth Immigrants and concerned individuals. However, the extra burden on local authorities with substantial populations of migrants from the new Commonwealth was recognized. Section 11 of the Local Government Act 1966 therefore provides that the Secretary of State may pay grants towards expenditure on additional staff to those 'local authorities who in his opinion are required to make special provision in the exercise of any of their functions in consequence of the presence within their areas of substantial numbers of immigrants from the Commonwealth whose language or customs differ from those of the community'.[1] Up to 75 per cent of salary costs of approved posts was payable. By far the largest proportion of this grant was used to fund posts in education. Thus, in 1986–87, of the estimated £100m Section 11 expenditure, 79.5 per cent went towards funding posts in education mainly as generalist teachers, ESL schoolbased peripatetic teachers and classroom assistants.

The next substantial piece of legislation covering race relations was the second Race relations Act in 1968. This act extended the powers of the Race Relations Board to cover employment, housing, education and the provision of goods, facilities and services, and the publication or display of discriminatory advertisements and notices. The board was also given the power to investigate suspected unlawful discrimination where there was no individual complainant. However, due to inadequate resources and the absence of any provision to tackle indirect discrimination, in practice the board's investigations were largely confined to individual complaints. The 1968 Act also established the Community Relations Commission and charged it with the responsibility for creating better understanding and harmonious relations between peoples of different races and cultures. The CRC in turn provided funds to local voluntary committees to employ officers to undertake work in pursuance of these objectives. Both the Race Relations Board and the Community Relations Commission did some very valuable work in tackling the difficulties experienced by new Commonwealth migrants.

However, by the early 1970s, it was apparent that the law needed widening to include indirect discrimination and strengthening to allow a proactive rather than a merely reactive approach to be taken to counter the continuing high levels of direct and indirect discrimination based largely on colour. It was also recognized that equality of opportunity and treatment could not be made conditional upon the total abandonment of cultural and ethnic identity by racial minorities, increasing proportions of whose members were either born here or had been substantially brought up in the United Kingdom.

---

[1] For a scrutiny of grants under Section 11 of Local Government Act 1966 final report December 1988 see Appendix 3.

The Current Law

With these considerations and the experience and lessons learned from the 1965 and 1968 Race Relations Acts, a new Race Relations Act was enacted in 1976. The Act merged the Race Relations Board and the Community Relations Commission to form a new body, the Commission for Racial Equality, with new and stronger powers for the creation of a society based on equality of opportunity for all racial groups. The commission has a duty of:

- working towards the elimination of discrimination;
- promoting equality of opportunity and good relations between persons of different racial groups generally; and
- keeping under review the workings of the Act and, when required by the Secretary of State, or when it otherwise thinks it necessary, drawing up and submitting to the Secretary of State proposals for amending it.

The 1976 Act gave a wider definition of unlawful discrimination to include traditional practices and procedures which, although they may not be intended to discriminate or disadvantage, nevertheless had that effect on ethnic minorities. A requirement or condition which although applied equally, or would be applied equally, to all racial groups constitutes unlawful indirect discrimination if:

- a considerably smaller proportion of persons of a racial group can comply with it as compared with the proportion of persons of another racial group;
- which cannot be shown to be justifiable irrespective of colour, race, nationality or ethnic or national origins of the person or persons to whom it is applied; and
- which is to the detriment of the person who cannot comply with it.

Thus unnecessarily demanding educational qualifications for jobs which do not require such high qualifications could be indirectly discriminatory. Similarly, unjustifiable dress or language requirements could constitute unlawful indirect discrimination. The 1976 Act also enables measures to be taken to meet the special needs of particular racial groups in regard to their education, training or welfare, or any other ancillary benefits. Additionally, the Act allows provision to be made for training and encouragement to apply for work in which particular racial groups are underrepresented. Actual selection for a job must, of course, be on merit.

Section 1 of the Act distinguishes two types of discrimination — direct and indirect. Direct discrimination refers to treating a person less favourably than another on racial grounds. For example, to refuse a student entry to a college because he or she was black would constitute direct discrimination.

217

Indirect discrimination involves applying a requirement or condition in a way that a smaller proportion of a particular ethnic group than others can comply with it. It has also to be established that failure to comply with the condition or requirement is detrimental and that the requirement is not justifiable on non-racial grounds. It is important to note that discrimination need not be conscious; it may be discrimination by effect, rather than by intention.

The two basic objectives of the Race Relations Act 1976 can therefore be stated as follows: firstly to regulate behaviour by laying down minimum acceptable standards which should govern relations between groups and individuals in any civilized society. The second objective is to encourage behaviour and actions necessary to overcome the effects of discrimination and disadvantage and thereby help to create a society in which groups and individuals enjoy genuine equality of opportunity. As both objectives aim to bring about a qualitative change in society their importance to educationalists cannot be overstated.

This then, is the broad legal context in terms of race relations, within which the education service has to operate. Detailed guidance on the implementation of the Race Relations Act with specific reference to every section is, of course, available from a variety of sources. Thus, for example, the Commission for Racial Equality's code of practice for the elimination of racial discrimination in education sets out the implications of every relevant section of the 1976 Act to help those involved with education to provide it without discrimination made unlawful by the Act. Other publications provide detailed guidance on important issues relating to the encouragement of awareness and initiatives necessary for the creation of an education service which is capable of meeting the needs and aspirations of a multiracial, multicultural and multifaith society. However, it may perhaps be useful to consider, albeit very briefly, one or two important avenues for making progress towards achieving these objectives within the framework of the Race Relations Act.

Multicultural Education

Clearly this has been, and continues to be, important in disseminating information relating to the culture, traditions and beliefs of various groups within society. However, the need is to build on the understanding and tolerance which will, hopefully, result from greater awareness of other ways of living by ensuring that the more positive aspects of different systems and values are identified and respected.

Antiracist Education

A careful and sympathetic review of teaching materials and methods is necessary to ensure that they are as free as possible of cultural and racial bias based on negative and/or stereotypical images and assumptions. Their replacement by appropriately based materials and methods will be helpful in promoting self-development and mutual respect amongst students and teachers. Encouragement can also be given to underrepresented groups to apply for work in the Education Service, especially in teaching posts. This would not only provide much needed role models, but may also be an additional cultural resource.

The National Curriculum

Implementing some of the initiatives discussed above within the constraints of the National Curriculum is inevitably going to pose challenges for both resources and commitment. As far as may be practicable, attempts should be made to ensure that teaching materials and methods in various subjects within the National Curriculum are such as to enable the various minority groups to understand and value their particular ethnic identities.

Finally, there are also other Acts which impose various duties and obligations on those involved in providing education. For example, the 1988 Education Reform Act with its provision for the local management of schools, opting out, the National Curriculum and the character of religious worship. All of these issues have racial as well as cultural and religious dimensions. Similarly, the right of parents to a school of their choice for their children poses challenges, which sometimes may be in conflict with obligations under other legislation. Consider, for example, the recent test cases in Dewsbury and Cleveland. In both, the High Court upheld the right of parental choice under the 1988 Education Reform Act, even though such judgments appeared to undermine the 1976 Race Relations Act. Under the terms of the latter, LEAs are not allowed to act in any way that would constitute racial discrimination. The parents won the right to have their children transferred to other schools from the ones to which they had been originally allocated. The parents were white and the schools had a high proportion of Asian pupils.

Section 18 (I) of the Race Relations Act 1976 as originally enacted made it unlawful for a local education authority (LEA) to discriminate racially in carrying out those functions under the Education Acts 1944 to 1975 which do not fall under Section 17 of the 1976 Act. The Education Acts of 1980 and 1981 updated Section 18 so that it covers functions under those Education Acts also. There is no similar reference in the 1986 or 1988 Education Acts. There is a suggestion that the words in Section 235 (7) of the 1988 Act that it 'shall be construed as one with the 1944 Act' are intended to deal with this point. But the position is not clear.

In addition to the requirements and expectations embodied in the Education Reform Act 1988, there is legislation relating to race equality in the Children Act 1989 as well as that contained in the Race Relations Act 1976. A number of the implications for practice have been set out in *Lessons of the*

Law: a casebook of racial discrimination in education published by the Commission for Racial Equality in 1991. The formal relationship between the Race Relations Act 1976 and the requirements of the Education Reform Act 1988 and the Children Act 1989 presents a number of issues that will require legal clarification concerning the rights and responsibilities of individuals and institutions. The complexities of these three pieces of legislation will almost inevitably create considerable work for members of the legal profession.

It should be mentioned that what we have learned as a result of twenty years' experience is that the law is a necessary but not a sufficient condition of solving the problems of race relations. The aims of legislation have to be translated into practice by various institutions in our society (e.g., courts, industries, universities, schools, politicians, employers and all citizens).

As with all laws, race-relations legislation must be kept under review to ensure that it addresses contemporary concerns adequately. The Commission for Racial Equality (CRE) undertook a review of the Race Relations Act 1976 in 1985, and made recommendations to which the government made no formal response. In the light of subsequent events, the CRE undertook a second review and published a consultation document in 1991 entitled *Second Review of the Race Relations Act 1976*. The review is in two sections. In the first of these, the CRE sets out proposals for changes in the legislation which it considers will improve the effectiveness of the law-enforcement process. The second part of the consultation document reflects on issues closely related to race relations and on ways in which society might better manage the many and varied tensions that occur across the boundaries of race, religion and sex, bearing in mind the implications of the move towards a more integrated Europe.

References

COMMISSION FOR RACIAL EQUALITY (1991a) *Second Review of the Race Relations Act 1976: A Consultative Document,* London, CRE.
COMMISSION FOR RACIAL EQUALITY (1991b) *Lessons of the Law: A Casebook of racial discrimination in education,* London, CRE.

Lists of ERA-related Publications

P.D. Pumfrey

Lists of Education Reform Act 1988 related publications (Primary-schools orientation): National Curriculum Council (NCC); School Examinations and Assessment Council (SEAC); Department of Education and Science/Department for Education (DFE) and Her Majesty's Inspectorate (HMI)/Office for Standards in Education (OFSTED).
(N.B. As from 1st October 1993, NCC and SEAC will be subsumed under School Curriculum and Assessment Authority: SCAA).

Section A: National Curriculum Council
(Adapted from the NCC Publication List)

Curriculum Guidance Series

A Framework for the Primary Curriculum July 1989	ISBN 1 872676 07 3
A Curriculum for All-Special Educational Needs in the NC.	ISBN 1 872676 09 X
The Whole Curriculum March 1990	ISBN 1 872676 14 6
Education for Economic and Industrial Understanding April 1990	ISBN 1 872676 19 7
Health Education July 1990	ISBN 1 872676 23 5
Careers Education and Guidance August 1990	ISBN 1 872676 24 3
Environmental Education October 1990	ISBN 1 872676 25 1
Education for Citizenship November 1990	ISBN 1 872676 30 8
The National Curriculum and Pupils with Severe Learning Difficulties March 1992	ISBN 1 872676 50 2
Teaching Science to Pupils with Special Education Needs March 1992	ISBN 1 872676 88 X

Consultation Reports

Modern Foreign Languages May 1991	ISBN 1 872676 52 9
Mathematics September 1991	ISBN 1 872676 61 8

Science September 1991	ISBN 1 872676 62 6
PE December 1991	ISBN 1 872676 74 X
Art January 1992	ISBN 1 872676 72 3
Music January 1992	ISBN 1 872676 73 1

INSET

Science Explorations March 1991 Book and Video pack	ISBN 1 872676 39 1
Aspects of English: English in the National Curriculum in Key Stages 1 to 4 September 1991*	ISBN 1 872676 55 3
Science and Pupils with Special Educational Needs (KS1+2) September 1991	ISBN 1 872676 42 1
Implementing Design and Technology at Key Stages 1 and 2 November 1991 3 Books and Video pack	ISBN 1 872676 60 X
Implementing National Curriculum History (KS1–3) November 1991*	ISBN 1 872676 53 7
Mathematics Programmes of Study: INSET for Key Stages 1 and 2 December 1991 Ringbinder and sections on planning, AT1, Communication	ISBN 1 872676 67 7
Information Technology in the National Curriculum (KS1–4) December 1991*	ISBN 1 872676 54 5
Issues in Design and Technology (KS1–4) December 1991*	ISBN 1 872676 76 7
The National Curriculum and Pupils with Severe Learning Difficulties March 1992	ISBN 1 872676 65 0
Using and Applying Mathematics Book A: Notes for Teachers at KS1–4 September 1992	ISBN 1 872676 95 2
Using and Applying Mathematics Book B: INSET Handbook for KS1–4 September 1992	ISBN 1 872676 96 0

Non-Statutory Guidance

Mathematics July 1989	ISBN 1 872676 04 9
English June 1990	ISBN 1 872676 21 9
Technology – Design & Technology Capability April 1990	ISBN 1 872676 17 0
– Information Technology Capability April 1990	ISBN 1 872676 18 9
History April 1991	ISBN 1 872676 49 9
Geography May 1991	ISBN 1 872676 51 0

---

* *The videos to accompany these books are no longer available from NCC, but may be borrowed from your LEA associate, subject adviser, Teachers' Centre or HE library.*

Modern Foreign Languages February 1992	ISBN 1 872676 63 4
Science (revised) January 1992	ISBN 1 872676 77 4
Mathematics (revised) January 1992	ISBN 1 872676 78 2
Physical Education June 1992	ISBN 1 872676 91 X
Music June 1992	ISBN 1 872676 92 8
Art June 1992	ISBN 1 872676 93 6
Mathematics 1989 and 1992 (revised and merged)	ISBN 1 85838 003 0
Science 1989 and 1992 (revised and merged)	ISBN 1 85838 002 2

National Oracy Project
(Occasional Papers)

Gathering and Presenting Evidence/Telling Stories in School 1988 Two accounts of sessions which formed part of the first workshop day for local coordinators of the National Oracy Project — ISBN 1 872676 35 9

The Play's the Thing 1989. The story of the 'Pied Piper Project', in which a group of primary-school children produced a play from inception to successful public performance — ISBN 1 872676 36 7

Who's Talking? 1991. An account of an oracy fortnight, describing a range of events organized within an inner-city primary school — ISBN 1 872676 37 5

Assessing Talk in Key Stages 1 and 2 1991. Advice on teacher assessment — ISBN 1 872676 41 3

Oracy and Special Educational Needs 1992. Case studies are used to show how talk helps pupils to learn across Key Stages 1–4, in both special and mainstream schools — ISBN 1 872676 94 4

Other National Oracy Project Publications (Not available from NCC)

Teaching Talking and Learning in Key Stage One 1990 — ISBN 1 872676 16 2
Teaching Talking and Learning in Key Stage Two 1991 — ISBN 1 872676 26 X
All titles in this series available from:
    National Association for the Teaching of English (NATE)
    Birley School Annex, Fox Lane Site,
    Frecheville, Sheffield S12 4WY Tel: 0742 390081

Talking I.T. Through 1990. A discussion document published by the National Oracy Project and the National Council for Educational Technology. Comprises nine case studies on talk and learning around the computer. — ISBN 1 853791 00 8

Available from:
NCET
Sir William Lyons Road
University of Warwick Science Park
Coventry CV4 7EZ Tel: 0203 416994

Talk and Learning 5 to 16 1991. An INSET pack on
Oracy for teachers. Published by the Open
University and drawing on the experience of
teachers in the Project throughout the UK.   ISBN 0 7492 3061 4
Available from:
Open University
OU Learning Materials Site Office
PO Box 188
Milton Keynes
MK7 6DH Tel: 0908 74066

Statutory Orders (HMSO)

English 1990	ISBN 0 11 270708 4
Technology 1990	ISBN 0 11 270709 2
History 1991	ISBN 0 11 270741 6
Geography 1991	ISBN 0 11 270736 X
Modern Foreign Languages 1992	ISBN 0 11 270750 5
Science (revised)* 1992	ISBN 0 11 270786 6
Mathematics (revised)* 1992	ISBN 0 11 270787 4
Art 1992	ISBN 0 11 270751 3
Physical Education 1992	ISBN 0 11 270752 1
Music 1992	ISBN 0 11 270753 X

Other Publications

The National Curriculum and the initial training of student, articled and licensed teachers April 1991	ISBN 1 872676 44 8
Religious Education — a local curriculum framework August 1991	ISBN 1 872676 59 6
Knowledge and Understanding of Science: Forces (KS1+2) March 1992	ISBN 1 872676 65 0
Analysis of SACRE Reports 1992 April 1992	ISBN 1 872676 90 1
Starting Out with the National Curriculum: An Introduction to the National Curriculum and Religious Education September 1992	ISBN 1 872676 98 7

NCC Free Publications

Newsletters

NCC news:	**Schools update for teachers and governors**:	**Talk**:
Newsletter of the National Curriculum Council	News from DFE, NCC and SEAC	Journal of the National Oracy Project
No 3 April 1990	No1 Spring 1992	No 1 Spring 1989
No 4 October 1990	No2 Summer 1992	No 2 Autumn 1989
No 5 February 1991	No3 Autumn 1992	No 3 Summer 1990
No 6 June 1991	(available from November)	No 4 Summer 1991
No 7 November 1991		No 5 Autumn 1992 (available from October)

Leaflets
Circular II: Linguistic Diversity and the National Curriculum March 1991
Education for Work: A Guide for Industry & Commerce April 1991
Aspects of National Curriculum Design and Technology December 1991
The National Curriculum: Corporate Plan 1992–1995 December 1991
Update 2: A guide to publications on the National Curriculum from NCC, DFE, SEAC and HMI March 1992
National Curriculum Technology: the case for revising the Order May 1992
Special Needs and the National Curriculum: Opportunity and Challenge, March 1993

Posters
'Technology in the National Curriculum
  Attainment Targets' December 1990 ⎫
                                ⎬ Maximum of
'Technology in the National Curriculum ⎪ 2 per school
  Programmes of Study' December 1990 ⎭
'Drama in the National Curriculum' March 1991

Section B: School Examinations and Assessment Council
(Adapted from the SEAC publications list)

SEAC Free Publications

	Reference
General	
Records of Achievement in Primary Schools 1990	RAB

LEA Information KSI
A Moderator's Handbook	KS1 MOD
Reference Notes: Core subjects tasks for 1992	KS1refnotes
Responsibilities of LEAs in 1991/2	RLEA

Exemplification KSI
Children's Work Assessed 1991	CWA
Children's Work Assessed: English 1992	A/014/B/91
English EN1: Speaking and Listening	EN1

Standard Assessment Task KSI
Core Subjects Task — Pupils' Pack 1992	KS1 SAT P
Core Subjects Optional task pack 1992	KS1 SAT O

School Assessment Folders KSI
School Assessment Folder 1992	SAF92KS1
School Assessment Folder 1993	SAF93KS1

Key Stage 2
Countdown to Key Stage 2	A/053/L/92

EMU (Evaluation and Monitoring Unit)

General
The Assessment of Performance in Design and Technology (APU DT)	D/010/B/91
The APU Experience 1977–1990 (EMU 77–90)	D/009/B/91
Decision Analytic Aids to Examining — The DAATE Report[†]	DAATE
APU Mathematics Monitoring Phase 2 — 1984–1988	EMU M2

EMU (Assessment Matters)
No. 1: *Graphwork in School Science*	EMU 1
No. 2: *Measurement in School Science*	EMU 2
No. 3: *APU Mathematics Monitoring 84/88 (Phase 2)*	EMU 3
No. 4: *Language for Learning*	EMU 4
No. 5: *Profiles and Progression in Science Exploration* (D/11/B/91)	EMU 5
No. 6: *Planning and Carrying Out Investigations* (D/012/B/91)*	EMU 6
No. 7: *Patterns and Relationships in School Science* (D/013/B/91)	EMU 7
No. 8: *Observation in School Science* (D/015/B/91)	EMU 8

[†] Only available from SEAC.
* Out of print.

EMU (Design and Technology Leaflets)
1: *Learning through Design and Technology: The APU Model*   EMU L1
2: *Negotiating Tasks in Design and Technology* (D/006/L/91)   EMU L2
3: *Structuring Activities in Design and Technology*   EMU L3

General SEAC publications

SEAC Recorder 3 Autumn 1989	REC 3
SEAC Recorder 4 Spring 1990	REC 4
SEAC Recorder 5 Summer 1990	REC 5
SEAC Recorder 6 Autumn 1990	REC 6
SEAC Recorder 8 Summer 1991	REC 8
SEAC Recorder 9 Autumn 1991	REC 9

Cyhoeddiadau ar gyfer Cymru — Publications for Wales

Cyfnod Allweddol 1 (Key Stage 1)   *Cyf.* (Reference)
Asesu Gwaith Plant: Dylunio a Thechnoleg a Thechnoleg
  Gwybodaeth   A/025/BW/92
  Children's Work Assessed: Design and Technology
  and Information Technology
CYMRAEG Cy2: Darllen 1991   CY2
  Welsh Cy2: Speaking and Listening
Plygell Asesu Yn Yr Ysgol (Ffeil)   SAF Welsh
  School Assessment Folder (Binder)
Plygell Asesu Yn Yr Ysgol 1991   SAF6–LW
  School Assessment Folder (insert) 1991
Plygell Asesu Yn Yr Ysgol 1992   SAF W 1992
  School Assessment Folder (insert) 1992
Plygell Asesu Yn Yr Ysgol 1993   KSI SAF W 93
  School Assessment Folder (insert) 1993
1993 (Pynciau Craidd) Tasg Asesu Safonol: Pecyn Yr
Athrawon   KSI SAT A 93
  1993 Core Subjects Task: Teacher's Pack
1992 (Pynciau Craidd) Tasg Asesu Safonol: Pecyn Yr
Athrawon   KSI SAT A
  1992 Core Subjects Task: Teacher's Pack
1992 (Pynciau Craidd) Tasg Asesu Safonol: Pecyn y Disgybl   KSI SAT D
  1992 Core Subjects Task: Pupils' Pack
D A Sau Technoleg 1992 a 1993   KSI SAT Te W
  1992 and 1993 Technology Standard Assessment Tasks
1992 (Pynciau Craidd) T A Sau Dewisol   KSI SAT OW
  1992 Core Subjects Optional Task Pack

Section C: Department of Education and Science (Department for Education at from 1992)

Key: NCSO = National Curriculum statutory Orders
      SI =   Statutory Instruments
      SO =   Statutory Orders
      C =   Circulars
      TGATR = Task Group on Assessment and Testing Reports

General Publications

DES (1985) *Better Schools.*
DES (1986) *Children at School and Problems Related to AIDS.*
DES (1987) *Task Group on Assessment and Testing: A Report.*
DES (1988) *National Curriculum Task Group on Assessment and Testing* (TGATR).
DES (1989) *Report of the Task Group on Assessment and Testing* (TGATR).
DES (1989) *National Curriculum: From Policy to Practice* (February)
DES (1989) *School Governors — How to Become a Grant-Maintained School, 2nd edition.*
DES (1989) *National Curriculum: A Guide for Parents.*
DES (1989) *Education (National Curriculum) (Temporary Exceptions for Individual Pupils Regulations (SI).*
DES (1989) *Education (School Curriculum and Related Information) Regulations* (SI).
DES (1989) *Education (School Curriculum and Related Information) (Amendment) Regulations* (SI).
DES (1989) *Education (School Records) Regulations* (SI).
DES (1989) *Planning for School Development 1.*
DES (1990) *Good Behaviour and Discipline in Schools* (revised).
DES (1990) *National Curriculum and Assessment.*
DES (1990) *Records of Achievement* (C).
DES (1990) *The Education Reform Act 1988: The Education (National Curriculum) (Assessment Arrangements for English, Mathematics and Science) Order 1990,* July (C).
DES (1990) *Education (Individual Pupil's Achievements) (Information) Regulations* (SI).
DES (1990) *Education (Special Educational Needs) (Amendment) Regulations* (SI).
DES (1990) *Education (School Curriculum and Related Information) (Amendment) Regulations* (SI).
DES (1990) *Education (National Curriculum) (Assessment Arrangements for English, Mathematics and Science) Order* (SI).
DES (1991) *Development Planning — A Practical Guide.*
DES (1991) *Education Statistics for the UK 1990 Edition.*
DES (1991) *School Governors — The School Curriculum.*

DES (1991) *Testing 7 year olds in 1991: Results of the National Curriculum assessments in England.*

DES (1991) *Your Child and the National Curriculum: A Parent's Guide to What Is Taught in Schools.*

DES (1992) *Curriculum Organisation and Classroom Practice in Primary Schools. A Discussion Paper.*

DFE (1992) *Education Statistics for the UK 1991 Edition.*

DFE (1992) *Education Europe.*

DFE (1992) *Education Observed: The Implementation of the Curricular Requirements of ERA.*

DFE (1992) *Time for School. A guide for Parents.*

DFE (1992) *Testing 7 year olds in 1992: Results of the National Curriculum assessments in England.*

Department of Education and Science

Religious Education
DES (1989) *Agreed Syllabuses and Religious Education: The Influence of the Agreed Syllabus on Teaching and Learning in Religious Education in Three Local Authorities.*

English
DES (1988) *Report of the Committee of Inquiry into the Teaching of the English Language.*

DES (1989) *English in the National Curriculum.*

DES (1990) *English in the National Curriculum, No. 2.*

DES (1991) *English (SO).*

Mathematics
DES (1989) *Mathematics in the National Curriculum.*

DES (1989) *Mathematics (SO).*

DES (1991) *Mathematics in the National Curriculum: (revised) Order and Circular.*

Science
DES (1989) *Science Policy — The Way Ahead.*

DES (1989) *Science in the National Curriculum.*

DES (1989) *Science (SO).*

DES (1991) *Science in the National Curriculum: (revised) Order Circular.*

Lists of Recent ERA-Related Publications

Technology
DES (1990) *Technology in the National Curriculum*

DES (1990) *Technology (SO).*

History
DES (1990*) History for Ages 5–16*, July, NCC Working Group Report for DES.
DES (1991) *History (SO)*.
DES (1991) *History in the National Curriculum.*

Geography
DES (1991) *Geography* (SO).
DES (1991) *Geography in the National Curriculum.*

Music
DES (1992) *Music (SO)*.

Art
DES (1992) *Art* (SO).

Physical Education
DES (1992) *Physical Education* (SO).

Section D: Her Majesty's Inspectorate

Key: CMS = Curriculum Matters Series

Each year, several hundred HMI inspection and survey reports are published by the Department of Education and Science. These contain evidence and evaluative comment relevant to schools' preparedness for, and implementation of, National Curriculum requirements.

The establishment of the Office of Standards in Education (OFSTED) based in Elizabeth House, York Road, London, SE1 7PH, in 1992, paralleled a government decision to devolve inspections of schools to autonomous teams of independent inspectors competing in a market.

General Publications

HMI (1985) *Quality in Schools — Education and Appraisal.*
HMI (1986) *The Curriculum from 5–16 (CMS).*
HMI (1987) *The New Teacher in School.*
HMI (1989) *The Curriculum from 5–16 (2nd Ed)* (CMS).
HMI (1990) *Education Observed 14: Girls Learning Mathematics.*
HMI (1990) *Standards in Education 1989–90: The Annual Report of the Chief Inspector of Schools.*
HMI (1990) *Special Needs Issues.*
HMI (1991) *Standards in Education 1990–91: The Annual Report of the Chief Inspector of Schools.*

HMI (1991) *Assessment, Recording, and Reporting.*

HMI (1991) *National Curriculum and Special Needs.*

HMI (1991) *Implementation of the curricular requirements of ERA: An overview by HM Inspectorate on the first year, 1989–90.*

HMI (1992) *Standards in Education 1991–92: The Annual Report of the Chief Inspector of Schools.*

HMI (1992) *Non-teaching Staff in schools: A review by HMI.*

HMI (1992) *The implementation of the curricular requirements of ERA: An overview by HM Inspectorate on the Second Year, 1990–91.*

OFSTED (1993) *Curriculum Organisation and Classroom Practice in Primary Schools. A follow-up report.*

Her Majesty's Inspectorate

Religious Education

English

HMI (1986) *English from 5–16* (CMS).

HMI (1987) *Teaching Poetry in Secondary School* (CMS).

HMI (1991) *English Key Stages 1 and 3.*

HMI (1991) *English Key Stages 2–4* (N-S G).

Mathematics

HMI (1987) *Mathematics from 5–16* (CMS).

HMI (1989) *Mathematics from 5–16* (2nd Ed) (CMS).

HMI (1991) *Mathematics Key Stages 1 and 3.*

Science

HMI (1987) *Science from 5–16* (CMS).

HMI (1991) *Science Key Stages 1 and 3.*

Technology

HMI (1987) *Craft, Design and Technology from 5–16* (CMS).

HMI (1989) *Information Technology from 5–16* (CMS).

Lists of Recent ERA Related Publications

HMI (1991) *Information Technology and Special Needs in Schools.*

HMI (1991) *Teaching and Learning of Information Technology.*

HMI (1991) *Teaching and Learning of Design and Technology.*

History

HMI (1988) *History from 5–16* (CMS).

HMI (1991) *Training Teachers for the National Curriculum: History.*

P.D. Pumfrey

Geography
HMI (1990) *Geography from 5–16* (CMS).

Music
HMI (1990) *Music from 5–16* (CMS).

Physical Education
HMI (1989) *Physical Education from 5–16* (CMS).
HMI (1990) *Physical Education from 5–16* (CMS).

Foreign Languages
HMI (1987) *Modern Foreign Languages from 5–16* (CMS).

Home Economics
HMI (1985) *Home Economics from 5–16* (CMS).
HMI (1990) *Home Economics from 5–16* (CMS).

Classics
HMI (1988) *Classics from 5–16* (CMS).

Drama
HMI (1989) *Drama from 5–16*.

Section 11 of the Local Government Act 1966: Background and Current Administrative Arrangements

Jo Jolliffe and Peter D. Pumfrey

Local Authorities have been assisted by a discretionary grant since 1967, through Section 11 of the Local Government Act 1966. This grant covers 75 per cent of staffing costs. Running expenses, accommodation etc. are not covered. Administered by the Home Office, this grant is intended to play a central role in the government's commitment to:

> the reduction of racial disadvantage which inhibits members of ethnic minorities from playing a full part in the social and economic life of this country . . . by helping local authorities to meet the costs of employing additional staff required to enable members of New Commonwealth ethnic minorities to overcome linguistic or cultural barriers and thus gain full access to mainstream services and facilities. (Home Office, 1992)

Although Section 11 grants have been interpreted as 'The only Government finance earmarked directly and exclusively for combatting racial disadvantage . . .' (Home Affairs Committee, 1981, para. 48), many aspects of the grant's operation have been criticized. The main criticisms of Section 11 grants include its low take-up by some local authorities and the absence of any monitoring of Section 11 funded staff by the Home Office.

In response to various criticisms of Section 11 grant, the government issued revised administrative arrangements for the payment of this grant which came into force on 1 January 1983. The changes in the arrangements were announced in the government's White Paper *Racial Disadvantage* (Circ. 8476) and were set out in detail in the Home Office Circular 97/1982.

The revised guidelines issued by the Home Office in 1982 were sound in principle, but were not taken in the same spirit by many LEAs. This was, in part, because of the 25 per cent of costs incurred. There was still a great deal of reluctance and inability to identify and account for Section 11 post holders at local and central-government levels.

Again in 1986, further guidelines on the administration of Section 11 grant were circulated to local authorities in Circular 72/1986. Although the new guidelines were more effective, there was some reluctance amongst local authorities to account in the required specific detail for Section 11 grant expenditure. In effect the new and progressively tighter monitoring procedures led to more clearly identifiable Section 11 post holders and Section 11 work.

The latest and most stringent review of the administration of Section 11 grant began in October 1988 leading to the publication of 'A Scrutiny of Grants under Section 11 of the Local Government Act 1966' which examined administrative efficiency and monitoring procedures. This scrutiny found that improvements were required in order that the grant was more effectively used within a more clearly defined framework. The main changes were:

- Section 11 to be cash limited;
- Section 11 applications must be for projects;
- Section 11 applications must be made in line with a regular annual timetable;
- Section 11 provision must fall within the new criteria for grant set out in the policy accompanying circular 78/1990;
- Section 11 approved projects must be monitored regularly against recognizable performance targets;
- Local authorities to be required to identify within their bids a proportion of provision for the voluntary sector; and
- Section 11 grant to be paid quarterly in arrears.

Subsequently, Home Office Circular 78/1990 was published setting out the new arrangements for the administration of grant under Section 11 of the Local Government Act 1966.

Introductory Timetable

October 1990 onwards	— Preparation and submission of project proposals under new arrangements for period 1 April 1992–31 March 1993.
	— Seminars/discussion by Home Office to explain new arrangements and assist in preparation of bids.
30 April 1991	— *Deadline for receipt of applications for April 1992 to March 1993*
May 1991–October 1991	— Consideration of applications for April 1992–March 1993
October/November 1991	— Applicants notified of decisions on project proposals for April 1992–March 1993.

1 April 1992 — *Funding under new arrangements commences*

Annual operational timetable

30 June 1992 — Deadline for receipt of applications for year commencing 1 April 1993.

January 1993 — Notification of grant available and project approvals for year commencing 1 April 1993.

1 April 1993 — Continuation of existing approvals and new approvals take effect.

30 September 1993 — Deadline for receipt of audited return of previous financial year's grant expenditure by recipient bodies.

Financial timetable introduction

30 September 1991 — Deadline for submission of final Fin Form C1 to Home Office.

October/November 1991 — Notification of grant available and project approvals for year commencing 1 April 1992.

November 1991 — Final full quarterly payment in advance to local authorities.

May 1992 — Remaining quarterly payment for posts under previous system to local authorities.

July 1992 — Submission of first quarterly return for period April – June 1992 and projected costs for remaining 3 quarters of financial year 1992/93.

August 1992 — First quarterly payment under new arrangements (in arrears) for period April – June 1992.

30 September 1992 — Deadline for receipt of audited returns on previous financial year's grant expenditure.

Full operation

January 1993 — Notification of approved provision for year commencing 1 April 1993.

30 September 1993 — See 30 September 1992 — detail to cover period 1 April 1992 — 31 March 1993.

July, October, January, April — Submission of quarterly returns.

August, November, February, May — Quarterly payments made to local authorities.

(same annual timetable applies thereafter)

This entire period of review of Section 11 engendered growing anxiety as well as great activity in local authorities across the country, culminating in their Section 11 bids in response to the new guidelines within the framework of the new policy criteria set out in circular 78/1990. The more rigorous monitoring and accountability for Section 11 monies were welcomed by Section 11 qualifying communities and Section 11 post holders alike. The need for quality assurance mechanisms, but also the risk of over dependency on this funding, were also important issues recognized by those concerned.

Ultimately, in December 1991, local authorities received notification of the success or otherwise of their Section 11 bids. Local authorities had been required to prioritize bids, but in some cases, those bids placed in higher priority failed to gain funding, whilst others with lower priority were approved.

Education Departments learned in the letter of 18 December that all successful education projects were to be subjected to an immediate scaling down of 15 per cent. Many authorities had submitted project bids based accurately on the researched needs of Section 11 qualifying communities. Projects thus most affected by this decision (which had no connection with proven need) were in local authorities where economics prevented further subsidy of Section 11 projects.

According to Home Office estimates, the 92/93 allocation was expected to fund 800 projects in total with 10,600 posts. Although this shows an increase in posts, the Local Authorities Race Relations Information Exchange (LARRIE) survey suggested that:

> This increase may be explained by an overall decline in the number
> of posts in higher grades. (LARRIE, 1992)

According to this survey, only 32 per cent of youth projects were approved, 81 per cent of projects to support E2L in schools and 52 per cent of education projects to support children and young people of African-Caribbean heritage were approved.

Projects approved in December 1991 started in April 1992. Morale was high as Section 11 workers and local authorities looked forward to three years and in many cases, five years of funding. Each post holder had a job description; objectives and targets were clearly stated; monitoring procedures set out. This was seen as a time to make unprecedented progress. Many local authorities, confident of funding, because of the letter of November 1991, appointed new Section 11 staff on permanent contracts. Then in a letter of 26 November 1992 the Home Office communicated a government decision to cut Section 11 Funding:

> the level of financial support which the Government is able to pro-
> vide by means of Section 11 grant crucially depends upon the
> economic circumstances of the country. The general economic

situation has changed markedly since Local Authorities were invited, in October 1990, to apply afresh for all Section 11 funding with effect from 1st April 1992, and since decisions were announced on the outcome of the subsequent applications round conducted during 1991. As you know, it has been necessary for the Government to review the whole of its public expenditure programme very closely in the changed economic situation in order to contain public expenditure within limits which the country can afford and to ensure adequate investment in line with the Government's strategy for sustainable growth in the economy. (Home Office, 1992)

The Home Office indicated that based 'on current best estimates' the rate of grant is now likely to be as follows: to March 94 at 75 per cent (no change); April 94 to March 95 at 57 per cent; April 95 to March 96 at 50 per cent. There was no indication in the letter of the future of five-year projects for the final two-year period. As a result of these unexpected cuts to Section 11 projects which have barely started up, 'thousands of teachers and community worker jobs will be lost over the next three years' (*Education*, 1992).

The Section 11 qualifying communities, who were previously consulted as to their needs, have not been consulted concerning the impact of the proposed changes in funding. At a time when access to the National Curriculum, the raising of standards and league tables have become so important in education, Section 11 support to pupils who are failing or those whose first language is not English, is being slowly but strategically withdrawn. Research has shown that ethnic-minority pupils can achieve in the curriculum once fluent in English. The latest Circular on Section 11 is being seen not just as a threat to Section 11 services but to the educational performance and the futures of young members of Section 11 qualifying communities.

Local authorities committed scarce funding to provide an enhanced service for qualifying communities. The outcome of the cuts will certainly have an adverse effect on staffing, recruitment and morale. In particular, this move will seriously affect the careers of many black and ethnic minority staff employed under Section 11. Provision for black and ethnic-minority communities will be adversely affected since it is unlikely that local authorities, already under massive pressure to cut mainstream budgets to essential services, will be in a position to have sufficient monies to make up the shortfall. These cuts must have a significant impact not only on educational provision for ethnic minorities, but also on the government's own long-term aim to provide equality of opportunity to all its citizens as promised.

It is clear from the above analysis that Section 11 was established to provide funding for use by local government as they interpreted and responded to the 'needs' of ethnic minorities. The types of expenditure incurred invariably differed from county to county. There is no doubt that Section 11 has had considerable impact on support for multicultural and antiracist provision for all pupils. In the current educational climate the continuing school-based commitment of governors and teachers, and political will at the LEA level, are crucial to translating multicultural and antiracist policies into practice, experience and achievement.

References

EDUCATION (1992) 4 December.

HOME OFFICE (1982) *Section 11 of the Local Government Act 1966, Circ. 97/82*, London, HO.

HOME OFFICE (1986) *Section 11 of the Local Government Act 1966, Circ. 72/86*, London, HO.

HOME OFFICE (1989) *A Scrutiny of Grants under Section 11 of the Local Government Act. Final Report December 1988*, London, HO.

HOME OFFICE (1991) Letter to Chief Executives dated 18 December, HO.

HOME OFFICE (1992) Letter to Chief Executives dated 26 November, HO.

LOCAL AUTHORITIES RACE RELATIONS INFORMATION EXCHANGE (1992) *Guide to Section 11 Funding: Research Report No. 3*, LARRIE.

Notes on Contributors

Alan Cross has taught both infants and juniors as a classteacher, as a deputy headteacher and as a teacher adviser. For the last three years as lecturer in education, Alan has led both science and technology courses in the School of Education at Manchester University. He has coordinated a number of initiatives related to teacher education and conducted research into science and technology as part of primary education.

Contact address: Centre for Primary Education, School of Education, University of Manchester, Oxford Road, Manchester, M13 9PL.

Julie Davies was a primary teacher and infant headteacher for thirteen years before moving into initial teacher training. Her present post at the School of Education, University of Manchester, includes work with PGCE primary students on the curriculum and methods of teaching English and history. She is on the Historical Association's Primary Committee and on the editorial board of 'Primary English'. She is currently researching aspects of the National Curriculum.

Contact address: School of Education, University of Manchester (*V.S.*).

Jo Jolliffe is head of the Section 11 funded Language and Learning Support Service in Manchester. She was formerly deputy head of Dick Sheppard Comprehensive School, Lambeth. Her research includes the language and learning needs of black and ethnic-minority children, the education and careers of Muslim girls and antiracist policies in schools.

Contact address: c/o Language and Learning Support Service, Palmerston Street, Ancoats, Manchester, M12 6PE.

Michael McLachlan has been involved in mathematics education for over twenty years. He is now the mathematics adviser for Stockport LEA with additional responsibilities for assessment and teacher appraisal. He has taught in primary and secondary schools and was a head of a mathematics department for eleven years. He spent three years as advisory teacher for mathematics for Sefton LEA before taking up his present position in 1988. He has published, through Causeway Press, the *What If? Pack*, a collection of activities to develop pupils' questioning skills. He is presently chair of the 'Greater Manchester Mathematics Challenge', a non-competitive mathematics event which attracts responses from over 30,000 pupils in the North West. He is a regional representative for the National Association of Mathematics Advisers. He has also recently been involved in a scrutiny of GCSE mathematics examinations as an independent consultant.

Contact address: Education Division, Stopford House, Stockport Town Hall, Stockport, SK1 3XE.

Prabodh Merchant is an employment officer. He works for the Commission for Racial Equality (CRE) and has extensive knowledge of race-relations legislation and its effect. Currently he is working in the North-West of England.

Contact address: Commission for Racial Equality, Maybrook House, 40 Blackfriars Street, Manchester, M3 2EG.

Philip Metcalf is an education consultant specializing in primary religious education. He was a primary-school teacher for nineteen years and now lectures at various institutions and leads primary RE INSET days.

Contact address: 'Spekelands', Oakhill Park, Broadgreen, Liverpool, L13 4BP.

Gillian Pearce taught for several years in a multiracial primary school before becoming a primary-science advisory teacher for Tameside Local Education Authority. She is now a senior lecturer in primary science education at the Manchester Metropolitan University.

Contact address: Primary Science Education, Manchester Metropolitan University, 799 Wilmslow Road, Didsbury, Manchester, M20 8RR.

Judith Piotrowski is a lecturer in education at the University of Manchester. Prior to this she was a primary-school teacher and a lecturer at Crewe and Alsager College of HE. She now lectures in primary education in English and art on PGCE, diploma and M.Ed levels. Judith is currently involved in a funded project looking at issues in art education in primary schools.

Contact address: School of Education, University of Manchester (*V.S.*).

Stuart Powell has twenty-years teaching experience in a range of schools, and is currently employed by the Metropolitan Borough of Stockport as an education adviser with cross-phase responsibility for the teaching of technology and art and design.

Contact address: Education Division, Stopford House, Stockport Town Hall, Stockport, SK1 3XE.

Peter Pumfrey is Professor of Education and Head of the Centre for Educational Guidance and Special Needs at the University of Manchester. His research and teaching interests include interethnic relationships, multicultural education, social psychology and race-relations research. He has published widely in these areas. He is author/editor/coeditor of fifteen books. *Educational Attainments: Issues and Outcomes in Multicultural Education* (1988) and *Race Relations and Urban Education* (1990) were edited, and contributed to, in collaboration with Gajendra K. Verma.

Contact address: Centre for Educational Guidance and Special Needs, School of Education, University of Manchester, Oxford Road, Manchester, M13 9PL.

Diane Rainey taught for several years in primary schools before becoming a lecturer in primary education at the University of Manchester. Her major responsibility is in work with PGCE primary students on the curriculum and methods of teaching geography.

Contact address: School of Education, University of Manchester (*V.S.*).

Rita Ray is a writer and part-time lecturer on the PGCE course at the University of Manchester. For her doctoral thesis she undertook research in aesthetics and education.

Contact address: School of Education, University of Manchester (*V.S.*).

Jill Scarfe is an experienced teacher and lecturer in music education. Her particular concern has been the development of strategies to introduce world music in the curriculum. She has worked in the USA, India, Pakistan and Trinidad. She has introduced steel pan and Indian music as part of the curriculum in schools in the UK. She is now a freelance music-education lecturer and consultant.

Contact address: 39 Church Lane, Barrow on Trent, Derbyshire, DE7 1HB.

Gajendra Verma is Professor of Education and Director of the Centre for Ethnic Studies in Education, School of Education, University of Manchester. He is also Dean of the Research and Graduate School, University of Manchester. Over the last ten years he has been responsible for directing over twelve national and regional research projects concerned with education, and the social and occupational adaptation of ethnic-minority groups. He has researched and published widely in the field of race in education, self-concept, identity; and was a member of the Swann Committee of Inquiry into the Education of Children from Ethnic Minority Groups. He has also served on a number of national committees concerned with the education of ethnic-minority pupils. He is author/editor/coeditor of over twenty books.

Contact address: Centre for Ethnic Studies in Education, School of Education, University of Manchester (*V.S.*).

Anne Williams is senior lecturer in education at the University of Birmingham, responsible for physical education and also for secondary postgraduate initial training across the whole curriculum. Primary-school physical education is a research interest, and she has taught physical education to Key Stage 1 and 2 pupils in various city schools on a regular basis. She is particularly interested in physical education as a vehicle for personal and social development.

Contact address: School of Education, The University of Birmingham, Edgbaston, Birmingham, B15 2TT.

Leslie Woodcock is senior lecturer in primary education at Bretton Hall College, University of Leeds, where he specializes in language. Before entering teacher-training, he was for many years a class teacher in primary education. His first degree is in music, and he holds an M.Sc in Education and an M.Ed in Reading. Currently he is researching the primary curriculum.

Contact address: Bretton Hall College, West Bretton, Wakefield, WF4 4LG.

Name Index

Subject Index

ability, 192, 193, 206–7
access to education, 50, 103, 122–3,
    158, 173, 237
  equality of, 21, 176, 180, 207
Access to Information on Multicultural
    Education Resources (AIMER), 5,
    52, 91, 131, 169, 196
accountability, 6, 41, 163
ACER
  see Afro-Caribbean Education
    Resource
achievement, 18, 48, 128, 237
Acorn (Percussion) Ltd.: address, 52
Action Aid, 168
adult life, preparing for, 21, 29, 103,
    158
advisory teachers/services, 46, 67, 121
aesthetic(s), 26, 81, 148, 151, 177,
    192
Africa, 119
African Video Centre, 52
Afro-Caribbean Education Resource
    (ACER), 52
Afro-Caribbean Groups/children, 200,
    203, 236
AIMER
  see Access to Information on
    Multicultural Education Resources
alienation, 4, 8–9, 43
'all white' schools, 129–30, 135, 163,
    165, 196, 205, 210
America/USA, 6, 18
Anglican schools, 44
Anglocentric approach, 18, 22, 151
antiracist
  education, 18–19, 41, 49, 121, 200,
    218–19

issues, 44, 131, 136, 166, 207–12,
    237, 238
policies, 160, 162, 163, 169–70, 203,
    206
AppleLink/Apple Macintosh, 92, 94n2
APU
  see Assessment of Performance Unit
Arabic, 9
art, 23, 26, 47, 109–12, 122, 189–99
Articles of Faith, 71–2
'artists in schools' schemes, 191, 196,
    198
arts council, 140
Asia/Asian, 19, 91, 179, 200, 203,
    204–5, 206–7, 210
assessment, 14, 22, 23, 45, 46, 48, 69,
    84, 185
  bias in, 18, 83
  history, NC, 148, 154
  Profile Components, 47, 133
  science, 121, 126, 128
Assessment of Performance Unit
    (APU), 76
assimilationist view, 18, 23, 25, 31, 81,
    145
Asylum Bill, 45
attainment, 48, 87, 192, 198
attitudes, 122, 126, 130, 158, 176,
    193
  and change, 17, 26, 40, 180–5
  and culture, 22, 62, 68, 190, 202
  teacher, 90, 160, 161, 163, 205
Attainment Targets (ATs), 45, 47, 48,
    65, 87, 133–4, 159, 167
  art, 190, 191, 195, 197–8
  history, 145, 146, 148, 150, 151, 152,
    153